In Spotless, *Sherman Yellen has brough*[...]
Reading his memoir is like watching a totally absorbing play: the characters come to vivid life and the events they experience register as first-rate drama. Bravo, Mr. Yellen! Bravo!

Sheldon Harnick, lyricist of *Fiddler on the Roof* and *She Loves Me*

This growing up story, in its unblinking view, makes us see ourselves and admit what we've avoided admitting: that the chaos and half-madness of any childhood, even that of a wealthy, "normal" childhood, must be faced, zits and all, allowed and forgiven. Spotless *is a story of family love trapped in the old world's hurricane of desire to share in American dreaming.*

Christopher Davis, author of
Valley of the Shadow and *Joseph and the Old Man*

I was stunned by Sherman Yellen's ability to recall his past so vividly. His autobiography is brilliantly told. I found it a unique and marvelous read. What a family! What storytelling! Spotless *is a feat of colorful and captivating detail by an admirable writer.*

Kenneth Geist, author of *Pictures Will Talk:
The Life and Films of Joseph L. Mankiewicz*

It's a wonderful book. Yellen's insights and scalpel-like honesty are very powerful and very moving.

Thomas Z. Shepard, Broadway cast album producer

David Copperfield, meet your New York cousin. Sherman Yellen's involving memoir, Spotless, *poetically delivers the right combination of gentle nostalgia with brutal honesty. As Yellen reflects upon his youth, it is apparent that, despite the challenges, he's the richer for having lived these experiences. Now, we're the richer for his having shared them.*

Stephen M. Silverman, author of *David Lean* and *The Catskills*
and former editor of *People Magazine* online

Told with wit, warmth, and wisdom, Spotless *brings to intimate life one colorful character after the other, even as it evokes a bygone era and makes the past the present.*

David Kaufman, theater critic and author of
Mary Martin: Some Enchanted Evenings and
Doris Day: The Untold Story of the Girl Next Door

Spotless

Memories of a
New York Childhood

Sherman Yellen

MORECLACKE PUBLISHING
New York City

Cover and puzzle design by Robert Armin

Audiobook available from Amazon, Audible and iTunes

For information, contact Moreclacke Publishing at
info@moreclacke.com or
325 West 45th Street, Suite 609, New York, NY 10036

First Printing: February 2017

Library of Congress Control Number: 2014914555
Moreclacke Publishing, New York, New York

ISBN-10: 0996016929

ISBN-13: 978-0996016926

Published in the United States of America

For my past and present: Joan

And a gift to my future:

Vivian, Zoe and Emily

The dead are notoriously hard to summon. I know this from personal experience. When I was a recent college graduate in 1953, the only job I could find was as an editorial assistant on *Tomorrow*, a quarterly journal of psychic phenomena published by Eileen J. Garrett, a stout, pretty sixty-year-old Irishwoman whose claim to fame was as a trance medium, one who called forth the spirits of the departed. Sir Arthur Conan Doyle, having abandoned Sherlock Holmes and embraced spiritualism, found and trained Mrs. Garrett as a "sensitive" in the years immediately following the First World War, when spiritualism flourished under the banner of psychical research.

In England, before Conan Doyle, Eileen was but one of many Irish country girls who wore Gypsy hoop-earrings, communed with ghosts and faeries, and impressed naïve authors and sober scientists. She soon owned a London tea room that was patronized by the novelist D. H. Lawrence ("a filthy-minded creature with mustard and bread crumbs lodged in his beard," she once told me) and other literati with cleaner beards and minds. But once the creator of Sherlock Holmes testified to her psychic powers, Garrett's fame spread across the Atlantic. She sailed to America in 1932, arriving, coincidentally, around the time of my birth. Despite the fact that she erroneously predicted for the waiting press the re-election of Herbert Hoover, she developed a sterling reputation among believers for foretelling the future and contacting the dead.

She had the "gift" and she used it with style. A famous hat maker, Lilly Daché, provided Garrett with a pleated silver-satin turban held together by a large paste diamond the size of an idol's eye. Her metaphysical hauteur was enhanced by her own sharp blue-green eyes which fixed their gaze upon you, checking out your aura, as her melodious Anglo-Irish voice commanded your complete attention. Among her believers were the novelist Aldous Huxley, the actress Gloria Swanson, and the Honorable Frances Bolton, a United States congresswoman and the widow of Oliver Bolton, the Ohio steel magnate. Mrs. Garrett brought the late, lamented Oliver back from the dead for conversations with his grateful, credulous wife, who took instructions from his spirit. It was Mrs. Bolton who, on the advice of the late Oliver, financed both the magazine and a serious scientific foundation for Mrs. G, providing the medium with her wealth and a lavish lifestyle that included an office building on West 57th Street in Manhattan, a Murray Hill duplex, and Le Piol, an estate in St. Paul de Vence in the south of France.

Imperious and demanding, yet capable of great generosity and kindness, Mrs. Garrett was modestly cagey in her appraisal of her own skills. "Madam" (as her clients and her worshipful secretary, Lee, called her) allowed that she could not do it alone. It took the assistance of her "control," one Abdul Latif, an eighteenth century Turkish physician who served as her guide from the spirit world and who would bring forth the departed from their repose.

Mrs. Garrett once told me that she could never be sure if Dr. Latif wasn't playing sly ventriloquist tricks on her, or if the dead were truly led by him to speak through her, their living instrument. When I asked her about the origins of her "supernormal" powers, she lifted a well-plucked eyebrow and shrugged in amazement at her own reputation, protesting that she was the last person alive who could testify to the veracity of these spirits or the authenticity of her gifts.

"Don't ask me if I'm real or a fake, Mr. Yellen! How am I to know? I am only the vessel through whom *the dead may speak!* What if these so-called spirits are nothing more than fragments of my own disordered personality?" she conjectured, thereby robbing her critics and a skeptical me of the best scientific argument against her powers. Since the spirits always arrived while she was in a deep trance, she could not testify to anything about them. Whatever they said, whatever they offered was out of her hands.

Lacking any psychic skills of my own, I have only my memory to call upon to summon *my* ghosts, and memory can be as ephemeral and suspect as Dr. Latif. It often magnifies the small everyday events of the past and diminishes the great ones. I am blessed, perhaps cursed, with what some might term "perfect recall." Nevertheless, my memories are subject to my imperfect humanity. At times we look at the past through the wrong end of our personal telescope. Even if we dislike our dead, they are always there before us in plain sight. They taunt us in death as they did in life, and will not lie easy in the grave. But what if we *love* our dead too much? Then we risk losing them to our sentimental portrait of their virtues. We see them pallid and lifeless, posed against a painted scenic backdrop, fading fast before our eyes. Who is that familiar stranger in the old family album wearing the odd clothes, the strange unflattering hairdo, flashing that fixed unnatural smile? Mother? Father? Sister? Never! Reverence, even more than time, kills memory. Praise for the dead can make them slip away like quicksilver, taking with them their humanity, all that is tasty, rough and impure, the very essence of life. And grief? Grief often leaves us "beyond words," dissolving memory in caustic tears. The way we grieve may tell us more about our *own* feelings than the nature of those we mourn. My own grief has often taken the shape of denial. Even after so many years, I cannot accept that my dead have died. I feel like John O'Hara, who upon hearing of the death of George Gershwin said, "They say George Gershwin died today. But I don't have to believe it if I don't want to."

In this memoir, my early life events do not march in lockstep through the years. I have made no attempt to provide an orderly progression from birth to maturity. Instead, I have allowed myself the liberty of randomness—the way memory works (at least the way mine does)—a literary scrapbook of how one boy felt as he was growing up during the 1930s and '40s. I move from the experience of a five-year-old boy who witnessed the burning of the Hindenburg, to the lives of my parents who helped to shape my own life, and then back again to that boy, preferring to write in my own psychological disorder rather than chronological order. As I write this it is more than thirty-eight years since my troubled father, Nat Yellen, died in his hospital bed, choking on a pill that a careless nurse had failed to monitor as he watched his beloved Yankees on television, twenty-nine years since my mother, Lillian, was killed in a street accident, twenty-three years since my beautiful, embattled sister, Simone, died of leukemia, and eighty-three years since I first appeared in the world and we all wove ourselves into that inextricable web of family. I shall try to pin them to the page, particularly my impressions of Simone, whom I knew best and longest since we shared a long childhood and were natural allies. I intend to convey some of her mischief, her wit, her beauty, her charm, her loyalties, her jealousies, her truthfulness, and her sly evasions, deceptions, and loving kindness. At the end of the day I will fail all of them, most of all Simone, but it will be worth my effort to spend time with them again.

All of us struggled, each in his or her own way, to build a good life out of the hard-earned scraps of wisdom and the bad nerves we inherited, together with the little learning we acquired. Each of us spent years taming our demons, not always successfully, hoping to shape better lives than the ones that chance had given us. What was most noteworthy about my family was our abiding affection for each other which survived our bad nerves and bad tempers, but also our good intentions. I am the sole survivor of that family and, like Mrs. Garrett, I am the chosen vessel through whom my dead can speak. And like Mrs. Garrett, I am obliged to question if they are real or only aspects of myself, projected onto them.

Time has only made me miss them all the more. We were not supposed to die. We were all to live forever. That was our unwritten contract as a family. And each in turn broke that contract. So this is as much an exercise in longing as it is in memory. What follows is my excursion into the past—a circling of it—tasting a bit, rejecting other parts, and somehow trying to find what was true in what *seemed* true during those early years. Much of what I write here comes from long conversations with my mother, who could never forget her own past; while quite intelligent, she lacked any real imagination, so I never doubted her memories. Some comes from conversations with my sister before her death, during which we spoke of our childhood and exchanged confidences, often laughing that our secrets were not secrets to each other. My father was more circumspect when I questioned him. He was, moreover, a born fabulist. But if one looked carefully, one could spot a morsel of truth peeping out from under layers of evasion and distortion.

I was fortunate in being the accidental witness to their lives and to certain remarkable events which gave me a jigsaw puzzle life—one in which I keep seeking the missing pieces that must be teased from memory. And so I start at the corners and try to fill in the middle as I go alone. Some of what happened then seems closer than events that occurred last week. It is the last gift of age to the mind. What follows is *their* world and *mine*, as I knew it, with all the distortion that time brings to long ago events. The boy you are about to meet is no stranger to me. He continues to take up residence inside me and, try as I might to shake free of him, he holds his own and will not let go.

Sherman Yellen
New York City

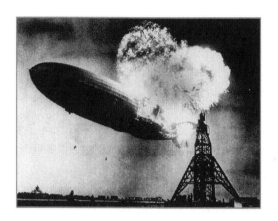

The Hindenburg and Me

M ost of us stumble into great events unaware that they have happened to us until we learn of their importance in the world. This was as true to a passerby on a clear day in downtown Manhattan on September 11, 2001 as it was to me, a small child in Lakehurst, New Jersey on a fateful evening in 1937.

My mother was a passionate believer in "a change of scenery," placing her faith in the healing powers of an ocean or a piney woods to cure my father's periodic depression, relieve my childhood asthma, and satisfy my nine-year-old sister's restless spirit. Although it was still May, and the school term for my older sister Simone would not be over for another month, my mother (who put first things first) announced that the family would be driving to Lakewood, New Jersey to spend a week away from the city.

Lakewood was then a winter resort, built around a group of small family-style hotels with one or two grand ones set in a pine forest that surrounded a lake. It was a place of rustic abandonment, first abandoned by the Indians and then by the Rockefellers, who had settled there for a while, now taken up by prosperous Jews as a resort close by the city. Looking back at this holiday I can only assume it came about because of my mother's effort to get my father to *snap out of it*. One of his moods had again put him in an armchair in our living room staring into space without appetite for his food or, more significantly, for his radio show favorites—*Vic and Sade, Lum and Abner*, and the always hilarious *Fibber McGee and Molly*. These were celebrations of small town life; a life he had never known growing up poor on the Lower East Side of Manhattan. He might sit like that for days with tears rolling down from his slightly bulging green eyes; tears which glistened on the stubble of his cheeks, for he had forgotten to shave, a sure sign of his despair in this fastidious man.

My father's moods could be read in his shaving habits: a close shave followed by the splash of a strong, aromatic Aqua Velva after shave testified that he was ready to face and fight the world. But the growth of stubble was a sure sign that his depression was now upon him. Of course, in those days it was called "a mood." My mother knew that the travel cure had worked for him in the past—a trip to the Thousand Islands in upstate New York had snapped him out of it early in their marriage—so she had hopes for it to do the trick again in early May of 1937. My father had in recent years started his own woolen business, one that had proven more successful than they had hoped in the Depression, and my mother was deeply concerned that his business partner, the shrewd and gregarious Max, would regret his decision to join forces with the unpredictable Nat, a master salesman when well, but a total loss when the mood possessed him. She knew that she had to act quickly to break this latest spell before it ballooned to an unmanageable size and threatened to destroy our newly prosperous lives. I was then five years and four months old, while my sister was nine.

Our Oldsmobile touring sedan was loaded with far too much baggage for the trip. Over packing is a family tradition that I carry on to this day—all those extra handkerchiefs and underpants, as if nosebleeds and incontinence were the consequence of leaving home. It was, at most, a four-hour drive from New York City, but given my father's propensity for getting lost, we arrived nearly six hours later at Light's Hotel in Lakewood, our retreat for ten days.

Simone, as ever, was carsick and exhausted from various stops devoted to what I even then considered her recreational vomiting along the roadside, where I was sent to perform a precautionary pee in the bushes whether I had to do so or not. There were few roadside amenities in those days and, if there had been, my cautious mother would not have trusted them for cleanliness. Having grown up in a world of filthy, crowded tenements and the illness and death that accompanied that world, she had made her god of *cleanliness*, the ideal being "spotless," and she worshiped it with Murphy's Oil Soap and Old Dutch Cleanser and scrub brushes with bristles hard enough to demolish any smudge or germ in sight. These were her incense and devotional candles, and she had as strong a faith in them as a devout Catholic woman might have in her rosary.

Arriving at the hotel at last and entering the lobby, my mother took the pen from my father's faltering hand and signed the register for the family in the modest reception area dominated by a painting on black velvet of a rabbi, eyes lifted heavenwards, lost in prayer, facing an equally large velvet painting of Hamlet contemplating Yorick's skull. I stared at the skull, fascinated, and my mother pulled me away, unwilling to start our holiday off with my contemplation of death on black velvet.

The elderly bellboy who told us that he was Annie Light's brother was so stooped with age that my father—a man of limitless compassion—was roused temporarily from his depression and insisted upon helping him with the luggage, which was then piled into a birdcage elevator, a space so small that it required that my father sit on our suitcases to make room for the operator. The conveyance of baggage and Yellens could not be accomplished without two separate trips in that noisy, jerky contraption. We entered into a two-room suite which my mother sniffed suspiciously for mold and eyed for signs of dust, but she was soon reassured when the small embroidered handkerchief she ran across the bureau top exonerated the suspicious-looking dark mahogany furniture, and she soon smiled, delighted by the room's fine view of the woods. Determining that there were no dangerous allergens in the room that could bring on my asthma attack, she put her alligator handbag down on the bureau—a sign that she was prepared to stay. Soon she rang for the housekeeper and, after giving the woman the decorative satin cushion with its picture of the pine forest and its stitched motto "Lakewood—land of health" (a pillow stuffed with pine needles and God knows what other hidden dangers), she was satisfied that the room was finally safe for me.

"It's exactly what you need, Nat!" my mother declared, although he could not have been unaware that it was *my* needs that were first attended to. He nodded, not knowing what he needed, least of all the sight of a pine tree. It was clearly what *she* needed, and even in his misery he knew that a vacation *with* him was not as welcome as one *from* him, and from what was then called "Nat's troubles."

The thought of being imprisoned with him within the apartment, not knowing when, if ever, he would become the familiar, cheerful, mendacious and angry Nat again, must have been terrifying for my mother. She had made her peace with what he was, for most of all he was "a good provider." This depression of his was stronger than her own fierce will and her talent as a wife and mother to transform such hard realities. She had dealt with all kinds of physical illness in her youth, illness that had led to the deaths of those she loved the most, but she was at a loss when confronted by mental illness, living as she did in a world where you "got over it," "forgot about it" or "put it out of your mind" with the ease that long practice in the art of survival had given to her. This was hardly the case with my father, who had suffered an equally impoverished youth, but who plunged into his depressions like a deep-sea diver cutting through the icy water to arrive at the depths and, having made it that far, was determined to stay until he found a treasure, that being the oblivion that might stop his ferocious and untamed worry.

Although they could have afforded the luxurious Laurel in the Pines, the premiere hotel of the area, and a few years later we would spend our holidays there, my mother preferred the smaller, unpretentious *hamish* Light's Hotel, run by Annie Light, a former actress in Polish-Yiddish theater; a resort where a man like my father, who seldom spoke, was okay as long as he did not turn away food (unthinkable); a resort where he would not attract particular notice given the odd clientele who inhabited its public rooms. That year the hotel was filled with Madam Light's fellow actors from the touring Yiddish theater company which was rehearsing for a performance to be given in the town for one night only at the local movie theater, a theater which had years before been a vaudeville house and had retained its proscenium stage and its velvet curtains. A poster of a distraught old woman with arms outstretched toward the heavens advertising *Queen Lear* in English, followed by Yiddish writing, was placed on the reception desk in the way of an advertisement.

Much to my mother's disapproval, the women of the acting company wore silk pajamas throughout the day, kept their tinted and waved hair in curlers and cobweb fine nets as they lounged around at the breakfast buffet, skipping lunch, but appearing again for dinner, where they gave my mother dark, dirty looks once they learned that she was not one of them, not a woman of the theater, and that her great beauty served no purpose but to bear two children and marry this silent, disturbing, unprepossessing man. My mother's great secret was that she had been a fashion model during World War I, something that was a source of shame rather than pride, one of those memories that were best buried alive.

For her part, my mother could barely hide her disapproval of these smoking, loud laughing, and probably promiscuous women in their Chinese silk pajamas, frog fastenings askew, flourishing ivory and silver cigarette holders; women whose breasts could be spied bouncing freely under their pajama tops, unadorned by brassiere or even a slip. Since I was too young and my father was beyond looking at vagabond breasts, my mother was more concerned by the influence these women might have on my nine-year-old sister, who had an eye for anything that passed for glamour, and was already indulging her dream of future movie stardom by wearing peasant blouses, exposing her shapely young neck down to her shoulders. What was hardest for my mother was that we had made our reservation on what was then called "The American Plan," which meant that three meals a day were included in the price of the room. This meant that there would be no escape from these dire influences at mealtimes if we were to get our money's worth.

Despite his silences, my father continued to read the newspapers piled up in the small smoking lounge; week old issues of *Variety*, a day old *New York Times*, and his favorite, *The World Telegram*. It was in one of these papers that he undoubtedly read that the great airship Hindenburg—the zeppelin of all zeppelins—was to make a landing the following day in nearby Lakehurst, where it would deposit its cargo of millionaire passengers traveling from Germany to America. It was a first luxury transatlantic crossing, advertising the smoothness of its ride in its beautifully appointed gondola, and bound to change the nature of transcontinental travel.

One of my father's great pleasures was being a witness to history. He took true pleasure in telling me how he had attended the great victory parade in New York City in 1918 led by General Pershing, which marked the return of our soldiers from France, and ten years later he had taken my mother to watch Lindbergh being celebrated on Fifth Avenue with a ticker tape parade after his solo flight to Europe. He would be in Yankee Stadium to hear Lou Gehrig deliver his farewell speech to baseball and life, and whenever he witnessed something grand in the company of others, it made him lose his terrible loneliness and feel one with the crowd. He would become cheerful—his natural state—and laugh for days afterwards, finding a comfort that was nowhere to be found in the humdrum events of everyday life.

Lakehurst was an hour's drive from our hotel and, based upon what I would later come to know of him, it would seem imperative for him to see the famous airship arrive and watch it being moored to its landing mast. Perhaps this would get him to snap out of it. The newspaper had assured him that this was an historic event, not to be missed, and his proximity to it was like an electric shock, stimulating him to rise from his lethargy and make a plan.

Why he lied to my mother that day I will never know, although I now suspect that he would be hard pressed to explain to my mother why he wished to greet the landing of an airship that sported large swastikas on its landing gear and cabin. By 1937 it was universally known that Hitler and the Nazis were bad for the Jews, that the racial laws were in effect, and that those few Jews who could manage it were trying to leave Germany with little more than their lives. None of these passengers would be escaping Jews. On board the commodious gondola of the airship would be the High German bourgeoisie who had voted Hitler into power, enjoying the historic luxury crossing that would put Germany at the top of world travel. It would be too hard to explain to her that he needed to see something remarkable, something greater than his own despair, in order to get through to tomorrow. So he told her that he wished to take me on a visit to an egg farm. At least the ovular shape of the zeppelin and that of an egg had something in common. The conversation between my mother and father, as ever, took the form of a skeptical question from my mother followed by a mendacious yet probable answer from my father.

"Why does he have to see an egg farm?" my mother asked.

"The boy should learn something about where our food comes from," he replied, stating that I was a city child and he did not want me to imagine that our eggs were hatched in the A&P.

He told her not to worry if we did not arrive back in time for the first seating of dinner. If we were going to be late, he would take me to a diner where I would have a malted milk and a peanut butter and jelly sandwich, my favorites. My mother was skeptical about this—given his mental condition—but she could not argue with him as she knew he would never do anything to injure me, and that he drove his car slowly and carefully.

"You'll be taking Simone too?" she asked, eager to get my sister away from the pernicious influence of those Yiddish theater actresses. She had caught my sister studying her own face in the underside of a spoon at breakfast that morning, and using a strawberry from the breakfast table to redden her lips. My mother feared that the vanity of these loose women was all too contagious. My father reminded her that Simone was carsick more often than not, and what would be a nice outing for Nathaniel and son would probably be a torment for his daughter.

"I don't know how smart this is," my mother said, still uneasy about our trip. "It looks like rain." My father made a dismissive gesture with his hand that carried the message, "Lil, stop the foolish worrying." She was so pleased by this sign of his spirits being lifted to an action, days earlier than planned, that she finally agreed to the outing. So it was decided that we would visit the egg farm as an all-male outing. And indeed we did.

Lakewood and nearby Lakehurst were magnets for European Jews fearful of city ghettos who wanted to start over in America in a simple, inexpensive, agricultural setting. They wanted dirt roads leading to small farms—Eastern Europe in New Jersey—and they found it there. Land was cheap and the purchase of a few breeding chickens, roosters and Rhode Island Reds was a small investment compared to the seeds, plough and help that a farmer, who depended on agricultural crops, good rain but not too much rain, sun but not too much sun, might need for his survival. Growing Jersey tomatoes was beyond their means and, besides, the chicken farmer felt connected to his old country in ways that the tomato grower could never be. Nobody in Poland or Russia grew tomatoes. Wheat? Okay. Corn? Maybe. But it was poultry that smelled and behaved in ways that made the farmer and his wife imagine, if only for the moment, that they were back in the village of their birth among farm animals who understood their language.

My father purchased a dozen large brown eggs at the first farm we visited, although looking back at that day it is hard to figure what he planned to do with them, since no cooking was allowed in the hotel's guest rooms. My mother, of course, travelled with a one-ring electric burner, to take the chill out of the glass milk bottle she kept on the windowsill, so that my sister and I should not suffer stomach cramps, but cooking eggs was out of the question.

After consulting his map and marking his route with a red pencil, we were soon driving towards the Lakehurst Naval Airfield. My father's eagerness to witness the Hindenburg when it docked there could not be contained. As we arrived at the airfield he soon took me into his confidence, telling me, "Son, I have a treat in store for you. You are going to see the largest airship in the world land in the airfield. It's something to stick in your memory book." He was a firm believer in the value of memory books and, as I write this, I have come to agree with him. Airfields meant adventure for me. Once, that past summer, he had hired the pilot of a one-engine biplane at Floyd Bennett Field to take us for an hour's ride over the skyscrapers of New York City. Amazingly, my sister was not airsick, and we were both thrilled by the ride, although we were obliged to promise not to tell our mother. When Simone broke that promise immediately upon our arrival home, my mother could barely contain her anger—and she was not an angry woman by nature.

"Were you crazy?" she asked him, although it was an accusation and not a question. "If I ever hear of you doing anything like that again I will never let you take them out for a drive," she exhorted. He nodded repentantly, but winked at me when she was not looking. I was hoping that something similar was planned for this evening, but there were no planes for hire on this field. Indeed, it was a field empty of all airplanes.

At the Lakehurst airstrip a small crowd, comprised of some spectators, a few reporters, and relatives of the passengers waiting for the arrival of the great airship, had gathered on the field. The landing field looked to me like a giant sandbox. Standing in the middle of this field was an enormous post which my father explained to me was the mooring post to which the landing gear of the great airship would be tethered before it settled on the sandy field to enable its passengers to descend on a portable staircase to terra firma.

Time passed; too much time for a five-year-old to tolerate standing still. I was growing restless and bored; the same feeling I had when I was obliged to sit through a doubleheader in Yankee Stadium which went well beyond its nine innings. A feeling that whatever was to happen had no end, that I was stuck forever in the middle of something I did not fully comprehend, as I watched my father cheer his team and I attempted to keep the scorecard of the hits, runs and errors for a game without an exit.

The airship was now an hour later than its scheduled arrival time and the sky had begun to darken. A light rain began to fall, at first as easy as a mist and then real raindrops hit our heads. My father opened his umbrella to cover my head, pulled out his pocket watch and looked concerned. He knew that if we did not return before nightfall my mother would worry, and he would have a hard time explaining his tardiness, particularly with the rain. He looked around for a pay telephone booth, but there was none in that field. As he started to walk with me back to the car, holding tightly to my hand, suddenly the great egg was looming above us, emerging from within the dark clouds in the silvery skin of the great airship itself. I was delighted. It reminded me of the great whale I had seen when my father had first taken us to the Museum of Natural History.

My father looked at the descending airship with undisguised admiration, shouting at me, "Look! Look! Look!" but the clouds had darkened again and smeared the sky with a blackish gray and the airship which now and again peeped out from those clouds seemed to hang above us uncertainly, a dim shape now barely discernable from below. I looked up at my father as he whistled to the airship to come closer as if he were summoning a dog. I knew at once that it was something wonderful, but to me it seemed less remarkable than the giant balloon of Popeye that I had seen floating down Thirty-Fourth Street in the Macy's Thanksgiving Day Parade, one that had dipped down, very close to my sister, and caused a commotion at the time. Suddenly I felt myself being scooped up from the ground and placed upon my father's shoulders so that I could see the landing from above the heads of the waiting crowd of friends and relatives of the passengers, a sea of fedora hats and gloved hands waving to their friends encased in the gondola on that chilly, rain-doused evening.

Later, many years later, I was to learn that the airship was obliged to make a sharp left turn at full speed because the ground crew had failed to prepare properly for the landing. It was about seven in the evening when, after a few more sharp turns, the mooring lines were dropped from the bow, just as static electricity began to move from the airship's underside to its hull. And then it happened. The airship was afire. The flames began to spread, moving forward, and the airship's back was soon broken, the red letters "Hindenburg" disappeared into the flames along with the swastika, the fabric skin burning away and swallowing the airship cell by cell, as it crashed to the ground nose first with a hideous, fiery verticality. I could hear the screams and the cries of the passengers, and the gasps of horror from those waiting below as the gondola hit the ground and the airship's skin was rapidly peeling away. It appeared to glow from within like a Japanese lantern, sparks flying everywhere, delightful for a child to look at, but ending in a fierce explosion lost in a thunderclap while a few fortunate passengers and crew started dropping from the airship gondola that was close to the ground. The waiting crew on the ground rushed towards the flaming wreckage.

I can still recall the sight of a man running towards us. He was immaculately groomed, pristine in his uniform, only his cap and his face were ablaze, and to my mind he looked more like a living birthday candle than a human being. My father hurriedly shook me off his shoulders and tossed me to a standing position on the ground. For a moment he pushed my face into his stomach against the hard metal buckle of his belt so that I would not see what was then happening. I felt him grab my hand and, like all the screaming, blazing figures around us, we too began to run as I was dragged along by him, my head turned towards the blazing man, hoping to get a better look, as my father pulled me towards our car. Most of all I wanted to see more of that fiery airship which had taken on the features of an immense dying dragon wrapped in its own flames. It was something that I found oddly reassuring because it meant that the chimeras that plagued my sleep with nightmares had their counterparts in the real world, and did not live only in my head. In a moment I found myself thrown into the rear passenger seat of the Oldsmobile, my head covered with the Turkish towels that were always placed there in the event that my sister should throw up without warning. These towels were to prevent me from witnessing more of the catastrophe. He started up the engine, making his getaway, and we raced out of the airstrip.

"Daddy, what happened?" I asked.

"Just fireworks," my father replied. "Only you mustn't tell your mother that we went to see them. You know how she is about fireworks."

I did know. The preceding summer when we were at Long Beach on Long Island she had refused to let me stay up to see the fireworks display on the Fourth of July. She had read about accidental explosions at such displays and did not want to encourage any of my incurable curiosity that might lead to danger. I was even forbidden to hold a sparkler, something my young friends had all accomplished.

After driving for a short while, as fire engines with screaming sirens passed us going in the opposite direction, my father pulled over to the side of the road and examined me. He took out his handkerchief, spat on it and proceeded to rub off some ash that had landed on my nose. Then, satisfied that there was no telltale sign of our disastrous outing, he proceeded to drive back to the hotel.

"Just fireworks!" he explained. "That's all it was, son." At five, I already knew that he was lying to me, that this was no simple fireworks display, but I also knew that there was nothing to be gained from asking him any more questions, other than having him lose his temper with me for distracting him from the nest of lies he was diligently weaving for my mother.

When we returned to the hotel an hour later my mother and sister were waiting. "Did you hear what happened to the big Nazi zeppelin?" my mother asked. "No," my father lied. And she proceeded to tell him of the awful accident that had been reported on the radio and was all the talk of the hotel. The next morning when Herb Morrison's recorded account of the airship disaster was first broadcast, Mrs. Light sneered when she heard him cry out, "Oh, the humanity!"

"He's wrong," she said. "Those were not humans who died. They were Nazis, and that was God punishing them for what they're doing to the Jews in Germany." It was then that my father presented Mrs. Light with the dozen farm fresh eggs and asked her to serve them to us for breakfast, graciously telling her to take some for herself and her brother.

I never again heard any discussion of the Hindenburg disaster at Light's Hotel, nor did I betray my father, knowing that what we had witnessed was a forbidden secret which we alone could share. Keeping that secret did not hang heavily upon my five-year-old conscience. It was better than those interminable doubleheaders. In time I would forget about that evening; all I would recall was the sharp metal of my father's belt buckle as he pressed my head into it to keep me from witnessing any more of the disaster, and the way he tossed me into the back of the automobile, the rough texture of the towels against my face and arms as we sped off like bank robbers in a getaway. But I never forgot the flames within the ribs of the airship and the burning man. Listening to the radio, a few years later, Clifton Fadiman on *Information Please* began to discuss the burning of the Hindenburg and I realized that I had witnessed it, but that I could never boast of it without betraying my father or, worse, being accused of lying. And strange as it seemed, the day after the accident my father appeared to have recovered from this bout of depression. Indeed, as my mother would later report to her sister Ida, "Nat finally snapped out of it. Must have been that trip to the farm. Leave it to him to find the freshest eggs in Lakewood."

Oh, the humanity!

Years later, as my father lay dying of pancreatic cancer in his hospital bed at Mount Sinai Hospital, I brought up the subject of the Hindenburg. I told him that I had such vivid memories of being present at that event, yet I could not be sure if it was a true recollection or a child's fusion of dream and reality. I recounted my remembrance of that day and he registered no emotion. Had we visited the landing field at Lakehurst *before* or *after* the event and had I only imagined the historic event that occurred there—a recollection that had lasted with me through the decades?

"Were we really there?" I asked him.

He looked at me, silent for a moment, and then for the last time in his life offered me the small, shy, turned up corners of his mouth that always preceded some guilty statement, and said, "Yes, son, I took you there. But for God's sake, don't tell your mother!"

Spotless

I Am Born

My arrival at that large red brick house with that high privet hedge on Andrews Avenue during that hard, cold February of 1932 was an unwelcome surprise to my older sister, Simone. She was a bright, pretty, wary and affectionate four-year-old who knew that something was afoot, but whatever it was mystified her—or so she would tell me years later as she described my entrance into the family. Strange things were happening all over. Simone had heard on the radio that it was so cold that week that Niagara Falls had frozen solid, and she had seen a photograph of that wonder in her father's newspaper, the great cascade arrested in its fall, its thunderous splash frozen in time in icy sheets. She had spied in that same newspaper the forbidding face of Hitler, who had just come to power, and listened on the radio to the terrifying news of the Lindbergh baby kidnapping, events that had little meaning in her protected world during the great Depression. But the one event that would most directly affect her young life went unspoken and unreported. A brother was just born. Me.

Until the day of my birth, she had heard nothing about my imminent arrival. It was an age when infant brothers or sisters arrived suddenly, lacking any preparation for their appearance. The era of home births had ended, sweeping away some precious information about life and death for city children. A pregnant mother disappeared into a hospital and with any luck returned with a living infant sporting a baby bracelet that spelled out his or her name on tiny celluloid beads. These, in pink or blue, designating the infant's sex, were placed at birth on the infant's wrist so that nobody took home the wrong baby. The "switched" baby was a much-dreaded bit of maternity folklore. Bassinettes and cribs were hastily purchased and installed *after* the birth, or borrowed from relatives whose offspring had outgrown their use; nobody invested too much hope or treasure in an infant who might not enter the world alive. And entering alive, the infant's luck (which meant life) could be poisoned by a display of too much pride in its survival. Nobody took the chances of a newborn's survival for granted.

My mother's older sister, Aunt Ida (pronounced Ann-Dida), cackling with joy, told her young niece that a brother was coming home from the hospital that day. Simone quite rightly refused to believe her. Aunt Ida, who dressed with so little sense of color or style, presented a problem in credibility. My sister was born with a sense of beauty and she instinctively knew that Ida had no taste and, lacking that, had no sense; for taste was a proof of judgment and beauty confirmed it. Arriving with her strong herring breath, which did not prevent her from planting unwelcome kisses on the girl's cheeks, Aunt Ida cast off her apple-green woolen coat with its large Bakelite pin of a Ubangi woman's head (complete with a multi-ringed elongated neck and hoop earrings), revealing her apron of printed bright-red cherries covering her cotton house dress with its riotous pattern of clusters of yellow bananas and palm trees, her stout legs adorned by heavy lisle stockings and scuffed, brown Dr. Scholl's lace-up shoes. Simone knew that such a woman, though "good as gold" as her mother said often enough, could not be trusted with the truth. Aunt Ida always managed to get the facts mixed up, her English trailing off into an incomprehensible Yiddish followed by a shrug of resignation and an apologetic smile which revealed her bright yellow teeth. Today she was babbling away about the "sparrow" bringing Simone a baby brother. Simone knew that her aunt adored her, but today she needed information, not adoration, to make sense of all the confusing whispers and silences.

She had no way to account for her mother's disappearance, something that had happened when she, Simone, was sleeping. The bony, pink-faced maid, Polish Mary, had smiled benignly as she blushed and, like Aunt Ida, retreated into her native language when asked about the whereabouts of Simone's mother. It was a subject no one wished to entertain, at least not in English. Her father, Nat, looked evasive as he always did when he was about to tell a fib, and she knew at four that he was a famous liar, a good-natured liar, a loving liar, but someone to be relied on for quarters, Mounds candy bars and Doublemint chewing gum, but never for the truth. She had only her mother for that, and her mother had disappeared, taking reality with her.

It was snowing heavily on the day I was to be taken home from the hospital, one of those blizzards that drifted down from Canada and settled on the city, clogging the roads, burying cars and slowing trolleys, concealing their tracks which were embedded in blocks of Belgian stone, as the otherwise unemployed day workers struggled with heavy, rusty shovels to clear the tracks for a few bucks a day. The transformative power of the snow covered all the dark brick apartment houses and the castle across the way that was the Salvation Army Training College. It wrapped the turrets of the castle and the barren trees in ever-thickening cotton whiteness, so that even the most unimaginative child could be transported back into a lost world of medieval wonders, a world of witchcraft and spells.

You could hear the stillness of the world then and see the shape of snowflakes falling—at least children claimed they could—and looking upwards, if lucky, you might catch the tiny, moist snow stars on your eyelids that melted as soon as they landed on your warm skin. Photographers in those days never tired of a winter scene, capturing its luminous stillness for the weekly magazines and photo journals in velvety shades of gray, black and white; creating their luscious gelatin silver and platinum prints. Tripods were set up, light meters consulted, apertures adjusted. Time—long, slow, careful time—was not just taken, it was lovingly spent; all before color film and fast lenses came along to spoil the beauty of a February snow. At a time when so much was going wrong in the world, a good snow helped one to believe in an orderly, beautiful world, at least until it melted and left the ugly slush that splattered your clothes as you waited to cross a street. But on *that* day, the snow was new, clean and, in my mother's favorite word, "spotless."

I can imagine my toddler sister looking out the window of our house, listening to the insistent hissing of the large exposed steam radiators, waiting for something remarkable to happen. It was an expression I would see many times in our long childhood. She would be watching the children playing outside in their thick, plaid, woolen snowsuits, scratched leather aviator caps flapping over their ears, bundled up in layers of sweaters so that their arms stuck out stiff as gingerbread men, flopping about in their rubber galoshes with flapping metal buckles undone. They had been sent out to play in the cold by child-weary mothers eager for some peace, the chance to wash and wax a floor and to hear a radio serial without a child ruining the climax of *Helen Trent* with a battle cry or stepping on the still wet surfaces of their kitchen. The liberated children embraced the cold, puffing proud clouds of winter breath as they shouted at each other in voices that had a new, crystalline clarity. My sister could hear the muffled screams of joy from her window seat as children, some no older than she was, went sledding down the hilly streets of Loring Place and Andrews Avenue, bumping into each other, landing in piles of wet woolen caps and mittens, fingers frozen, faces exhilarated and stunned, limbs impervious to injury. She knew she was a princess, but she was a princess stuck in a tower of her mother's making, one that was built to protect her from all the dangers outside, along with all its pleasures.

The large empty lots that existed between the apartment houses remained undeveloped because of the Depression, when residential building came to a sudden halt. Signs advertising the soon-to-be movie theater or elegant modern apartment dwellings would never deliver on their promises. The lots were now a level battlefield for snowball fights and the perfect place to start a snowman (although nobody ever had the patience to finish one or find coal for its eyes or a battered hat for a head covering). In a world where there were rules for everything, suddenly, wonderfully, thanks to the new, fast falling snow, there was a world without boundaries. Simone watched this and waited for her parents' return, knowing that mother—who fretted about colds and chills and wet clothes and the contagious, unclean coughs of other people's children—would never let her outside to play in the marvelous snow.

Coming Home

Having spied under her high, iron hospital bed a collection of dust balls and a wad of pink chewing gum with its castoff Juicy Fruit wrapper, its tinfoil undergarment gleaming with menace, my mother, Lillian Yellen, determined to quit the hospital at once. Nothing could keep her from taking me, her newborn, home to that haven of hygienic safety. She had in the past days developed the deepest suspicion about the cleanliness of the hospital nursery. She could sniff the ammonia of the urine in unchanged diapers, and saw that the used rubber nipples of the baby bottles were tossed carelessly into a common jar to be sterilized by God knows who? God knows when? You should know that the highest praise that my mother could give was "spotless." How often as a child I would hear my mother speaking to her sister Ida on the telephone during their review of the past day to commend a friend, a maid, a restaurant, a floor, a dress, a kitchen, a bathroom, a character, with that synonym for perfection, "spotless." Clearly the hospital was anything but, and its dangers must be fled before the dreaded microbes contaminated her infant. She believed in microbes as she believed in God, an unseen force that wreaked havoc on the unwary unless steps were taken.

My mother was a genial, loving woman, in whom kindness abounded. It was spontaneous and easy for her and, like a great athlete, it was her natural gift. It had its good seasons and its bad seasons but, in the main, it was a stellar goodness, equal to most of the challenges life had put in her path. Her goodness was genuine and rare, but it was tempered by a hard childhood and a fierce will. She saw the best in most people, and when she couldn't, she stopped looking, unless their presence was imposed upon her life and they refused to leave her field of vision, in which event she turned her back on them forever. Rather than see the worst, she simply wouldn't see them again. But in the case of my father's family, exiled for her lifetime to far-off Flatbush in

Brooklyn, they defied her system—she did not see them, yet she constantly saw the worst in them. My father now knew that her good nature was more than matched by her amazing stubbornness, for once an idea had entered her head there was no way to pry it loose. She might smile, nod, and agree at first, but in the end she went her own way, my father following behind reluctantly.

Leaving the hospital at once was her big immutable idea for the day. My father had tried to convince her to stay on until the storm subsided, claiming that it was impossible to find a cab that would take us home in a blizzard and, anyway, it was a dumb idea; it was dangerous to go out into that storm with a newborn child. He tried teasing her into compliance, stating that she was like her namesake, the silent-screen star Lillian Gish, cast off with her baby into a wild storm in a melodrama like *Way Down East*. She shook her head, not a bit amused, and ordered, "Nat, go find a cab. I mean it." He called several taxi companies and they all declined with variations on "Mister, are you nuts? Don't you know there's a blizzard out there?"

After eight years of marriage my father knew better than to hope to change Lilly's mind once she had made it up. He could rant and rail, cajole and threaten, as he often did, but he knew that beneath her warm smile and gentle manner was an iron will that could not be bent or broken by his strongest, most rational of arguments, or even his most irrational rages. So my father, in defeat, telephoned my mother's younger brother, my Uncle Frankie, who was at home taking a day off during the blizzard from his work as a deliveryman. Frank agreed to dig out his buried Ford van, the rusty *Mother's Friend Laundry* truck he used to deliver and collect laundry, and to collect us. There was nothing that the genial Frank would not do to please his older sister, the one who had raised him after their mother had died. If Lilly wanted it done, Lilly should have it done. If she was ever wrong, she was wrong for the best of reasons—her own. Nat knew that there was no point in complaining to her family, none of them would have believed his complaint, or if they believed it, they would have thought her in the right.

Frank drove with mother and baby up front, seated beside him on the only passenger seat, while my father crouched uncomfortably in the back on bundles of laundry, muttering about the stubbornness of my mother, his complaints ignored by his wife and her brother as if they were nothing more than the harmless rattle of the old truck's muffler.

Driving us home slowly through the swirling snowdrifts, Frank was making admiring noises at me, the swaddled infant whose face barely peeped out of the layers of blue wool baby blankets, jesting that it was fortunate I had not inherited my father's "shnoz" and that I had arrived with the Horowitz good-looks intact. A handsome man himself, he knew his own looks were compromised by the tic in his right eye, which he tried to coordinate with his smile so that it could pass for a sly wink. He would stop every so often to wipe the snow off the windshield, the old creaking wipers defeated by the burden of the ever-growing blizzard. He drove with great caution, not just for the safety of the passengers within, but to avoid hitting any of the children playing wildly in the streets, the snow having erased all boundaries between street and sidewalk and any idea of a world of caution and fixed rules.

There were few private cars in the Bronx in those days; few could afford them and few needed them. The city's public transportation was in its heyday and everyone used the trolleys for local travel and the elevated trains to reach the outer boroughs. There was, therefore, little traffic for Frank to avoid. But the trolleys trudged through the worst of storms, and the horse-drawn milk carts continued to service their customers, making their way through the blizzard, the steaming horse droppings marking a trail in their slow but steady progress, the hard metallic ring of the cart's bells a warning to motorized vehicles, and a welcome sound to all who heard them, so preferable to that rude blast of horn with which cars announced their presence.

Snow meant a holiday from school in those early Depression years. It was not necessary to announce a public or parochial school closing; it was assumed by all that weather had to be respected. It was, after all, God's will. The local shops enjoyed a brisk business in neighborhood trade despite the winter weather. Since most of the shopkeepers lived above their stores in two-story buildings called taxpayers, they kept their doors open for the nearby customers who might brave the weather for a half-dozen Danish pastries, a navel orange, or a quarter-pound of yellow sweet butter carved fresh from a wooden tub.

Life went on at a far slower pace. All travel plans were postponed, except by my mother who needed door-to-door transportation and, as always, she got what she needed. So in this way, I was taken home to our house on Andrews Avenue, covered with my uncle's praise for my button nose and a few random snowflakes on my blue cotton cap, together with the bundles of undelivered laundry, and the bassinet that Frank had kept in the back of his truck with a full month's supply of clean cloth diapers. Once home, Frank assembled the crib and carried the changing table to the maid's room near the kitchen, which I would share with Polish Mary for a few months. The furniture was scrubbed by Mary with a strong disinfectant—one could not be too careful—and I was set up to begin my life.

The Princess Simone

Until my arrival, my sister Simone had been the brightest star of a very small universe in which my parents were the sun and the moon, and various Hines and Horowitz relatives their close and adoring satellites. All of them were held in orbit by my mother's astonishing beauty and my father's new wealth, which in those early Depression days seemed miraculous among those who were desperately struggling to get by. As far as my mother was concerned, my father's family was not even a part of our solar system.

My father doted on his daughter and when he saw the scowl on my sister's face as she first laid eyes on me, he assured her that at last her wishes for a brother had finally been answered. He pretended that the new baby was her idea, kissing her cheek and patting her hand, figuring that telling her that she wanted me so much would put her halfway on the path towards believing it. He was a superb salesman and if anyone could sell her on this infant Sherman, he could. But she was a tough customer and she was buying none of it.

Her father now offered me up to her as a living doll; someone to love and be loved by; her guaranteed friend for life. "No more lonely afternoons from now on, sweetheart." I would be a world of fun and pleasure as soon as I grew a bit, walked and talked, and she could help me towards all of that by teaching me the ropes. It did my sister no good to reply that she was never lonely, that she had no wish for this Sherman, and that I didn't look much like a doll or anyone's idea of fun. Worse, I looked incapable of learning anything and cried often, loud, and fretfully. She turned to my mother for a better explanation for my being there, but nothing was offered except my mother's smile, which Simone had seen too often to value. For everything else her mother had a good, plain, honest reason, but on matters of birth or death she remained silent. In my mother's world nobody was born and almost nobody ever died. Those who did *pass on* were spoken of in hushed voices, and rarely before the children. The origins of life and death were dangerous secrets to be kept out of a child's hands, like a sharp pair of scissors. Such secrets might overwhelm a fragile child, as they had so often overwhelmed my mother in her own childhood. To understand this, one must look back to Lilly's early life.

Libby / Lilly

As a child in the years preceding the First World War, my mother, Lillian Yellen, then Libby Horowitz, had watched the agonizing "white death" of her own mother Sarah on the Lower East Side. It was followed by that of an older sister—the beautiful, gentle Rebecca—and that of her tall, handsome brother Sam, both of whom had ended their tubercular lives in a sanatorium in Colorado while in their late teens. These deaths were a bitter lesson in the impermanence of life and the power of a grief that sometimes arose within her like a rogue wave in a calm sea threatening to pull her under. There were days when she felt herself drowning in that grief, unable to catch her breath for the two siblings who would never return, and for the mother she lost when she was twelve.

The child had watched silently, fearfully, as her mother's brow was covered with feverish sweat, the woman coughing fitfully and turning her head into her pillow, hoping to conceal from the children the tiny red pansy stains of blood that spotted her bedding, irrefutable news of her forthcoming death. She was not yet forty, but she was weighed down with the shame of dying young and abandoning her children. Libby was a veteran mourner before she was out of her childhood. Grief had taught her the indestructible nature of love; she would never stop thinking of her mother, or that lost brother and sister, but it had also taught her bitter lessons on the impermanence of life.

She began to feel that her love had put those she most loved in danger; her love needed to be concealed from the angry god of families, who showed no mercy to those who wore their affection or their sorrow openly for everyone to see. The cheerful face she assumed was a mask she forced upon herself to cover her sadness, until it became her true face, her armament against life's betrayals and uncertainties. Lilly's smile, which showed a perfect set of teeth, animated her dark classic beauty and became her signature expression as she grew older, drawing people to her, while allowing her to distance herself from them. "Love me, admire me, yes, yes, that's okay," it advised. "I don't mind that, since you're very nice I'm sure, but not too close, please, I require air and distance." That smile did not invite intimacy. Those who mistakenly assumed that it did, soon learned that her true affection was reserved for the sole use of her surviving family who now needed all of it; what was left over for the world was a genial courtesy. As far as her own needs went, the greatest was for privacy, something she had none of in her youth, sharing a bed with two older sisters and a tiny tenement flat with three brothers. That need for privacy developed in her a respect for the privacy of others, their right to behave in any way they wished, as long as it did not touch upon her own life. This allowed her to accept in others much that was condemned as immoral or irregular in the narrow judgments of the ghetto. How many times as a child I would hear her say, "It's his business." Or, "if she likes doing that, why should we care?" Privacy was the great luxury, and she was determined to obtain it at any price and she knew instinctively that she could not get it without giving it to others.

As a child, Libby/Lilly had maneuvered the crowded streets of the ghetto turning a deaf ear and a blind eye to the coarse cries of the peddlers chanting their second-hand bargains; these angry combatants fighting for the small amount of cash that would get them through another day. She resisted the warm delicious pretzels held up for sale by men in torn woolen gloves, whose grimy fingernails peeped through the frayed finger holes, touching the crust of coarse salt. It was a time when old women with huge goiters could be seen roaming the streets of the ghetto; few had teeth, many had collapsed chins. Scars and warts decorated worn faces. Beggars with mutilated smiles and rasping voices appeared waiting in door-ways. Ugliness ruled. It was the order of the day. This only made true beauty more remarkable and strange and people stared at it with a rudeness usually reserved for looking at the wonder of freaks. Libby/Lilly was the recipient of such stares and she determined to pass through this ramshackle world, filled with dirt and dung and splinters, and remain untouched by it. It would not define her or confine her. She knew she was born to get out of this place and to endure it not a moment longer than necessary.

Unlike the wooden shacks of the rural Russian village she left behind as a child of three, these tenements were made of bricks and mortar, built to last forever in the mid-1860s by skilled German contractors, with stone lions, cherubs, and garlands decorating the facades provided by Sicilian stonecutters who had mastered the art of disguising the narrow airless rooms of the slum within. But to my mother, it all looked like the stone carvings of a graveyard. These were domestic prisons, some with fanciful terra cotta ornaments, cruel mockeries of the uptown brownstones, the better to entrap those who lived crowded within them, stacked in their narrow, airless rooms. Armed with that brilliant smile, my mother kept her eyes open for the way out of this place where grief was forever waiting to ambush you and rob you of your small treasure of hard-earned joy.

She knew she had already escaped the worst that the Old World offered—death by rampaging demons. In Russia, as a child of three, she had hidden in a coal cellar with her family when the Cossacks rode into the village to entertain themselves with a riotous pogrom of looting and rape. She never forgot the impenetrable darkness of that cellar, or the sound of wild, drunken voices above, followed by screams drifting down, or the reassuring pressure of her mother's hand as they waited out the pillage taking place in the world above them. America had to be better. Arriving in New York with her family she soon learned that there were no state-sponsored pogroms here, but there were other, less obvious dangers for a growing girl among a world of strangers.

The crowded streets with the pushcart merchants were her only refuge from the noxious tenement rooms. Walking out in those streets she could not keep people from staring with admiration or speaking rudely, but she didn't have to listen to what she didn't want to hear. This selective deafness was an early habit that lasted her lifetime, entering her DNA so that she passed it on to my sister, Simone. Lilly had quickly learned how to tune out the indecent proposals of strangers who regarded her youthful beauty as an erotic opportunity. What others took for flattery, she regarded as an intrusion. Having miraculously escaped the tuberculosis that cut down those she loved the most, she managed to hold at bay that devouring, monstrous grief that every day threatened to swallow her alive. She trained herself not to think about it. If she could have done so, my mother would have scrubbed her memories with Murphy's Oil Soap until they gleamed like the linoleum on our kitchen floor. But the memories were ineradicable. They were far from spotless. So present were they in her later life that they spilled out of her from time to time, the past unceremoniously breaking in on the here and now. Unlike so many who rose in the world, she was not ashamed of her early poverty. Poverty was the heart of her story and she saw no reason to deny it. When she spoke of her past to her children, it was not as a moral lecture to make us grateful for what we had—she thought we deserved only the best—but as a lesson in the miraculous nature of life, where anything could happen and often did.

Running out of nursery rhymes and picture books as she tried to feed a sickly child with a small, finicky appetite, she told me stories of her past, unedited and unexpurgated, feeling that I would not understand all the parts but I would get the gist of their common moral: get through the bad times and the good times will follow. What she needed was to create an endless flow of talk to distract me from that gruel-laden spoon that I was pushing aside with my quick rebellious tongue, aided by my small, furious, protesting hand. And for this reason, I am now able to recall and preserve so many of these, her recollections.

With her own mother terminally ill by the time she entered public school, my mother's beauty made her the pet of her first grade teacher, Miss Salina Stokes, a "colored woman" teaching in the public school system and assigned to the Lower East Side where it was assumed that no one among the undesirable immigrants would dare object to or even notice her dark skin. When she discovered that there were three Libbys registered in her class, Miss Stokes renamed her polite, attentive new student Lady Lilly. When she learned of the child's dying mother, Miss Stokes treated Lilly with a grave affection and, upon learning that it was her birthday, she gave the grateful child the first and only doll she ever received. It was a blonde rag doll fashioned with a printed cloth head and yellow wool hair, stuffed with cornhusks that crinkled as you squeezed it. The doll wore a long gingham skirt that could be turned over to reveal an upside-down black baby underneath, dressed in a similar outfit but sporting a polka dot headscarf. Lilly saved it for years, but like all the scattered debris of her life it disappeared during one of several moves.

The New York Times and other newspapers of the day often condemned the slums with their hordes of unwashed, diseased Eastern European Jews, brawling drunken Irish, lecherous Italians, and ignorant blacks, calling them public health dangers; miscreants, filthy in body and mind, criminals in the making, and demanded a halt to the new waves of immigration from abroad and up from the South. But this child was no street Arab begging pennies or hard candy of visiting journalists, her face grimy and her hair a nest of lice, the subject of so many editorials to "improve their lot" by diminishing their numbers. She was always well-scrubbed in the kitchen sink by one of the older children and neatly dressed, even in the made-over clothes of her older sister, Rebecca. Until she was thirteen, Lilly had never known the luxury of wearing a dress of her own. Her dark, thick hair was brushed to a silky shine and tortured into long thick curls by one of the women in the family. Before she was sent to Colorado to die, Rebecca, aware that she might never return, restyled her own best dresses for little Libby, the needlework supervised by Tante Mary, a professional dressmaker and a proud divorcée, the one who had worked long hours to bring the Horowitz family over from Russia, knowing that her handsome but feckless younger brother could never accomplish that monumental task on his own.

My mother's clothes were washed and ironed daily by her older sister, Ida, who saw to it that Lilly wore a shiny red satin hair-ribbon to set off her long dark curls as she went off to school. She was the family flagship sent off with the assurance that she could sail with the best of them, *them* being the pampered children of natural-born Americans, forever flaunting their pale, privileged watercolor faces and blonde curls in silent films, newspaper advertisements and illustrated school books, but nowhere to be seen on the Lower East Side.

Thanks to the care of her sisters, there was nothing about this child that declared her a waif of the Jewish ghetto. The admiring Tante Mary told her that if one did not know better, Libby could be the love child of a Brazilian dancer by an Italian Count, or possibly a Frenchie, even the daughter of a Czarina, God forbid. Indeed, she somewhat resembled the young Princess Anastasia. She was, in fact, whatever an admirer chose to read into those enormous dark eyes, the small-sculpted nose, and the perfect oval face. Italians, Germans, Poles, Russians, Irishmen, each spoke to her in their own language, convinced that it was their own homeland that had produced such beauty. The only thing certain about her was that she did not belong there, in that place. And she soon came to accept that as a fact of life.

My mother had little vanity. She rarely looked in a mirror and then only to brush her hair and apply a bit of lipstick, but she knew that her good looks assured her the chance denied to most of her friends, plain girls who would be stuck in factory jobs; girls who still wore the dark woolen immigrant *schmatas* and the downcast expressions born of the Eastern European villages from which they came. At seven, Lilly found her first place of refuge, the local public school. She loved its orderly world and its simple uncomplicated rules—be clean, be quiet, be obedient, and learn. It was a haven from the turmoil of her family, with its constant illness and its ceaseless poverty. She had the secret hope of becoming a grade-school teacher, encouraged in this by Miss Stokes, who found her bright, neat and attentive, and praised her for her superior penmanship and excellent spelling, the sign of a girl with a brilliant future. But once her older brother and sister became ill, there would be no further schooling and the future was compressed into the here and now.

One morning as she was going off to school, her father stopped her and told her that her school days were over. Everyone old enough to push a broom or sew a button would be obliged to work to help pay for the Colorado sanatorium. The dying, but ever hopeful, Rebecca sent her favorite younger sister weekly postcards filled with tidbits about life at the "San," sending regards to friends—"tell Selma Segal I've taken my autograph book with me to Colorado and I laugh at what she wrote in it"—and offering advice to the child—"be nice but not too nice. You can't be better than the world and survive."

The last card Lilly would receive stated that Rebecca was so happy. She had been allowed to see their brother Sam at a birthday party for one of the inmates and, best of all, with a reduction in their fevers they were permitted to go unmasked, so they could look at each other's faces and brush their flushed cheeks against each other for the first time in months. Rebecca died a week later and brilliant, handsome Sam followed her to the grave within the month, taking with them my mother's youth.

After the funerals and the gravestones were paid for, there was little left over for the living. Though their world was cheap, it was still too expensive for the Horowitz family, sinking deeper and deeper into poverty. Miss Stokes came to the tenement to find out if Lilly was sick and, if not, why she had not attended school for weeks. She was met by a wall of Russian speaking relatives, all frightened of government authority, all shrugging, looking confused, and saying nothing, using their confusion as a declaration of their innocence. Lilly was out of the flat on a shopping mission and when she arrived a half-hour later she discovered that the concerned teacher had refused to leave before speaking with her. Miss Stokes asked her to return to school. She would give her special tutoring to make up for the lost time. The child's face revealed her longing to go back to class, but her words made it clear that there was no way for her to continue with her education. There were laws to keep a child in school, Miss Stokes warned, but they both knew that such laws did not apply to the Lower East Side. My mother told me that for the first time she wept for her future, surprised by her own tears, which were formerly reserved for the past. But she knew she was needed at home and there was nothing to be done about it. As the schoolbooks taught, you should not cry over spilt milk, and her education like her childhood was certainly that. Gone, hopelessly spilled, with no looking backwards.

When the family had to deal with the rent or the butcher, a job that had been Rebecca's, it was Lilly who was now sent to accomplish the task. Her older sister, Ida, looked like an Asian peasant with her high Tartar cheekbones and yellowish skin; clearly some Mongol horseman had had his way with some Horowitz woman in Russia generations before, rendering Ida's looks of no use in an emergency. Her cracked voice and sing-song speech had no appeal; her smile, which revealed a jumble of crooked overlapping teeth, was worthless currency in an emergency.

It was Lilly who was sent to beg time from the rent collector, Otto Miller, an old German Jewish immigrant famous for his melodramatic heartlessness. It was as if he had patterned his cruelty on stage performances of villains he had enjoyed in Yiddish theater, and his refusals were well-rehearsed performances. He would hear no excuses for unpaid rent and would quickly turn a wretched family out of a tenement flat into the street (along with infants, cast iron beds and torn bedding), deaf to all appeals. Families standing stunned on the sidewalk amidst their few belongings, carrying the latest bawling infant in their arms, were known in the neighborhood as "Miller's people." Some claimed that he was heartless so no one would suspect he was a Jew. Lilly alone could ask for an extra week to find the money for the rent, and he could not turn down her request. "This time only, little girl, this time only," he warned, time and again, unable to refuse her.

When the family was too broke to buy meat, she would be sent to the butcher's shop to beg scraps for the "dog," a time honored ruse which the butcher easily saw through.

"Who do you think you're talkin' to, girlie?" the butcher asked derisively, educating her on the fine points of lying to a butcher.

"You tell me you got a nice clean cat to keep down the mice in the flat, understand? I can believe in a cat, especially if you give it a name. Call it Goldie. Yes, Goldie, that's a good name for a cat. But you're telling me it's for a dumb dog? A *meshuggah hundt*, never! What kind of story is that, child? Dogs are useless. No Jew likes dogs! Worse, no dog likes Jews! Why should I give anything to a worthless anti-Semitic beast? Here they call him man's best friend. For what man is he a friend? No man I know!" The butcher went on to advise her that hounds were the known companion of the peasant anti-Semites in all parts of the Pale of Settlement (that part of Czarist Russia where the Jews were permitted to live). Nevertheless, the butcher always gave her the unsold kidneys and the leftover calf's liver for the hungry "Goldie," and the chopped beef which had turned too brown for sale to sharp-eyed housewives, as well as the soup bones from which her older sister, Ida, would make a tasteless but nourishing meal.

For a short time, Lilly helped Tante Mary in her dressmaking business, her sharp young eyes threading needles for the older woman and sorting out the various colored spools of cotton thread and buttons to match the gowns on which the proud, stout, magnificently corseted woman worked. The Tante attempted to teach her the trade, but she soon saw that the girl had no gift for needlework; she was constantly pricking her fingers and making stitches that wandered aimlessly across a hem as she daydreamed, forcing the Tante to go over her work, undoing the uneven stitches and sighing deeply, "You better stick to darning the holes in socks and looking pretty," an assessment followed by a wet kiss on her cheek. Wet kisses were the currency of family love in those days.

Lilly was a tall child for her age, growing rapidly, showing curves that no twelve-year old could safely possess. It was a fact well noted by the Tante as she surveyed the young girl's body, for which she fashioned a makeshift remedy: an elastic bust binder topped by a boned corset to conceal the burgeoning breast problem. But the corset only thrust the bosom outward, defying the Tante's camouflage. Try as she would, it was impossible to conceal the young girl's maturing beauty. Determined to make good but respectable use of the child's undeniable assets, Tante Mary had her model dresses for her private clientele, those who made appointments for a fitting, not the off-the-street people, the drop-ins who climbed up the rickety wooden staircase to the second floor; clients who were regarded suspiciously by the Tante as uninvited guests who had crashed her exclusive dressmaking party. When she was not showing off the Tante's finely tailored garments, Lilly was put to work folding bolts of cloth, measuring trimmings, sorting buttons, and delivering packages to the paying customers, many of whom had prospered, moved uptown from the Lower East Side, but still came downtown for their clothes.

One day Lilly delivered a dress to a woman who lived in the West Eighties off Riverside Drive. Upon answering the door, the woman stared at her for a long time, saying nothing, then took her by the shoulders to draw her nearer, grabbed her face in her hands, studied it long and hard, pinched her cheeks and shouted, "Are you real? You're too pretty to be real. Too pretty, Miss Pretty. That's a face. A real face you got there." This had been said to her before, too often to surprise or flatter her, but never with such peculiar gusto. The woman told her that she should not waste such beauty delivering parcels for a Lower East Side seamstress. My mother grew suspicious. She had been warned about white slavers who lured you with flattery and promises of high-paying work and then shipped you off to South America to be lost forever in a brothel where you would die alone of some terrible disease.

The woman made her meaning clear. Lilly, should work as a showroom model for a dress wholesaler, assuring her that there was good money to be made that way for a girl with her looks. The buyers liked to see the clothes they ordered worn by a pretty young woman. And this girl looked good in all the bright colors, red, blue, yellow, even Kelly green, which no Jew could possibly wear. All she had to do was walk and smile, and she saw that the girl had a talent for both. The woman took a few steps backwards, surveying the girl. "You're a perfect ten," she claimed. That was the model size in those generously proportioned days. The woman would ask her husband to give the girl a modeling job in their dress business. The salary was an amazing forty-five dollars a week, more than twice what Lilly's own father earned as a night watchman, but of course it meant that she had to help out in the stock room by packing and taping down boxes for shipment when buyers were not visiting the showroom. Nobody had one job in those days, not even the boss who worked alongside his stockroom boys when shipments were made.

When Lilly returned to Tante Mary and reported what had happened, the Tante agreed that this was a fine opportunity, but she cautioned her niece to tell no one her real age. She was not yet thirteen but she must pass for a wised-up sixteen; moreover, she must never tell anyone outside the family what she was doing for a living. "Anyone asks you, you tell them you're a stockroom clerk." Stupid people might misunderstand and, misunderstanding, gossip if they discovered that she was working as a model, confusing her with those wicked girls who took off their clothes for lascivious artists and lay about languorously on velvet sofas, rather than Lilly, who would be virtuously putting on clothes for respectable customers and walking about, back straight, legs turning, and showing her excellent posture.

More important, she was to let no man see her in her undergarments as she changed outfits in the back room, and she was to avoid all unnecessary contact with those lousy bosses who employed her; the most dangerous threat to a girl was from those closest at hand. If any impropriety was attempted, she was to leave work at once and report it to Tante Mary who could deal with it by confronting the man and brandishing her enormous walking stick with its lethal carved ivory lion's head handle. The older woman demonstrated her outrage in a practice run, threatening some invisible masher as Tante Mary drilled into Lilly's young mind the necessity of saying, "Stop it! No more of that! I will tell my Tante Mary, a large and violent woman who is happily married to an angry Irish policeman," a limited but useful threat if delivered in a firm, loud voice within earshot of strangers.

Before she was thirteen, Lilly bobbed her hair in her effort to look older; she learned how to apply lipstick so that it filled out her thin upper lip, she brushed rouge in her soft olive cheeks, powdered her short, straight nose and weeded her dark eyebrows to a perfect curve with her dead sister's eyebrow tweezers. Now plucked, buffed and polished, she was ready for the great world.

Her first job didn't last long. Her employer's business failed within a month of her being there, but she easily found work in another showroom. She was soon modeling gowns in various showrooms and dress shops in the newly flourishing garment district during the years of World War I, sometimes helping to sell fashionable clothing, but eager to end her modeling days. It was one thing to be admired by strangers in the street, quite another to put yourself forward so that people praised you. Like many natural beauties she thought beauty overrated because she had it in abundance, found it wanting, and wished for more than admiration. What more she was yet to discover, but certainly more than the witless stares and stale praise that her appearance provoked. She wanted a family of her own to replace the lost ones, and a husband she could depend upon so that their children would be safe from sorrow in a dangerous world. Hers was a seven-year apprenticeship; then at twenty years old she was offered the job of a retail clothing store manager on Broadway in the theater district, an enormous step upwards in earning and responsibility. The absentee owner regarded her as a great asset in a street of competing shops. The war was over; it was a time of celebration and general prosperity. And she, Lilly, knew that she looked like the girls in the magazines, those who advertised cigarettes and automobiles. That she was poor and struggled to add and subtract numbers did not inhibit her. With her small, straight nose, large dark eyes, and ten fingers on her hands, she knew she could get by. Beauty allowed her to make choices that birth and circumstances would not. By the time she was twenty, it brought her romance, and four years later marriage, but not together.

Harris, the Handsome Intern

When my mother's youngest brother, Ally Horowitz, an angry, fractious terrier of a boy, was injured in a Stanton Street gang fight one Saturday afternoon, a fight where flying fists were quickly replaced by bites, kicks and lunging pocket knives and the jagged edges of broken glass bottles, he was cut deeply on his forearm, bleeding profusely as he ran home to his sister Lilly to be patched up. When she could not staunch the bleeding, she wrapped the wounded arm tightly in a clean kitchen towel and rushed him to the emergency room of Bellevue Hospital in the first taxi she had ever taken. It was there, she told me, that she first met a handsome young intern, Harris Goldfarb, a blond Jew with blue eyes and those long eyelashes that everyone declared were "wasted on a boy." Harris cleaned the wound with a stinging witch hazel, lavishly painted the cuts with a burning iodine, finished it off with a splash of mercurochrome, stitched whatever torn flesh needed stitching, wrapped the arm in bandages, and packed ice on the boy's bruised face, devoting far more time to the wounds of the penniless miscreant than hospital policy dictated.

Harris could hardly keep his eyes on the bleeding boy and off his beautiful older sister. She was perhaps a few pounds heavier than the current fashion in svelte flapper perfection, but as he told her later, her looks might have carried her onto the silent screen if she aimed in that direction. When he heard she was a showroom model he told her she should be advertising cigarettes and Packard motorcars in magazines, not wasting her beauty on buyers in showrooms. A moviemaker would see her picture and offer her a contract. He assured her that this had happened to others and it could happen to her. She was every bit as lovely as the late Olive Thomas; indeed she closely resembled the young film star who had recently died in Paris, the reports saying that she had mistakenly taken some poison, although he believed she was a suicide. He loved Olive Thomas pictures. Did she? Lilly did, but she was tired of men telling her she should be in moving pictures and that she resembled so-and-so. Theatrical aspirations required a mind filled with vanities, not the necessities that filled her day, and suggested loose morals, while she knew her own to be spotless and firm. A few flirtatious photographs of her teen years survive but they were rare expressions of the playfulness that leads to a theatrical career or a love affair with the camera. With her large dark eyes looking mischievously at the world, thumb coyly resting in mouth and pushing out a pouting lower lip, she reveals a young girl's imitation flirtation with the lens; an imitation of seductive playfulness, not the real thing. A moment of fun snatched from the everyday reality of life.

My mother and Harris soon walked together in Central Park on one of his rare days off, and Harris held her arm gently as he guided her through the park, leading her to a bench near the Bethesda Fountain, where they sat and talked about their past lives. Or, at least, he spoke of his, for he was a great talker and not much of a listener. No more than five-foot-seven, an inch taller than she was, when seated he could look directly into her eyes as he spoke and she liked that. It kept him on her level, one she could control. Most of the small men she had known were scrappy and difficult to control, but Harris was so personable, educated and interesting as he talked about himself and his dreams of a great career in medicine. He never asked her about herself, which was all right with her. She took no pride in where she lived and what she had suffered. It was too painful to be interesting and she saw no good in sharing her pain with an admirer. Only good news and big plans were interesting. This was what the world wanted, and she had little of this to offer.

Harris assured her that he was heading for a successful practice in dermatology, the medicine of the future. As my mother recalled it years later, he mixed his praise for her with praise for his prospects. "Not all women have your perfect skin," he told her. "So, Lilly, Doctor Harris Goldfarb will be there to deal with the splotches and the pimples and the rashes that plague your average well-to-do woman today. They eat too many sweets, drink too many cordials. Worst of all they smoke cigarettes. All of it is murder on the skin. Murder," he continued. "More accurately, epidermal suicide. There's big money in it," he assured her. "Big!" And he had big plans to get that big money. He would not be one to waste his talents on impoverished patients in a clinic, or sitting by bedsides watching fevers rise and fall as he rubbed alcohol soaked towels on sweaty heads. He was planning to establish his practice on Park Avenue, where the faces of the rich would come to him for soothing lotions and expensive repairs. He himself had perfect skin, except for a small mole at the side of his left eye that, strangely, only made him better looking for it. He cut a handsome figure, dressed in well-fitting suits and a check jazz-bow, the newly fashionable bow ties that only the smart-looking men wore. You could see at once that his clothes were his alone, no hand-me-downs from a father or older brother.

Arriving at the movie, Harris paid for her ticket and, once safely inside the dark theater, he held her hand. On their second date he surprised her by kissing her lips just as the heroine of the movie was being kissed, stirring within her feelings that she could not enjoy *because* she enjoyed them, suspected them, and felt unsafe in their presence. He didn't seem to mind her lack of response, considering it a sign of her inexperience, a guarantee of her virtue. There were nurses galore in the hospital for his other needs. He wanted her as she was— innocent, naïve, *spotless*. Harris courted her whenever he was free from the long hours of his internship, and a month later he told her that he wanted to marry her. It was not a proposal but a statement of intent. They would someday marry, but that could not happen for at least four years. He would first have to establish himself in a medical practice.

"You'll wait for me?" he asked rhetorically, knowing she would.

"No. I don't have time for waiting," she replied, astonishing him with her flat-out, unromantic refusal.

"But I love you" he protested, stunned by her refusal. Wasn't he good looking? A doctor? The waking dream of every immigrant Jewish family? Not just his own proud mother, but the Irish nurses in the hospital and the girls in his Brooklyn neighborhood had made him aware of his attractions, and he had every reason to believe that Lilly should feel the same rush of pleasure that he felt when he saw himself in the mirror. He challenged her to tell him how she felt about him, sure that she would confess her hidden passion and *that* would put an end to her absurd rejection. Getting his way was his way.

"I don't know what I feel," my mother replied. "I only know that in four years who knows what *you'll* be feeling. Worse, in four years who knows what I'll be doing? I can't live another four years as I've been living. I want a family of my own. Children, not customers."

"We can be engaged," he offered. My mother told him about her friend, Muriel Levy, who had been engaged for three years to a young lawyer, helping him pay his way through law school, and the feckless fiancé who, upon passing the bar, passed Muriel as well, marrying a legal stenographer he had recently met. Long engagements were for romantic fools and she, Lilly, was no fool.

Harris protested that he was no philandering attorney but she could not be persuaded. More pressing than her need for love was her desire to start a fresh life in a new place, where the complaints of the living and the cries of the dying would be distant memories, lost in new sights and new sounds. She needed more than hope and promises and romance. She needed a clean, well-tiled bathroom of her own, not some stuffed up hole in a tenement hallway that made her retch every time she approached it. She needed fresh air and tree-lined streets, free from the noxious odors of unwashed peddlers and rotting vegetables. She needed a lover who would not ask her to wait any longer. And she needed it *now*.

Her reckless brothers were growing up in ways that she could not control. Ally seemed devoid of any moral sense; for him right was what he could get away with and wrong was what happened when he got caught. All the sweet nature that had belonged to the dead older brother, Sam, had gone into little Frankie, together with a blinking right eye that marred his natural good looks. They both required a strong, controlling hand, one that could not be offered by their father.

Meyer was a handsome, placid night watchman and janitor who swept a bit with a stiff straw broom and slept a lot while guarding a factory at night, and by day dreamed stupidly of a lost Russia where he had served with distinction in the Czar's army. Being a Jew, he had been taunted by his superior officers and was denied a commission. This, more than anything, had driven him to emigrate, aided in this by his sister Mary. Misfortune had been his loyal companion for the past thirty years. The promise of a better life in America had not been kept, but he did not blame the new country. He blamed himself for "buying a bill of goods" from the fools in Russia who told such ridiculous stories about life in New York. He felt his life no better here than in Minsk, where at least he was surrounded by friends and family, and failure was expected, not scorned. And here, in America, he had suffered so many losses—incomprehensible ones, if one was to believe in a just god, for those taken had been good and kind and beautiful. But how could one believe in any other kind of god? Surely there was a higher meaning to his misfortune. But whatever it was, that meaning eluded him, and he became more religious in his efforts to suppress his doubts.

At home the man wept between prayers for his dead wife of twenty years who had ruled the family with grace and a stern affection. When not asleep or in prayer, he poured over his copy of the *Jewish Daily Forward*, his only comfort being the misery of his fellow immigrants. In the evenings at dinner he gave thanks to the God who had taken his beloved wife and two eldest children in the hope that the Almighty might pass his surviving children by with this show of unquestioning acceptance. "Enough, Lord, enough!" Lilly had once heard him cry out in the middle of a prayer shortly after he learned of his son Sam's death. It was the closest he ever came to protest.

She loved her father's wonderful calm consistency. He never smiled, never laughed, never raised his voice to her, never hit her, never cursed her, always struggled and always failed to put enough food on the table. She watched as he turned to God for answers to questions his dull mind could not even formulate. In her school years he signed her report cards without looking at them, unable to read the English reports with their praise of his child. But after her mother died, he seemed like a silent boarder in his own tenement flat, hopelessly confused by his failed life. He was not like some of the other refuge men, fathers of friends who absconded from their families in disgrace, driven up North or out West by their shame when they failed to provide for their families properly. Lillian understood that her father would stay put, but would always be pushed about by a fate he could not control; a man who lived for the plain meals that Ida, his homely married daughter, prepared for him on a one-burner stove from her own flat above, while my mother provided the extra cash she earned through her modeling jobs and through the small commissions she now made from clothing sales in the Broadway store she managed.

The Arrival of Nat

S hortly after she refused the engagement of Harris Goldfarb, my mother was introduced to my father, Nat Yellen, by her public school friend, Muriel Levy. It was the lawyer-abandoned Muriel who told her about Nat Yellen, a showroom salesman with a high salary working for George Washington Knitwear, a large manufacturer of wholesale woolens for children. This Nat was a good-natured and fun-loving guy, a jokester, a catch, twenty-eight years old, without a known girlfriend and looking for a wife. Nat, Muriel explained, had already taken an interest in Lilly. It had all come about by chance.

Nat was standing on a street corner, conversing with Muriel one early Saturday night, when he saw Lilly emerging from the Canal Street subway on her way home from work. He watched her greet Muriel with a brilliant smile and a friendly wave of her kid-gloved hand, one that indicated, "I'd love to stop and chat but I'm too busy to stop now." As soon as she disappeared from view, he asked if she was single, and that Muriel arrange an introduction to her friend for him. Muriel cautioned him that Lilly was out of his reach, this was clearly a future doctor or lawyer's wife, but he insisted that Muriel do her best.

"Just give me a chance," he pleaded.

"Okay, but you're wasting your time," she warned him.

Muriel went to the Horowitz flat and showed Lilly Nat's recent photograph taken with a group of friends while cavorting at the beach, announcing, "This is the man for you, Lil. I know… I know he doesn't photograph well," Muriel explained, "but he's smart as a whip, funny as hell, and he's got a good heart. Kind? They don't make 'em any kinder. The man's a Jewish saint. He's the oldest son of a big family, been working his tail off since he was ten years old to support this no good family with a lazy gambler father and a hump-back mother who never stops breeding, and he never complains. And to top it all, he still managed to get himself graduated from High School with honors in writing."

Lilly studied the photograph. His gaunt face looked intelligent. His ears stuck out a bit more than necessary, but not alarmingly. His nose was large and curved, but well-shaped, a good, strong, assertive nose, and his beanpole body with its narrow sloping shoulders and long bony legs seemed ascetic, unassertive and comically likeable in the tank top bathing suit. There was none of Harris's vanity and muscular sensuality about him but, of course, that would have been impossible. His receding hairline, hawk nose and shy smile did not attract her but it did not repel her. And best of all, he looked spotless. The teeth were white and straight, set in a nice, shy smile. He was well-shaved, well-combed, and well-manicured. It was clear to her that he made the best of what little he had in the way of looks; he had not surrendered as some might to the bad hand that nature had dealt to him. She would think about it. But it could only be a group meeting, not a formal date, she insisted. On second thought, no, not even that. This was a man longing for love. It was written all over his gentle, homely face. He was one catch it would be hard to toss back should she decide she did not want him in her life.

A week later, Muriel showed Lilly a thank you note written by Nat in appreciation of her failed attempt to arrange the meeting. The grammar was good, the sentiment refined, the spelling was dictionary perfect, but it was the handwriting that won my mother's consent to a meeting. This was no faltering immigrant scrawl, but a polished, elegant hand, the kind she had seen in school books as penmanship models, the kind of writing she had mastered herself with great effort but to a lesser effect. His was an undisputed American-born handwriting, fit for the signature on an engraving on a dollar bill, not an ink spot anywhere to spoil the flawless rhythm of its line. Her own pretty penmanship with its round, giddy loops was nothing compared to Nat Yellen's perfectly proportioned copperplate letters. Muriel joked that theirs would be the mating of two fine handwritings and, best of all, his was the signature of a great artist but without the burden of an artistic temperament that might drag him down in the world. This man was going places and a smart woman would go along with him. Everyone said he was sure to own his own business in a few years. Muriel swore she would try to get him for herself if he wasn't so smitten with Lilly, calling her "that Jewish Venus emerging from the subway sea."

Lilly's first meeting with Nat confirmed the obvious. He was no Harris Goldfarb, but he was polite, modest, well-dressed down to the gray spats that covered the tops of his highly shined brown shoes, and to her astonishment he asked her about herself and her family, a rarity among the men she had met who, after first acknowledging how pretty they found her, went on to talk only of themselves as if she had been waiting a lifetime to hear their story. He spoke little about his own life, as if it had just begun with their meeting, and hung on her every word as she told him about her living brothers and sisters and her dead Sam and Rebecca. When he learned of her mother's death and that of her brother and sister, he lowered his voice theatrically, made a sympathetic tsk tsk sound with his tongue (a bit exaggerated, but it reflected true sympathy), and he told her how sorry he was for her losses, that she had suffered much, but that life would be better for her in the future, you only had to look at her to know that.

"So, now you're a fortune teller?" Lilly asked, so trapped in her present that she had little time to think about her future.

"No. But it doesn't take a gypsy to know that you are going to have a good life. You're a good and beautiful woman. Why should it be otherwise?"

Despite his encroaching bald pate, which he attempted to cover with the remaining strands of black hair (optimistically doused with Vitalis hair oil), despite his large, thin, aquiline nose and the slightly protruding green-gray eyes, his was a genial face, intelligent and kind. A pleasant face. If not a hero's, that of the hero's best friend. The genial character actor who stands by the heroine in her misfortunes when the no-good hero has gone off and betrayed her. She quickly appreciated him for his natural good humor, his quick mind, his genuine sympathy for another's pain, but most of all, for his resolute ambition.

This man was no dreamer. He told her that for years he had been saving towards owning his own business, and although it had taken him longer than he liked — having his family obligations — he was only a few years away from meeting his goal of ten thousand dollars in savings — an enormous sum — enough to start a wholesale sweater business with the right partner of his own. He was tired of bosses who did not take his advice. Jacquard designs were in. You had only to go to the department stores, as he did once a week, to study the newest styles and know what was selling—yet his boss had refused to make them or any of the novelty items he had suggested. You had to keep up with the current fashions; better yet, anticipate them. He would stay ahead of the competition, for to stand still was to fail. Owning his own business, he could profit from his awareness of trends in fashion. "You go to the movies," he told her, "and see what the actresses are wearing. You look about you in the streets and see what your average working girl has on." Turtle necks? Crew necks? V necks? Sweater sets with pearlized buttons like they make in Scotland, Jacquard sweaters with matching skirts like they showed in the fashion magazines, it was all there to profit from if you cared to look and learn. He took her to Gimbels Department Store and pointed out the sweaters that would sell and those that would soon end up in the half-price sales bin. She admired his enthusiasm for his work and his knowledge of his business. He could point to any sweater and tell her the exact amount of wool it took to make the garment, the quality of the wool, its wholesale cost, and its retail value.

Added to this expertise, he was as neat as he appeared in his photograph, spotless. In the weeks he courted her, she never saw him without that close shave, topped with a scented talcum powder finish that made his face pale and his hazel eyes seem darker. He always had a manicure that gave his nails fine shiny white spotless moons, and the soft well-shaped hands of a thinking man, fingers fit for page turning, sure signs that he was prepared for whatever challenge the world would present. His brown pin-striped suit was neatly pressed and the crease in his fedora was just so, his patterned silk tie neatly knotted and showing no food stains; he wore a gold tie clip with his initials NY on it, and carried a matching money clip that was stretched wide with dollar bills that graduated in value from singles to twenties. Sharing his initials with the city of his birth somehow made him all the more pleasing, a man in tune with his world. He had a warm American voice, and a shy way of looking at her that she found disarming in its silent adoration. All the admiration of the world was in that look, all the desire to protect her and honor her. It was the adoring look the Beast gave to Beauty in the illustrated storybook that her teacher Miss Stokes had given to her years before. It could break your heart if you let it do so. She realized after a short time that she liked him, trusted him, and enjoyed his company, but she would not be pushed into marriage. She knew she did not love him, though she believed that she should have, if she was only a better person.

Although Nat did not make her forget Harris, or the past with its ineradicable sorrows, he was a master salesman and he sold her a future at a terrific discount. She could have safety, prosperity and privacy married to him, and it was not necessary for her to give him romantic love in exchange for all that or make declarations of affection that she did not feel. Children loomed large in her mind. She wanted children of her own, children who would have a childhood that was denied to her on the day she was forced to leave grammar school and the loving attention of Miss Stokes. What did it matter that she did not love him the way people loved each other in the movies, the way she had almost loved Harris? Her life would be a bridge to the future; her children would live lives that were larger, freer, more accomplished than any that she or her husband could contemplate. Her children would know a happiness she had only briefly glimpsed before death had taken those she loved the most. Her children would be bright and talented but, if necessary, she would make sure they could afford to be fools. She would make certain that they would be immortal, guarded against the rough world by love and well-scrubbed rooms and plenty of money. Money mattered. She was no gold digger, she knew that, but she needed a man who could insulate her and her future family against the bad luck that came into everyone's life, and especially into the lives of those poor who could least afford it.

When Nat told her about his plans, she understood that this man would make something of himself, and she could make more of that something if she helped him. Best of all, he was no greenhorn. The oldest son of Russian Jews who had emigrated to America after a long stopover in London before the turn of the century, he, their eldest was born in America in 1899, and he wore his casual American ways—that relentless ambition and optimism—with an appealing ease. But she had doubts. He needed too much from her. He was constantly trying to please her in ways she found annoying. He felt that he must amuse her, and she disliked being amused, and she sensed an anger coexisting with his sweetness, an anger that would need a tight rein on it. There was an extravagance to this man that surprised and sometimes confused her. His stories were exaggerations with a punch line. Even his sneezes were larger than life; huge sneezes, demanding an immediate "God bless you!" in order to give them the recognition they deserved.

Lillian suspected that she would soon marry Nat, but she soon discovered that there was a shadow hanging over this otherwise decent man—that of his family, the abominable Yellens. When she learned their story, it was like a dark fairy tale in which my father—the child hero—had suffered greatly. It was clear from what he let slip as he spoke of them, that *they* lacked all that *she* valued—pride, kindness and truthfulness—qualities that abounded in her own family, even in her renegade younger brother. After Nat's terrible childhood, one of exploitation and abuse, she would be obliged to be his happy ending, and it placed a burden on her that she had not been prepared to carry.

The Prince of Pinochle

When my father, Nathaniel Barnett Yellen, was born at the turn of the century, in the seventh month of his mother Esther's pregnancy, it was thought that the baby would not live and, if he did, he would forever be a burden to his parents — scrawny, fretful, perpetually hungry, and assuredly doomed to a tiny coffin. Isaac and Esther Yellen, a young married couple who had emigrated from Russia by way of England to New York's Lower East Side, had hoped for the best, while expecting the worst. The problem was not, as one might have thought, the infant's weight — a mere four pounds. It was the infant's nose. It was inordinately large. So large, my father told me, that it dominated the tiny, red, screaming, shrunken face. And such a nose, if not a birth defect, bordered on the far side of normalcy and spoke of trouble ahead. How would those miniature lips grab the mother's teat when the small, sharp scimitar hung over the lips and blocked the door to nourishment and life?

Esther soon learned to manipulate the obstruction, to pull the nose up gently, pressing the soft tip upwards with her finger, thus allowing a clear passage for the buttonhole mouth to seize her nipple and greedily suck. And so Nathan lived. As he grew and flourished, the large nose found its way into an otherwise commonplace face and, though conspicuous, it was not so outstanding that it could not be called Roman or noble and the new parents were pleased when, at last, their son could be regarded as strong featured but nondescript. He might be teased as "Nate the Nose" growing up, but he would live to tell the tale.

Handsome but diminutive Isaac's surprising marriage to the hump-backed Esther Slavin resulted from a vow he had taken in his native Russia upon being refused in marriage by the local village beauty, Tovah Gerstein. As he lay on his deathbed, having lived a century of life, he enjoyed retelling the story of his marriage. When Tovah rudely dismissed his offer, stating that he had no prospects, that he was a not-so-secret gambler and, worst of all, though handsome enough — with those large green eyes and excellent even white teeth — at five-foot-one he was far too short for her five-foot-five beauty. She would not spend her life looking down on a tiny tailor, the source of mocking smiles among the villagers.

"I won't marry a little Jewish thimble," she said, rejecting him disdainfully. Isaac replied that her refusal was of no importance to him. "I don't love you. The only reason I asked was that my dear mother just died, and I felt it was time to marry." The advantages of marriage—the cooked meals and bedtime companion—had finally outweighed the solitary pleasures of his bachelorhood. Isaac hated cooking, but he loved eating, a conundrum that could only be solved by marriage. As for other pleasures—ones he infrequently purchased in a local brothel—he preferred to confine such pleasure to his own clean bed. While making love to a prostitute in Minsk, he had seen a large red roach crawling along the floor marching toward the bed, and it had quite interfered with his pleasure. Any clean woman would do for his purposes now. He announced to one and all that "I'll marry the next unmarried woman who comes into my shop or God strike me dead."

As luck would have it—and with Isaac it rarely would—into that shop on tiny birdlike steps skipped Esther Slavin, the humpbacked daughter of Asher Slavin, the village cantor and sometimes blacksmith. Esther was carrying her mother's old black woolen dress that was to be taken in and made over for Esther for the High Holy Days. This in itself was something of a scandal, because the Slavins were known to be people of substance. Esther's mother had been the daughter of a lumber mill manager who had progressed to mill owner, and the Slavins could well afford a new holiday gown for Esther. The Slavin family claimed that Esther's hump was the consequence of the infant Esther having been stung by a poisonous spider while placed on the grass by a careless relative, and it was generally agreed that the burden she carried behind her would keep any man from loving her. And without a great dowry—in her case, any dowry—she was doomed to a spinster's celibacy.

With her crooked little body balanced on two small, skinny legs, her strong curved beak of a nose, set between tiny, bright and bulging black eyes, and her gleaming black hair, Esther was as close to a small, shiny feathered crow as could be found in a young woman. It was a rather pretty crow, as crows go, sleek and clean, but still a crow. That ornithological resemblance was only enhanced by the feather boa her mother forced her to wear at all times, in the mistaken belief that it concealed the odious hump but instead looked like a set of wings folded before flight.

At twenty, Esther had settled into the life of the permanently unmarried daughter in her parent's comfortable home. In Little Minsk, a God who kept careful accounts did not regard such an affliction as hers as an accident of birth or the random mischief of venomous spiders, but a judgment upon the sins of the family. Rumors abounded about the dubious piety of the Slavin family. Despite Asher's soaring, operatic cantorial chants, it was reported that shortly before the birth of Esther, Asher had been seen conversing with the local priest, Father Thomas, famous as a spoiler of Jews with his secret Salvation mongering. Worse yet, Asher Slavin had been far too familiar with the married women of the congregation. He was known as a winker, a laugher, a cajoler, a hand patter, preening before the female world with his luxurious red beard and that soft velvety voice of his, sure to attract the admiration of some foolish women, but more certain to attract the wrath of God Almighty.

Isaac was true to his word. He approached the bride's parents, made his offer, and was accepted at once by the astonished couple who could not determine at first if this was an act of madness or some vile jest of the little tailor's. But whatever it was, it must be snatched first and examined later. They would be losing the daughter who was a source of shame and comfort to them, an unpaid household worker who rarely complained of her lot in life, but her very acceptance of her lot was a reproach to her parents. Asher made it clear to the suitor that there would be no dowry. "We never thought she would marry so nothing was put away for her," he explained. "You want her? Then you take her as she is. Your passion, if that's what you call such craziness, will not impoverish us."

Isaac agreed that he would marry Esther without a dowry. And so Esther brought to her marriage neither a rough linen sheet or a dinner plate or a gold coin. The local gossips noted that if not for those selfish parents, there would be a remarkable array of household goods for the young couple to begin their married life; gold-rimmed dishes of the finest German porcelain, not just your dinner and dessert plates for twelve, but a grand array of embossed gold leaf covered serving dishes, meat platters, and soup tureens, undulating silver teapots, and dainty tea cups, accompanied by large crystal goblets, cut so deep and so fine, that the light caught their prisms like so many African diamonds, casting rainbows around any room where they were placed. "One could be blinded by such goblets," Rebecca Levy, a neighbor, exclaimed after having once been shown the goblets by Esther's mother, who held one up to the window, spit on it, polished it with the skirt of her woolen dress, and claimed that she would go to her grave content in the knowledge that these goblets would never be used.

And so the Slavin treasures had come down through the years, cradled in sawdust in their original wooden packing crate from the bride's grandparents, people of wealth and importance, owners of forests and lumberyards, before they had been killed in a pogrom by Cossacks, hate being the great leveler among the Jews. They had hidden their treasure far better than they had hidden themselves. There was the silk bedding, if not all silk, cotton so fine and shining that it might have been spun for a Czarina's pillow sham. Although none of this would be offered to Esther, Asher Slavin and his wife did not stint at the wedding feast. Wine was imported from Moscow and the bride's gown was made from a stiffened white satin, so that it appeared to have a life of its own, an orthopedic casing for the deformed bride rather than a dress to reveal her beauty. Alas, her vigilant mother tossed the white feather boa over Esther's hump just moments before the bride marched down the aisle. The mocking Tovah Gerstein said that Isaac, married to that *meeskite*, would never need a pillow; he could rest his tiny handsome head on his bride's commodious hump. People laughed, but nobody was more surprised than Tovah when weeks later she found herself lying in a pool of sweat on her own drenched pillow, dying of typhoid fever after a trip to Poland to visit her married sister. Nobody had ever warned her that God preferred to tell the cruel jokes and punished those who intruded upon his prerogatives.

A few weeks after the wedding, Esther asked her husband to approach her father in the hope that he would reconsider the dowry question. "How would it hurt them to give us a few plates? A couple of goblets?"

Isaac did as Esther asked and Cantor Slavin brusquely explained that these would never go to Esther while her parents lived.

"What kind of fool do you take me for? We all know about the vow you took. You married my poor daughter because she happened to pass through your door that day. How long will you honor that vow? It is one thing to marry a woman because you fear the wrath of God, but how long will you stay with her? Will you abandon her when you think that God is not looking and take the precious plates and goblets with you?"

My grandfather told me that it was then that he decided to leave Russia and settle in England, where his second cousin, one David Jacob Seltzer, had established himself as a tailor in St. Charles's Lane in the East End of London. D. J. Seltzer—"King of cuffs and collars," as he announced himself to customers—offered Isaac a place in his shop, his own window to work in (albeit a back window facing a narrow alleyway, but a window nonetheless), his own sewing machine, and a chance to make something of himself if he only followed the pattern that Seltzer himself had cut for success: diligence, thrift and abstinence from all drink, whoring, religion and gambling.

According to Little Grandpa, as he was known to my family, before arriving at cousin Seltzer's he had walked across the face of Europe, a wandering tailor, a minstrel of the needle, mending clothes for food or a night's shelter, from Little Minsk to the Austrian border, crossing that by night and making his way to Hamburg where he took a freighter to the port of London.

The months of separation had been hard ones for Esther, who was obliged to deal with the gossip that passed for sympathy afforded an abandoned bride. Before Isaac she knew nothing of sex. Her parents had assumed that it would be useless knowledge to her, another burden she didn't have to carry, and the wedding night came to her as a revelation. Parts of her body which she had never viewed as anything but shameful were declared beautiful by her groom as he explored them in the candlelight and showed her the several points of pleasure that were hidden there, his small, soft, almost girlish hands touching her gently and stroking the pleasure out of her, making it rise to the surface of her skin, ending with such a splendid surprise. He admired her well-shaped breasts, her tiny feet, her fine round stomach, and the nether parts which no one but her own mother had ever seen, and no sane person would consider beautiful. It appeared that the presence of the hump never challenged his belief that she was beautiful. Not only had she loved her new husband with a fervor released by their union, but she alone never feared that he would abandon her after having left the village.

"He will send for me," she told her parents, and she said it so often that it infuriated her mother, who wished only to prepare her love-crazed daughter for the loss of her illusions, so she could take her proper place in the village as a betrayed bride and household drudge. "You don't send for a worthless burden," her mother declared. "You drop it and run. And he did." Esther refused to respond to the sad, knowing looks that people gave her when they asked how Isaac was doing and had she heard from him. Was he well? When did she think he would call for her? When she hung back shyly and refused to answer, she was bombarded with myriad tales of abandoned wives, all told to her as a form of comfort. "You're lucky you have no children," the comforters assured her. Even a beautiful woman would have had cause for concern as weeks turned to months without a word from Isaac. When she discovered herself pregnant with my father, she was both joyful and despairing, fearing that perhaps "they" were right and she would be abandoned with a baby to care for alone. But one day a letter came. Stuffed within it were forty pounds sterling, a train ticket to Cherbourg, France, and a paid boat passage from Cherbourg to England on a packet boat, *La Ventura Suprema*. Esther wept with joy, as people did in those days, before such expressions ceased to represent true feelings, or before such feelings disappeared. She had not been forsaken. She was not left behind to live alone, loveless and mocked as one of God's mistakes. She had been sent for, as only the most beautiful and loved wives had been sent for. Bulging bird eyes, sharp nasal beak, feather boa, hump and all, sans dowry, sans dishes, sans goblets, sans hope, sans a miracle, she had been sent for. She, Esther Slavin Yellen had been loved. My grandfather enjoyed the telling of his wife's conflict with her mother, since it showed her spirit and her love for him.

"So you mean to leave us?" her Mother asked in a matter-of-face fashion, without tears, recriminations, or a proper maternal show of sorrow at her loss.

"Yes, I am going to join Isaac in London. And I will be taking my dowry with me."

"What dowry? You have no dowry."

"What do you call the embossed gold German plates and the cut crystal Austrian goblets?"

"Are you crazy, crazy girl?" her mother asked rhetorically. "That matter was settled already. He married you without a dowry. Ask your father."

"I want them. I want to take them to my husband in London," Esther stated calmly.

"You are crazy!" her mother cried out. "Elena Kopf, the village lunatic who speaks gibberish to invisible demons has nothing on you. We offered him no dowry. You know that. He knows that. When we're gone — and with God's mercy, that will be many years from now — then, they are yours!"

"Poppa may have got the best of Isaac, which is not hard to do, but you cannot get the best of me. I'm your daughter, flesh of your flesh. I know you," Esther responded.

"You know nothing. They're too valuable to travel. These dishes do not leave Russia."

"I won't join him without them!" Esther declared. "He sent for me, but I won't go without my dowry."

"Who are you fooling? You've spent the past months waiting for his letter. You carry his child. Now you think I can be gulled into giving you what was never offered so you can bribe him into sending for you?"

"Deny me what is mine and I'll tell the world that you have kept me from my husband by your stinginess and dishonesty."

"But he married you without a dowry," her mother pleaded. "Who gets a dowry after?"

"I do!" Esther stated.

"Don't you know why he married you?" her mother asked

"He was blinded by my beauty," my grandmother replied without a trace of irony in her voice. "My beauty may not last, but a dowry will!"

"I told you, when I'm dead they'll go to you."

"When you're dead, Poppa will remarry in a month and the dishes and the cut crystal glasses will be used by the new Mrs. Slavin, someone younger, prettier and smarter than you are. She won't keep them crated in sawdust, but toss them about like a clumsy street juggler, smash them for her pleasure, laughing at your ghost as she does so. Is that what you want?"

The war over the dowry continued for another week, but the Slavins knew that public opinion was turning against them. Esther was now looked upon as an object of sympathy, not for the husband who had abandoned her, but for the parents who had denied her a bride's rights. When Rabbi Levinson remarked to Cantor Slavin that this was fast becoming a public scandal, endangering the Slavin's place in the community, the argument ended.

Arrangements were made with Fyodor Pavel, the Russian man of all jobs, to fortify the wooden storage boxes which would accompany

Esther on her voyage from Russia, and repack them with the necessary paper and straw to hold the dowry securely. When her mother tried to hold on to the matching Dresden tea set, sequestering it in a blanket chest, Esther hunted it down with dog-like determination and insisted that it be packed with the rest. "They drink a lot of tea in London," she said. "And I must be prepared to entertain all the Lords and their Ladies when they come visiting."

"You're worse than crazy. Go on this way and they'll lock you up forever. Be careful. They got madhouses in London—a place called Bedlam for people like you." The threat of oncoming madness was now part of her conversational litany when talking to her daughter.

"So I'm crazy. More reason for you to humor me. Who needs a crazy pregnant daughter in their house? Crazy daughters kill, they bring disorder and disgrace!"

The tea set was included in the packing crate.

When Esther arrived in London with her four large crates of eighteen carat gold-rimmed china, cut crystal, and fine lace embroidered sheets (which she also demanded from her mother in a final fillip of demands), everything had survived the journey without a chip, including Esther's love for her husband. He was as handsome as ever, and if he had not grown an inch, he was more perfect than ever in his smallness; a diminutive delight with his smooth shining apple cheeks, his bright green eyes, and his perfect matching teeth.

Initially, London, with its new smells—the kerosene lamps and horse dung mixed with the heavy fogs and relentless drizzle—plus its impenetrable language, confused and frightened her. Esther felt herself drifting through a damp, soiled world of alien voices and unfriendly faces, but she was far too clever to turn a temporary discomfort into worthless nostalgia for the wretched Russian town from which she had escaped. Esther took easily to her husband's trade and proved to be as fine a needle worker as he was, possibly better, but modesty forced her to miss a few stitches so that she would not put his needlework to shame.

Soon, working diligently together, they had acquired enough money for their steerage passage to America, where Isaac had heard tales of prosperity that did not require the endless sewing of hems and cutting of patterns, days upon days huddled over a machine, and always facing, at the end of the work, a critical customer who wanted the waistline let out, the hem lengthened, or the seat of the pants taken in a bit more. Isaac's even stitches were so admired that it was predicted by David Jacob Seltzer that should he stay in London; he could end up a bespoke tailor on Saville Row. If he polished his English and his graces, with his good looks there was nothing to stop him from having a West End tailor shop of his own. Others spoke of leaving for America to find still greater opportunity, but Isaac had a secret he dared not share with Esther or anyone else. They would soon set out for America, but he alone among the immigrants, he later confessed to me, was not going to America to find opportunity; he was going there to escape from it. He knew that opportunity was just another word for backbreaking work, for the days, the weeks, the years lost in endless toil bent over a needle and scissors; a bad gamble with life, holding out the promise of ease in one's last days, but grueling labor in one's best days; a sucker's bet with mortality. He had seen the photographs of the milling crowds on the Lower East Side of Manhattan and it struck him that there, among all that peddling, shouting, scheming, malodorous humanity, he could be lost, and being lost, find himself. Not as a tailor with a thimble welded to his index finger and a needle piercing his heart, but as a man with an art.

Isaac Yellen had another secret. He could count. Not just numbers in his head or the give and take of coins that came his way. But with one glance he could figure the precise number of stitches it took to tailor a coat. With another glance, he could closely estimate the number of the myriad beans in a glass jar, and with another glance, most importantly, the number of aces remaining in the deck during a game of poker. He recognized this as a rare gift, and he was determined to use it for pleasure and profit.

Arriving in America, the Yellens settled in on the fourth floor of a six-floor tenement on Rivington Street on the Lower East Side, where my father, Nathaniel Barnett Yellen, he of the majestic nose and tiny body, was born. Isaac Yellen himself was reborn there as a street gambler, or as he was known on Rivington Street, "The Prince of Pinochle."

I know very little about pinochle, or any card game for that matter, so the torch was not passed on to me, although it was passed on to my father and he struggled with it uneasily throughout his life. What I do know from my father is that the trouble with gambling, even for a card counter, is that knowing what cards are in the deck or what cards were held in one's opponent's hands is fine for a start, but it is not enough to guarantee winning. One must also be dealt good cards. One must have luck, and it was here that Isaac failed miserably. He considered himself an honest man, and he knew that a well-shuffled deck was no friend of his. Card counting was a skill, a talent, even an art, but he would never descend to sleight of hand, palming cards, stacking the deck, dealing from the bottom; never would a card come in contact with his sleeve and rest within it, nor would he indulge in any other trickery. And so he lost as often as he won, taking with him his meager earnings as a tailor, and those of Esther as well.

Esther, suckling her baby as she worked her sewing machine, had finally confronted her husband with their need for more money. She had done all she could, taking in piece goods to sew, renting out the small hallway of their tenement flat to boarders, bargaining ruthlessly with the grocer, buying the cheapest scraps of animal innards from the butcher that she would make into a stew, offending God for abandoning kosher meat in favor of these cheap cuts, begging time from the landlord for the late rent payment, but all her efforts could not keep the family together unless Isaac gave up his gambling. He swore he would mend his ways but he broke his promise so often that Esther now knew that this was worse than her worst fears. She realized that this was worse than losing him to another woman. A man will tire of a beautiful mistress, but the cards were more compelling than any woman and as much a part of him now as his handsome features.

He would go off to his gaming neatly dressed, every jacket button buttoned, cravat neatly tied, walking his odd little walk which gave him the spirit of a humorless Charlie Chaplin, but there was no taking the well-dressed Isaac for a tramp. It was necessary for him to have a pressed coat and a clean collar. There must be no whiff of poverty about him. Nobody wanted to play cards with a bum. And every day that she saw him go, she feared he might not return.

It was a time of mass abandonment in the Lower East Side. Hard times weighed heavily on the unemployed husbands of these immigrant households. It was easier to find your feet and run off alone to another city, some cold, hard place, with dirty coal-stained snow, a smaller, meaner New York; a place where the horse piss turned to streams of yellow ice; a Rochester, a Syracuse, a Buffalo; far easier to run away from failure and face oblivion than find a job in New York City that would provide for your family. Esther knew that she did not wish to raise her children alone. If Isaac was no help, he was still Isaac, the prize that she had won in a game of chance. And the gambling that took him from her and stole their treasure was the very gambling that made him marry her. Such was life. Demons buried deep within angels, waiting to spring to life in those angels, albeit destroying angels. She would keep him no matter what.

Esther was pregnant again, and would be six more times, all living children. But with this one, a daughter, Ruthie, the dowry began its slow disappearance from their flat. At first a dessert dish vanished, possibly the work of a boarder, if not a professional thief who had waited his time for Esther to leave the flat to buy provisions for the evening meal. Who knew? But then the dinner plates disappeared, and one by one the beautiful gold-rimmed covered dishes were gone from the shelves of the kitchen cabinet. Esther was determined to guard her goblets, placing them under her bed and checking them every evening, pleased to find that the boxes had not been disturbed.

One fine crisp October morning, while out marketing on Essex Street, Esther saw five of her cut crystal goblets on sale in a pushcart. She did not have to ask the peddler where they came from. It was all too clear to her. Isaac, her husband and my grandfather, alone knew their secret hiding place. He had stolen them to pay his gambling debts, or worse, stake himself to new games and new losses.

"How did my goblets end up on Moses Finkel's pushcart?" she asked him.

"You think you're the only one with crystal goblets?" her husband queried dismissively. He denied all, claiming that he would never sell her family heirlooms, but... but if he ever did... Yes, yes, let's say that he did, what right had she to question his judgment? And weren't those goblets his as much as hers as part of the dowry? Such was his confession, and Esther knew that there was no hope to be found in her husband as a provider. He would waste whatever small treasure they had gained faster than she could amass or preserve it. Seventy years later, as he told this story on his deathbed, he showed more pleasure than shame in his ability to turn those treasures into ready cash for his gambling.

My father knew that his mother would need an ally in her struggle to survive, an ally who could protect her family, someone who could provide for the family that was, and the family that would be. That ally would be himself, her first son, her eldest child, Nathan.

When I was a boy I once asked my father what he enjoyed as a child. My father replied that he loved watching baseball games in the park, or joining in a handball game against a building wall, but that he had no other childhood pleasures he could recall. "It was okay," he would tell me. "They hadn't invented childhood then, so who knew better?" His large nose had made him sensitive to the odors of his world; the smell of meat bones in the soup cooking in the hallways, mixed with the smell of urine clinging to the stairwells from the common toilet, and in the streets, the sweat of the crowds, workers, peddlers perfumed by the dung from their horse drawn carts, strong decent odors that dominated the indecent ones and made life bearable.

One day, making a delivery uptown to Fifth Avenue, he became aware of the fact that there were clean, orderly streets, indeed, whole neighborhoods that did not have these smells. There were servants to scrub down the sidewalks and clean up the pavement with buckets of soapy water, and lives lived where an opened window let in a spring breeze rather than the stench of excrement.

Happiness? Yes, he knew that it existed. It meant being taken out of one's own small life and joined to a larger, more agreeable world, like watching a handball game or a pretty girl pass by. There was the odd game of stickball on the streets or a rare afternoon sitting on the piano bench with his cousin—the prodigious young lyricist Jack Yellen visiting from upstate—as he sang his early Tin Pan Alley songs (which would later include "Ain't She Sweet" and "Happy Days Are Here Again") while Nat turned the pages of the music, as if they were a holy book, amazed at his cousin's witty words. What it all came down to was a short supply of pleasing memories: a stickball game and a tune, and after that, work and more work. The endless sweeping of barrooms, stables, grocery stores, followed by the hauling of large boxes at the pier, a hauling that would forever weaken his back but spark his ambition. No one had to tell him that if he did not come to the table every Friday afternoon with his salary intact, his family might starve. He did not have to read Horatio Alger to know that hard work was the way out, although he never believed the myth that there would be some rich benefactor to steer his course, and "the way out" didn't mean mansions and riches but a full belly and a soft bed to sleep in, alone, free of his tossing younger brothers. He knew that he had to continue working ceaselessly, not only to feed his family, but to gain the love from them that he had never known. Esther had rarely kissed him or thanked him; instead she had regarded him with disgust whenever he had fallen short of her expectations.

The rage Esther felt against her handsome husband could never be expressed. He had, after all, married her, saved her from spinsterhood, saved her from slavery as her parent's unpaid servant, given her healthy children, and for that she must ever be grateful. But that rage born in his gambling, his waste of their small treasure, was vented on occasion against her oldest son. "Your pay envelope is short this week!" she would state, accusingly, as if he had squandered *her* money. This was often followed by a sharp slap across his cheek. Her rage, which she tried to keep in check, broke out whenever Isaac had committed some new crime against the family's well-being, and Nathan was the recipient of it. It mattered little to her that Nathan had spent the money on a birthday gift for one of his brothers or sisters, or had used it to buy some necessity for himself, like the hair tonic and aftershave scents he loved, in the hope that they would make him more acceptable. It did not take long for my father to understand that he must always give, and give all, now and forever, and someday perhaps he might be rewarded with gratitude, if not love. He had no greater expectations of his family or the world. He knew they could not love him for himself, but God help them, they would need him.

At last, after many small pickup laboring jobs sweeping and hauling, there was work for a woolen merchant, packing scarves, hats, gloves, mittens and sweaters, repackaging returns, shaving off the pilling that clung to aging sweaters with a handheld razor blade, "freshening the stock," as they called it. All this was done as more and more children were born to Isaac and Esther; first Ella, known as Pretty Ella. Then came Ruthie, Greedy Ruthie, so rapacious as an infant, known as Ruthie the *schnorer*, borrowing, cajoling her brothers and sisters, eyes darting, nervous fingers flying, jealously fondling the fabric of someone else's gown through her long, hard lifetime; Louie, later so prodigiously handsome like his father, only tall, well-muscled and lazy. My own mother once remarked, "Louie's muscles are for show, not work." He was forever Louie the Bum, and when he joined the peacetime army years later in the early 1930s, the name was considered prophetic. There was nothing about him that his family admired, particularly the *shiksa* bride he attracted and later divorced, and nothing would be expected of him other than the mistakes that a good-looking man could make. There was Harry the Hustler, a miniature version of Nat, and Benny the Baby, all depending on one eleven-year-old boy to exist. His parent's fecundity was always one baby ahead of my father's capacity to provide for them, but he never doubted his ability to somehow put food on the table.

My father did not have to be told that *his* father had lost the small earnings he made as a tailor and had squandered his wife's dowry. It was clear from their meager lives that the captain wasn't steering their ship, but the ship's cabin boy was in command as their mother navigated the roiling waters. When the last child was born, there was only a hand-blown milk glass egg cup, the sole survivor of that dowry, which my grandmother kept hidden inside one of her button-up shoes, to be taken out every Passover for the Prophet Elijah, and used as a shoe stretcher between High Holy days. Crossing Rivington Street one September morning, a speeding newspaper delivery truck struck Nat. His small, frail body was hurled into the air, landing on a pushcart that held silk piece goods. The impact was broken by the piles of soft cloth remnants, probably saving his life. As he tried to get out of the cart, he discovered that he could not stand on his leg without great pain, so he was wheeled in that very pushcart to the Holy Mother of Mercy Hospital on Essex Street. His fractured leg was set and he was placed in a charity ward for a week because one of the nuns thought that the undernourished boy with the large nose and the bony frame was starving and could do with a week of hot hospital food before he limped towards damnation with the other Jews. This was the *only* rest he would know in his childhood.

In the hospital, Nat was visited by his mother and sisters who brought him two packets of chewing gum and baseball cards, which he generously shared with the burned boy who occupied the hospital cot next to his own. The family tried to ignore the scarred child and the crucifix with its bleeding Jesus on the wall behind my father's cot, but by the end of the week they had failed to make another visit. They had grown impatient with his hospital holiday, so he returned to work, hobbling on his crutch, attending to the sweeping up of a grocery store and never missing a day.

Once, years later, when he was reading aloud to me from an illustrated edition of *A Christmas Carol*, he pointed to the picture of Tiny Tim on his crutches and proudly claimed, "That was me, son! Me!"

He had fallen into the role of family provider, a boy saint, and he did so without complaint, and with unconcealed pleasure. But in him brewed dreadful rages, storms that came on without warning, rarely exhibited to strangers, but when they arrived, such storms held terrors for all who experienced them.

My father was an intelligent boy who knew that he had been cheated of his youth by his father's gambling, his mother's fertility, and the world's indifference, and that boy remained within him as he aged, seeking some sign of love from those he provided for. It was still there at his death. His was an unrequited life, until his grandchildren arrived to redeem it.

Nat was elevated to the chief salesman of George Washington Knitwear, working long hours in a world of brightly lit showrooms and dusty stockrooms, a world of exposed pipes, stippled caramel-colored walls, black lava soap in the dingy tin sink of the bathroom and harsh brown paper towels, where he became the young man in the vested suit and neatly knotted silk tie, with an ever ready smile to greet the buyers. My father had mastered the art of schmoozing the buyers who came to the showroom, "Let me see the latest pictures of your beautiful children. Movie stars, all of them." He knew how to praise the virtues of a dying parent he had never met, and offer condolences for a newly dead one, tears welling up in his large green bulging eyes. And backing up that talk were the gifts—never to be confused with bribes—impressive cream-colored ceramic wedding gifts from Ovington's Department Store, vases ringed with filigree silver decorations, and when all else failed, envelopes filled with hard cash, new bills, fresh from the bank. So genial was he, they might have placed orders with him because of his easy smile, his handshake, the light of pleasure that showed in his eyes when they entered the showroom, but it was his mastery of the kickback to the buyer, never too much, never too little, that allowed him to rise in the world of woolens, and harvest his monthly commissions.

It was while working as chief salesman at George Washington Knitwear that he met Max Rosensweig, a clever, dour man of mountainous girth, the chief clerk in the production part of the firm, and my father's future partner in the woolen business. The Max of the huge behind, the loosened necktie on the white-on-white shirt, the unlit cigar stuck in his down-turned mouth, the snarling voice, a living model for those cartoons of the garment district that appeared at times in *The New*

Yorker. That Max who, with a perfect knowledge of how much wool it took to make a single sleeve or a dozen sweaters, would become my father's natural ally in a world of natural enemies. Max saw more in my father than that perfect salesman who could charm any buyer into taking out her yellow pad and scribbling orders on it.

I suppose my father learned early in his life that truth was not his friend, not in his personal life or in his work. There was no wiggle room in it, and he needed a larger space than reality provided in which to move his restless spirit. Truth bound you tightly inside its confines. It was often escape proof. Good enough, perhaps, for boys who wished to be President, but useless for boys and men who wanted to prosper in the smaller world, the world of everyday living. Nat could lie about an unshipped order to an enraged customer who had been promised early delivery without betraying the smallest twitch of the lips. He could pretend that the order of red sweaters which had arrived with a purple cast was the newest, most fashionable shade, lying with such innocence in his face, and such apology for the inadvertent delay, or the misunderstanding, all of which could pass for sincerity in their world. The partners saved and plotted; they ingratiated buyers, and they found a mill in Philadelphia that would manufacture their sweaters on credit. Together, this odd pair roamed the aisles of Macy's and Gimbels buying sweaters to copy, which Max's wife would later return, as the men dreamed of becoming the bosses of their own company.

My father was a great newspaper reader and a dedicated moviegoer, and he used this to advantage in his business. He devoured the fashion columns and knew what woolens the movie stars were wearing, how the Olympic ice skater and soon-to-be movie star Sonja Henie had arrived from Norway with her hand-made knit sweaters, those woolens with their stepped antlers and snow-clad Christmas tree ziggurats to be worn as a cardigan set in green and yellow, red and blue, with matching knit cap, copied by my father on a clever, newly designed Jacquard knitting machine, ready for wholesale at three dollars a set. It was a time when the sweater was still regarded as something to cover up a woman's breasts and provide warmth in winter, rather than an acceptable way to reveal the body, as it was later in the Lana Turner forties, and my father knew the point at which modesty and economy met. His sweaters were never so full that good money was thrown away in extra wool, nor were they so tight that a young girl might feel herself immodestly exposed.

When my father was twenty-two, his only experience of women had been a hasty encounter with a stout, aging Spanish prostitute in Harlem, one whom his much younger and more daring brother Benny had set up for him. He told me this as a cautionary tale as I entered my own adolescence; he so feared the disease that he had so luckily escaped. There were no girlfriends, no dates, he told me; he was the guy who went out with the group to Coney Island, who was never paired off, who seemed to accept his role as extra man without complaint. Then, at twenty-six, he met my mother Lillian Horowitz. My father would tell me that she was the most beautiful woman he had ever seen, and although I had learned to distrust the accuracy of all my father's claims—the salesman's exaggeration marked his speech—there was nothing to contradict that statement in her early photographs.

The Courtship of Lilly

Nat struggled to entertain Lilly with his small jokes, the kind he collected from columns like Franklin Pierce Adams' *The Conning Tower* in the daily newspapers he loved. *The New York Times* was only read for business news and to be carried about as a sign that he was a man on the rise. Every morning, over coffee, he scoured six of the New York papers—the *News*, the *Mirror*, the *Sun*, the *Telegram*, the *Post* and the *World*. He mined them for jokes to tell the female buyers in the showroom at the sweater factory where he worked; short, dainty jokes, easy to digest morsels of humor fit for a tired working lady with an order pad and no time to waste. Lilly disliked packaged humor. She saw no point in it. Life was so filled with the ridiculous, why make up stories that could not compete with the everyday nuttiness of real people and the foolishness that she observed daily? So she merely smiled at what she assumed was the punch line, often turning away in the middle of a tale, disinterested in a story that she could not connect to her own life, and disapproving of anything that dealt with a lusty widow Cohen and her unseemly questions to a Doctor Levine.

Having taken her to a vaudeville show once at the Variety, Nat watched as she sat stony faced through a Marx Brothers act, hating the anarchy of their horseplay, only coming alive when the headlining Irish tenor sang a sad ballad that touched her deeply, tears running down her cheeks as he sang of his long dead mother and then, wondrously, sang the same song in Yiddish for his Jewish audience. Nat knew she could laugh; he had heard her laugh when her brother had told her about some ridiculous misadventure, some near escape from disaster that the boy delighted in bragging about, sending giggles of relief through her, but he never, in their long marriage heard her laugh at a comedian. Years later as she patiently sat through the radio shows of Jack Benny and Eddie Cantor, Fibber Magee and Molly, she never so much as laughed at a joke, although she allowed a smile when Fibber Magee opened that closet and everything fell out, as he did week after week. While her husband slapped his knee with delight, threw back his head and roared, she watched him in silent bewilderment. She much preferred the soap operas with their serial calamities, never fatal, never resolved, but moving from one arresting disaster to another by actors with gracious theatrical diction offering the promise of a better world for everyone.

He understood that she would not give her laughter away to a suitor who had, as yet, failed to win her with his warmed-over punch lines and devoted looks. Prepared to wait out her indifference, he offered to be of help in her work and advise her on how to deal with the problems of her family. She knew he was smart—smarter than Harris—and hers if she wanted him. And the good part was that unlike Harris, Nat loved her so much that it would be unnecessary for her to do anything but accept that love, which revealed itself in sighs and darting glances. He asked so little in return. His feeling for her was large enough to cover a courtship for both of them. A lover would have frightened her, but a suitor pleased her immensely.

He never pressed his lips against her cheek or her lips, never stirred anything uncomfortable within her; content to grab her hand in his own from time to time, overwhelmed by his adoration of her. Occasionally, he would plant a kiss on the back of her hand and then watch her immediately take his own neatly folded pocket handkerchief (with its monogrammed NY in bold modern lettering) from his jacket pocket, handing it back to him seconds later after daubing dry the moist residue of his kiss. He was steady, loyal and adoring as he helped her tally the complicated accounts of the day's store sales, balancing her books in her shop after his own long day's work was over as chief showroom salesman at G. Washington Knitwear. His way with numbers impressed her deeply; it was like watching a magic trick that she could not master, and there was no way not to admire the magician. No matter how she tried she could never get the gist of it. He could carry over a number without writing it down, multiply three figures by four figures in his head and, best of all, help her to keep her position as a store manager, always in peril because of her limited fourth grade arithmetic.

Tank Tops and Bowler Hats

I t was early in July when a large Italian woman with an alpine bosom came to the store my mother managed on Broadway in order to buy a bathing suit. The large woman requested a black woolen tank top and bottom, the norm for women's beachwear in the mid-twenties. The shop assistant, Molly, advised my mother in a hushed voice that they had run out of tank tops in the woman's extra-large size, and the new shipment was not expected for a few days. Lilly could see that this customer was hell-bent to get to the beach and would not wait for the new shipment. Clearly, she would go across the street to *Feingold's Famous Fashions* to make her purchase.

Business had been slow that week and my mother knew that she had to make her quota of sales to satisfy the shop owner who begrudged her small salary—her "draw"—and obliged her to get most of her pay in commissions. He had suggested that on slow days she stand outside to lure customers in, promising bargains, or sit in the window to attract customers, something she would never do. She had heard that the prostitutes in Mexico did that in the red light district, and no decent woman would imitate that form of salesmanship. In desperation to make the sale, my mother chose a nearly identical woolen top in the same large size from the shelf of men's bathing suits. She took a celluloid rose from a damaged straw bonnet in the fifty-cent sale bin and pinned it to the man's tank top with a safety pin, hoping to make it more feminine in the process. Since the laws of hygiene and modesty forbade the trying on of bathing suits in a shop in those days, the woman made the purchase and departed the store ready for the beach that weekend.

Unfortunately, the man's bathing top was cut lower in front and deeper under the arms than a woman's would be, and this woman's large breasts swung out of their loose container, flopping about freely when she raised her arms in the waves of Coney Island. Finding herself exposed, she was forced to throw her wet body upon the sand to cover her breasts until she could reach her towel lying halfway up the beach near the boardwalk. People stared. Several laughed. She had been shamed before strangers. The following Monday the woman came back to the dress shop in a fury, determined to return the top for cash, and hang about until she could get my mother fired from her job, demanding to speak to the boss who, fortunately, at the time was away at his other shop, but would be back later.

My father stopped off from work in the early evening, as was now his courtship habit, to help my mother tally her sales and balance her books, and thus make a better case for his courtship. He walked into the store just as the woman was berating my mother, threatening to call the police and have her arrested. Nat claimed to be the store owner, listened to the woman's complaint sympathetically and went on to calm her as he explained that the lower cut was the newest fashion, that it was the rage of the Riviera, perhaps a bit daring for Coney, Brighton or Bath Beach, but worn everywhere on the beaches of Europe, the Lido, Nice, and the Costa Brava. He asserted that he had just returned from a vacation that covered the better beaches of Europe and he could attest to this from personal experience. In his magnificent salesman's rhetoric, he even named it "the French swoop cut." He spoke with such authority of places he had never seen, and of bathing suit fashions of which he was completely ignorant, that my mother stood in awe of his performance. She now saw in action a genius for selling that she had only known by hearsay, a mind so inventive, so equipped with telling details stored away for use in just such an emergency.

Although it was both against the law and store practice to exchange bathing suits, he offered her the "American model" — found in the newly arrived shipment of women's tank tops — exchanged it for this risqué European model, and she left the shop satisfied, thanking him profusely for his help, warning him against "pretty employees" such as my mother who didn't know their job, leaving my mother's job and sale intact after this encounter. It was then, for the first time, that my father saw my mother laugh. For five minutes after the woman left the store, she would laugh, break it off, and laugh again, repeating his phrase, "the swoop cut." He soon joined her in laughter, realizing that he had finally pleased her. It was their first duet. For her it was a laugh of relief, a laugh of triumph, and for him, at long last, a laugh they could share.

His performance with the bathing suit showed her that he was a naturally gifted liar, a weaver of grand personal myths, and a master of everyday dissembling. As time passed she saw that he never lied to hurt anyone, to trick, or to cruelly deceive, only to improve his own reality. His lies were betrayed to her by his small secret smile, one that passed over his thin lips, the corner of his mouth twitching involuntarily as he repackaged some ridiculous used falsehood and offered it up as fresh goods. She loved the truth and was surprised to find that she found this skill, in him, strangely endearing. She understood that in Nat she had an ally in her difficult world, one who would be there for her when she needed him; a man who was clever, imaginative, a survivor in a world of victims, one who might lie about bathing suits but would never lie about his intentions or his obligations (as Harris might have), a man who would only lie about the unimportant stuff that made a sale or improved a story. Unlike Harris, the tempter, he was living in the here and now, not asking her to wait for a future that might be the biggest lie.

Nat came to her rescue once again when the police held her fractious kid brother Ally overnight in jail for shoplifting. Nat provided the bail and volunteered to defend the clumsy crime that the wild, teenaged boy had committed, an informal arrangement allowed by the court for juvenile first-offenders.

"Imagine, stealing a bowler hat two sizes too big and thinking he could walk out of the store with it perched on his head," my mother lamented. "Why, it fell down over his eyes and the crazy clown stumbled right into the store policeman. I could kill him if I didn't love him so," my mother added. Nat used the very clownishness of the crime as a successful defense of the boy.

"Your honor, he was just trying to show off the way kids do. He didn't mean to steal the hat. He was just using it to make himself look funny." He then planted the hat on Ally's brow and the Court watched it fall down to the tip of the boy's broken snub nose. The judge laughed and dismissed the case, fining the boy the cost of the hat (which my father paid) and warning the boy against any future clownish tricks with other people's property. Lilly looked at her suitor with new admiration that afternoon. She even let him kiss her on her cheek afterwards without grabbing his handkerchief.

Lilly agreed to marry Nat when he presented her with a small round diamond ring over dinner at Gold's Kosher Dairy Restaurant on Sixth Avenue, together with a detailed plan for their future. "Once married," he stated, "we will move to Brooklyn to be near my family in Flatbush. Rents are cheap there, and we could save towards a business of our own. She noticed that he had said *our own* rather than *my own,* and that tipped the scales heavily in his favor. Nevertheless, she rejected his plan immediately. There would be no Brooklyn in her future, she announced, no proximity to somebody else's relatives. She commended him for loving his family (from what she had seen, it took a lot to love them), but she had no intention of making a life surrounded by these Yellens. She had a better idea. A recently married friend had moved to the Bronx, and claimed that it was beautiful, convenient, and cheaper than Brooklyn, a refuge from the noise and tumult of the city, with new homes, apartment houses, and parks where only a decade before there had been farms. A few farms remained on the outer reaches, but in the newly developed West Bronx, castle-like apartments had been built, some with working fountains set deep inside landscaped inner courtyards, in imitation of the grand apartments of Park Avenue. My mother admired the new buildings. Some were modernistic structures of curved white brick, with casement windows and smart canvas canopies, sporting elegant bronze Bauhaus style numbers, while inside the flats had modern kitchens and sunken living rooms, all for half the cost of a flat in Manhattan.

In the boom years of the early twenties, the Bronx was advertised as "The country in the city." It offered hilly streets and parks, nearby zoos, Fordham and New York University, Edgar Allan Poe's cottage, and movie palaces like the Loews's Paradise on the Grand Concourse with sparkling electric stars imbedded in their dark-blue high ceilings and pipe organs that pounded out their own celestial tunes. There were walks with views of the Harlem River and it was only forty minutes, at most, to the City via the Jerome Avenue elevated train. They traveled up to the West Bronx together to examine it and, compared to any other place she had seen, it was spotless. He agreed that they should begin their married life there. Her enthusiasm for the place was infectious. She even liked the way the old men and women sat in front of the brick apartment buildings, bundled up in dark woolen clothes to catch the sun. Safe in their great age and free from all the concerns that plagued the old in Russia and on Rivington Street, they would exchange stories of their successful children who had arranged for this haven for them, plucking them out of the tenements and placing them in these neat apartments. Some wore Persian lamb coats and pretty hats, attesting to the existence of those wealthy children who doted upon them and relocated them to this salubrious place where they could brag away their idle days.

Best of all, she liked the new apartment buildings, their red bricks held together with thick white mortar, like a Christmas fireplace in an advertisement for cigarettes. And the private homes were even more wonderful. Several were big English Tudor affairs, set back in gardens, although most were smart-looking two-family houses, set close together, separated by driveways that led to garages in the rear. The couple then visited a friend who had rented an apartment on Burnside Avenue; most streets were named for Civil War generals in the Union Army. It was a tree-lined street near the uptown campus of New York University and the Hall of Fame. They toured the Hall of Fame, a walk high over the river with busts of dead notables set amidst the colonnade; great men whose very existence no one could remember, but a beautiful Greek inspired walkway. Best of all, this was only a trolley car and an elevated train ride away from Manhattan, and the finest apartments could be rented for forty dollars a month. This, she knew, was what she needed, the perfect place to raise a family. She wanted children of her own, children who could live the life she had been denied, secure, confident, and innocent. Lilly's plan was simple. Nat would work hard in his job as chief showroom salesman at G. Washington Infant's Knitwear and she would continue working in her shop until the first child came. If they were prudent and managed their money, saving half of their salaries, they would soon own a business of their own.

All this conformed to his plan. He had already found a business partner in the plant foreman, the barge-bottomed Max "Rosie" Rosensweig, a grumpy but honest man who wore his pants high, held up like a barrel by thick red suspenders. My father joked that it was unnecessary for Max to wear a necktie or change his shirt, since they would all be covered by those shoulder-high trousers. Max was the "inside" man who ran the factory, chomping a fat cigar in cartoon fashion, while my father worked as chief salesman in the showroom, dazzling the buyers with deals and promises and funny stories, and placating them with promises he couldn't keep should an order be delayed or come in the wrong sizes and the wrong colors. Together, he and Max plotted a future of their own—a Ro-Nat Sportswear, which combined their names and their fortunes—all to take place when they'd saved enough to rent a showroom and buy goods from a factory.

My mother knew that her young brothers would soon be out of school and on their own, a relief to her father, but a great concern to her and to Tante Mary, who could not work and keep an eye on them. Their skimpy educations had prepared them for nothing but mischief, petty crime, or backbreaking labor. She had promised her late sister Rebecca as she was departing for the West, that she would not leave the boys to the mercy of the streets or in the care of their good but stupid sister Ida. Ida could teach them little, and the streets had already taught them far too much. In the case of Ally, it taught him to view the world with contempt as he scrapped, stole, and bullied his way through his youth. It had given her good Frankie a tick in his eye, a cigarette habit, and a sweet acceptance of his life, the desire to live in the day and never plan for tomorrow, an innocence that was dangerous in a boy. He had seen his brother steal from the pushcarts, fight for the sheer joy of harming another boy, and yet he, Frankie, stronger and better looking, blinking as he smiled, remained a holy fool, an innocent when it came to the world. From girlhood, Lilly's love for her brothers had been a constant. She could not stop loving her dead brother and sister or her lost mother, so she transferred all this love to the younger brothers. But try as she could to be fair, she knew she favored Frankie. He was so good, so generous, so decent, she feared for his life. These boys were her inheritance from the dead. Ida and her father were helpless in setting them on a proper course, so the task fell to her.

Her father Meyer was about to marry Augusta Zaro, a shy, crumpled spinster whom he met while she was working as a night cleaning woman in the factory he allegedly guarded. She was so reticent and gentle, it looked to my mother as if the poor woman was trying to make her head disappear into the high collar of her dress in imitation of a dime store turtle. Lilly saw "Gussie" as a decent woman, a religious woman with a tiny terrified goodness, scared to death of God, Meyer, and his daughters; a perfect wife for her father, the only woman in the world who could fear and respect that handsome nebbish.

Gussie met Meyer's primary requirement—she was meek, quiet, had no children of her own, and was willing to marry at once. His oldest daughter Ida had already married, neither wisely nor well, but married, and Libby was sure to follow soon. Meyer needed a reliable woman to cook his meals, warm his bed, and keep his home dusted for him. He found in this aging spinster someone who was prepared to accept his unruly sons and indifferent daughters, cook a decent kosher meal, cover her head with a shawl, light a candle and welcome the Shabbat for all of them. They married in a tiny storefront shul where my grandfather prayed. This prompted my mother to marry my father a few weeks later; she was determined to accept this woman who had replaced her mother, but never to live under the same roof as her, and living on her own was out of the question. She never called her new stepmother by her name. "Gussie" would be disrespectful, "Tante" (Auntie) was already taken by Tante Mary, and "Mother" would be impossible. But she managed through their lifetime to treat her with respect and sympathy without ever giving her a name.

Lilly married Nat at City Hall, wearing a light cream-colored satin-collared silk suit she had borrowed from the shop and planned to return later. The stiff cardboard price tag, sewn to her inside collar to hide it, scraped against her neck during the ceremony. She carried a spray of camellias on her wrist and covered her hands (her least pretty part) with a pair of fine kid gloves with pearl fasteners, a match for her first real pearl earrings. Earrings were her fashion weakness. She would have them for every outfit and never feel dressed, even sitting on the beach, without her ears dressed up for the world.

It was a simple ceremony, witnessed by her friend Muriel, her sister Ida and Ida's husband Mike, her younger brothers, her father, her new stepmother, Tante Mary, and that pack of unhappy-looking Yellens, who saw in this marriage the loss of their family breadwinner. Years later she told me she did not want the expense of a wedding gown, or to feed those Yellen freeloaders more than courtesy required, so there was only a meager wedding feast of cold meats and cheap kosher wine, all presented on the lace-patterned oilcloth covering of the table in her father's kitchen, with a bowl of fruit as the centerpiece, and a dozen Danish pastries and a few shnecken piled on top standing in for the wedding cake. Of my father's family she only liked his mother, a small, hunchbacked woman, quiet and dignified, who seemed pleased that her eldest son Nat was now doing so well that he could afford to marry a beautiful woman, beauty being a useless and expensive attribute for a wife and mother, and thus a sign of success.

The Abominable Yellens

As much as she loved and indulged her own younger brothers, my mother despised the full range of Yellens; brothers Harry, Ben and Louie, sisters Ruthie and Ella. She watched this large, healthy, grasping brood approach their older brother with outstretched hands, begging for the money, the chocolates and trinkets he would give to them. She had raised her own younger brothers to be independent and plain spoken, even if it led them astray from time to time. Remembering her brother Ally's crime and comparing it to the Yellen beggary, she commented to her sister Ida, "Better a thief than a beggar!" to which Ida readily agreed. Ida's husband, Mike, had once been known as "Little Jeff" in the gangs and had been arrested once for possession of stolen goods. Although he had long ago put aside his life of crime in favor of backbreaking work as the owner of a small hand laundry (a business with dark Mafia connections), Ida was sensitive to his criminal past and took my mother's remark as a compliment to her husband.

These Yellens, male and female, seemed to my mother like a nest of greedy birds; chirping, demanding starlings waiting for their generous brother Nat to arrive, laden with treats and money that they would grab with feigned gratitude, never to be satisfied, always coming back for more breadcrumbs. Oh, they covered him with kisses and flattery, a sure sign of their deceitfulness, for mother knew from her own experience that he did not inspire love, thus their motives were mendacious. She asked her sister Ida, "How could they love him as much as they claim? They never gave him so much as a rabbit's foot keychain or a monogrammed pocket-handkerchief for his birthday in September. Shame on them. He has supported them all since he was a boy. He gives and gives and gives and they take and take and take, and the poor man doesn't seem to mind. This has got to stop!" The tension between my mother and my father's family that had begun during his courtship would increase during their early marriage, and last for a lifetime.

My mother's real animosity towards the Yellens started with my father's sister, Ruthie. Ruthie had been married for a year and was already too pregnant to bend over and clean her own apartment, so she begged my mother to help her straighten up her untidy Brooklyn tenement rooms on Flatbush Avenue "for the Holidays." Ruthie had mentioned to her sister Ella that she was surprised that the beautiful Lillian would agree to help out. Perhaps their brother had made a more practical choice of a wife than they had believed.

When mother arrived at the flat, she looked about for an apron and found none. She looked for the cleaning materials in the cupboards and the broom closet and found none. All she found was dirt and disorder and the lazy bloated Ruthie. It was evident that Ruthie was far from spotless. Displaying a pregnant woman's confusion, Ruthie sent my mother out to buy the Murphy's oil soap, a scrub brush, and a cotton apron, but failed to offer to pay for them when my mother returned to her small flat with them. My mother decided to swallow the loss, but worse was to occur. Ruthie neglected to thank her for the day's heavy housekeeping, one that included, at Ruthie's request, the scrubbing of floors and the washing of windows. My mother now judged Ruthie as both dishonest and an ingrate. She pitied the poor children who would be born to such a mother. She was never to change her bad opinion of this woman, only to have it fortified when Ruthie's husband Moe went to prison for a year after embezzling funds from a World War I veteran's club where he was the treasurer. My mother now told her sole confidante, her sister Ida, the hanging Judge, that Nat needed to be protected from this pack of ingrates and thieves, and she, Lilly, was the only one to do it.

Nat's sister, Ella, was not sly, flattering and dishonest like the others. She asked for nothing, expecting all to be given due to her superior gifts. Ella was open in her contempt for her brother's choice of a wife and quick to express her opinions. Ella had been through the twelfth grade, thanks to Nat's determination that Ella, the brightest of the girls, should be properly educated and not sent out to work before she had graduated from High School. Elegant and intelligent, if no beauty, Ella carried herself as a superior being, and with her husky, cigarette-darkened voice and her sharp, observant eyes, she was a formidable figure to my mother. Ella had read Freud and Marx and favored hifalutin words and abstract ideas that my mother distrusted and could not understand, and Ella looked downright pleased when my mother seemed confused by some obscure reference Ella made to a character in a French play. Ella had appeared as an ingénue in a garment worker's amateur show, and was full of a haughty theatrical pride, looking like the young Bette Davis and speaking in an imperious voice that she modeled on that of Stella Adler in her early Yiddish Theater days. Wearing a fancy velvet cape, a wide-brimmed felt hat with a peacock feather on it, and long kid gloves, Ella employed her deepest, most affected theatrical voice whenever she saw my mother. In the event that the theater failed her, Ella had her eye on a fledgling stockbroker and had dreams of Wall Street wealth, an apartment on Park Avenue, and a chauffeur-driven Packard limousine, none of which she would acquire, but she *would* come close to it in her suburban married life.

Alone among them, Ella was no beggar, but my mother knew that Ella often disparaged her to Nat, citing his wife's lack of education and the poverty of her family. Shortly before my parents married, Ella had asked Nat in a troubled voice, "Are you sure you want to marry her, darling? Think it over carefully. Is she good enough for you, Nat? Pretty is good to look at but it isn't good enough for you. Why, she never made it to the sixth grade, if that! Have you ever heard her say a clever word? And she smiles too much, not because she's all that friendly but because she wants to show off her perfect teeth! Yes, I'll grant you that she's beautiful in a somewhat conventional way, but so is a sunset over Brighton Beach, and you wouldn't marry a sunset over Brighton Beach, you look at it with admiration, pack up your beach towel, kick the sand from your shoes, and go home."

Ella's envious sister Ruthie, forever eager to spread discord in the family, reported this conversation to my mother, who deeply resented being compared to the sand in a beachgoer's shoes.

My father replied that his Lilly was more than beautiful, she was good, she was kind, she was generous, and what Ella took for ignorance was innocence.

"Nat, she's twenty-four? Nobody is *that* innocent at twenty-four! Particularly a showroom model!"

He turned and told her sharply to "Shut up!" He would not hear another word against his Lilly. His faced flushed with rage as he insisted that Lilly was spotless. He looked so angry that even the impertinent Ella heeded the warning, at least while my father was about, although disparaging Lilly was soon to become her favorite indoor sport.

Ella now stepped to the head of the line of the abominable Yellens. Slow to anger, Lilly could never forgive or forget in the way her schoolbooks advised. If she had doubts about marrying my father, the opposition of his haughty sister satisfied those doubts. Here was a girl who lived off her brother's bounty, didn't work, yet felt herself superior to the world. My mother had seen him secretly slip dollar bills to the most unsavory beggars, a sign of his virtue, for helping out-of-luck strangers was godly. But she had to get him away from this pack of family *schnorers* who had encouraged in him a foolish, wanton generosity. By marrying Nat, they would rescue each other.

The newlyweds, Lilly and Nat, went to Macy's to purchase a suite of solid mahogany furniture (bought on time), a Sheraton-style sofa with boldly striped maroon and silver satin upholstery, and a Hepplewhite drum table with a tooled green leather top and space underneath for bric-a-brac and books. She admired some heavy, wine-colored silk velvet draperies for the living room, topped with swag worthy of a small theater, and he insisted she buy them. She was drawn to a black Dutch pottery lamp with an abstract design on it, and knew that she must have it. For the walls, she found an oil painting of nuns crossing a bridge at Bruges at dusk; some small plaques for the kitchen with scenes of Dutch family life molded in bas relief, and some hand-painted ivory miniatures of French noblemen and women at play on flower entwined swings. For the two private modern bathrooms in their apartment, she purchased two identical oilcloth shower curtains decorated with silver bubbles in graduated sizes. Most important, she bought twin beds. Having slept with one sister or another for most of her life, she vowed to sleep alone. Moreover, she had no intention of enduring her husband's amorous attentions for long. It was okay for now, a necessary part of the scheme of things, but as Ida advised, "You put up with it for a little while and hope they outgrow it." The primary drawback to marriage as my mother viewed it was not the physical obligations of a wife, but my father's unwavering devotion to that large, grasping and unendurable Yellen family, a tough habit for him to break, but she felt herself up to that challenge.

My parents had a brief honeymoon in a boarding house on the Thousand Islands in upstate New York, with a side trip to Niagara Falls, during which Lilly bought a half-dozen scented pine pillows and picture postcards of the Falls for her family. The newlyweds then paid a visit to Sam and Esther Kaplan, cousins of my mother who lived nearby in Gouverneur, New York. The prosperous Kaplans had settled there upon arriving from Russia in 1900, working first as peddlers selling to the local farmers their bales of brightly-printed cheap dress cloth and fancy trimmings, and then as the owners of Kaplan's Quality Department Store. It was a general store, selling everything from overalls to tractors to the rural families. It was during this visit that my mother procured a job for her younger brother Ally as a sales clerk in their store, thus disposing of one of her most troubling obligations and setting this shrewd but unruly brother on the path to retail success and riches. After the week's honeymoon, the newlyweds immediately returned to the apartment they had rented on Tremont Avenue in the West Bronx, providing a greater distance from my father's family (a full hour-and-a-half by elevated train from the Bronx to Brooklyn), and they settled in a new, freshly painted apartment building atop a hilly street, its large windows offering a view of a nearby playground and handball court. Everything was spotless. The open skies seen from their third floor window seemed redolent of health and a new beginning.

Nat's First Tantrum

When the furniture set they had ordered from Macy's failed to arrive on time, leaving them for several weeks without the sofa and chairs my mother admired, they went to Macy's where the salesman dismissed their complaint without an apology or a true remedy. He advised them that such things happened, delays were unavoidable, the store would provide them with a replacement off the floor if they could not wait, but there was little he could do to accelerate the speed of delivery. There had been a strike in the North Carolina plant where the furniture frames were made, delaying delivery. The salesman made it appear a matter of their impatience rather than the store's failure to keep its promise.

My father as well as my mother knew all about a salesman's tricks and evasions, having practiced some of these themselves. Both Nat and Lilly suspected that the factory had overlooked the original order. They viewed the matter as the salesman's fault. Any decent salesman would follow up an order with the factory to make sure that his customers were satisfied. Nat said that they did not want shopworn merchandise in place of the new furniture ordered. The salesman turned away from them and walked towards a new customer. It was then that my mother saw my father explode with rage, his white face turned a deep crimson, his gentle voice was transformed into a sharp, loud growl, this would be the first of his lifelong eruptions that she was to witness and endure. Berating the salesman, he called him a "goddamned liar who didn't know his job, his customer, or his ass from his elbow." There was no strike in that factory, he claimed, demanding an honest answer. When the salesman turned away, as if from a bad smell, my father went about creating a scene; shouting, cursing, demanding attention, which brought both the store detective and a small crowd of shoppers to a full halt, the customers were now the attentive audience to my father's outburst.

It was the heyday of the department store as a consumer cathedral and it was unheard of for anyone to carry on in this fashion against the papal authority of this powerful institution. My mother calmed my father down and got him to leave the store at once, fearful of a run-in with a store detective. Amazingly, the furniture arrived within the week, but she now knew that there was a fury inside this man that could be released at any time, and must be controlled by her, but not so much as to destroy his ambition, for that same rage spurred him on and got things accomplished.

Among the first visitors to the newlyweds was my father's tiny, lazy, gambling father, Isaac Yellen, whom everyone called "the Prince of Pinochle," although my sister and I would later call the sweet-natured and cheerful old man "Little Grandpa." Isaac had forged the template for the beggary that all but Ella used on their older brother. Although the old man would always be welcomed in her home, my mother had little use for this toy-sized patriarch who barely touched five feet and never shaved close enough to remove the gray stubble on his hollow cheeks, and although he never gained a pound, ate his own weight like some jungle animal every time he came to visit. She forced herself to lean over and kiss him when he paid his monthly visit, merely brushing his straight, iron gray hair with her lips, and offering him her over-boiled coffee in an heroic effort to be polite, knowing that my father would be slipping his father a fast fifty bucks before the afternoon was over and before she could relieve him of the loose bills he kept fastened by a money clip in his pants pocket.

My mother understood what my father refused to accept—that his childhood had been cruelly stolen from him by this gentle old man with the gambling habit, as her own youth had been stolen by her feckless father's inability to provide for his family. Nat had been sent out to work to support his parents' growing family at ten years old, and the burden of providing for them had taken its toll on the bright, affectionate boy. He soon believed that the only way he could get love, or even deserve it, was by providing for his younger brothers and sisters. The more he gave to them, the more they demanded, and the less they honored his sacrifice with any show of gratitude. He understood early on that his homely looks did not inspire love or respect from his family, and that to be loved he had to be perfectly groomed, always genial, hardworking, friendly and generous. Any departure from this formula, he believed, would consign him to despair and loneliness. Thus, the suppression of all the anger for all the abuse and insults he had received from those he loved would, in later life, return as a raging inner despair, a demon that would break through its chains from time to time in appalling ways. My mother observed that the sudden flare ups, the howling rages, came when her husband was challenged in his authority, when he was made to feel small, helpless or ignored—when he was reduced to that ten-year-old boy sent out into the world with an impossible task—"bring back some money or we starve." And so she considered it a mitzvah, a blessing, to remove him from this family who had seeded his rage with their constant demands and only gave him their perishable flattery and counterfeit affection. The Bronx—so far away from the dreadful Yellens—might calm him, if it could not cure him. He would spend his lifetime starved for a love he did not believe he deserved because the very demands that the world placed upon him proved to him that he could not be loved for himself alone. Only with grandchildren and animals did he feel himself loved. Walking a dog, or taking a grandchild for a stroll, one would see a man who was at peace with the world, one who was not on a quest to prove himself, but who knew he was someone worth loving. But that would be years ahead. Now, early in their marriage, with Simone on the way, my mother determined that her husband would be saved from the abominable Yellens. Her first line of attack was to prevent him from giving them his hard earned money. She knew there would be no talking him out of this, he would only lie and swear he no longer did so. When it came to his family he was like the village drunk, and the only way to keep him sober was to remove the supply of liquor. In my father's case, it was to keep him from having any surplus cash.

It did no good to ask him for it. He gave her most of his salary on his payday, but she knew he held back twenty dollars and change in case someone from the abominable Yellens came to his office for a handout. There was no way she could prevent that. He would only lie and swear that he had ceased to support them now that he had a wife of his own and a child on the way. It was a plausible story, but not credible to her. A few months into her marriage she learned the art of the domestic pickpocket. She had seen light-fingered people ply their trade in the Lower East Side. The Tante had shown her how it was done and what she should look out for. Diversion, the Tante explained, was at the heart of it.

Distracting Nat was simple; she drew him a hot bath and collected his cast off clothes to hang up in the bedroom closet. After his bath, as he sat in his new silk robe, the one he had bought at J. Tripler for his honeymoon, she sat him down in front of the new Emerson radio—the one with the green eye that slowly lit up as the crackling sound of the broadcast gradually came on—poured a glass of Harvey's Bristol Cream Sherry for him, and told him to relax. While he listened to Rudy Vallee or Russ Colombo singing, she made a thorough search of his pockets, overcoat, jacket, and trousers, even his shirt pockets. No place was left unexplored. Whatever she could take from his pockets without risking discovery was taken. She knew that he was so free with money that he rarely knew what he had in his pockets, and she left just enough so that he never suspected her. Five years after they married, when he started up his own business with Max he was short five thousand dollars of his share in the partnership. Max told him that without it, he would be obliged to look around for another business partner. There was no question of taking in a third partner; the fledgling business could not afford so many slices of what would be, at first, a very small pie. It was then that Lilly produced the needed five thousand dollars from her hiding place in a white ceramic jar. Nat was astonished. "Where did you get this money," he demanded. "I borrowed it from a fool who was going to throw it away," she replied. He did not press her further on it, and he was now in a business of his own.

Nat and Lilly were soon followed to the Bronx by her married sister Ida, now Mrs. Mike Hines, who took an apartment nearby on Sedgwick Avenue. Her brother Frank, working for Ida's husband's hand laundry as a truck driver, lived as a boarder with Ida until his own marriage to his girlfriend, Sue, a few years later. Frank had, in his early youth, impregnated an Italian girl on the Lower East Side, information that Ida was only too pleased to pass on to Sue, his fiancée, who, to Ida's astonishment, showed no shock at this news and did not call off the marriage, a black mark in Ida's book against Sue's own morals. The birth of my sister Simone came in 1928, two years after my parents had married, and then four years later, in 1932, I appeared.

I Settle into the Family

When I finally arrived home in that February blizzard, a plump, squalling bald baby, Simone knew from the moment she laid eyes on me that I could not possibly be her baby brother. She was beautiful; I was not. She knew that she was not beautiful in the way that our mother was beautiful with those storybook features set in a smooth olive skin, but then who could be that beautiful outside of a photograph? Simone regretted the slight downward turn of her small nose, and the sprinkle of freckles that carelessly bridged it. She would often put her finger to the tip of her nose to lift it, but it always came down again, discouragingly. Still, she felt herself to be superior in looks, spirit, and wit to anyone of her own age who was not a movie star. My mother, who loved movies, had taken her to see any film with a child actress in it—the Baby Peggys and Baby LeRoys and Little Shirleys who inhabited the screen. Indeed, if Simone squinted in the mirror or caught her face reflected on the curved back of a silver tea spoon, something she did often as child and woman, she could picture herself as a Gloria Jean or a Deanna Durbin, or at least a Peggy Ryan, one of those lesser child stars, darkly imperfect compared to the mythical blonde Shirley Temple, but a child star nonetheless.

Simone's vanity lacked all cruelty, and indeed it inspired her generosity. She was so sure of her own charms that she took no pleasure in the fact that others were plain or stupid. She felt sad for those who lacked looks and wit, a little guilty for having swallowed up the small allotment of charm that was given out in the world, and she treated these unfortunates with a special kindness, as close as a child could come to *noblesse oblige.*

Although she laughed easily, she did not laugh or snicker at her older cousin Gertrude's foolish remarks, or her Aunt Ida's awkward immigrant ways. Without being told she knew that this would be forbidden by her mother and disapproved of by her father; besides, she saw no contradiction between loving them and finding them ridiculous. From her mother she learned that one must carry one's superiority very carefully, without a show of snobbery, for the one vice her father could not tolerate was snobbery. Although every day her eyes revealed that she was superior, her ears told her—by way of her parents—that "everyone is equal." Simone's vanity was founded on the agreeable image reflected in that teaspoon and in her parents' pride and love for her. She did not triumph over her small friends who did not share that beauty, nor did she flaunt herself before strangers, except at the behest of her father who could not contain his pride in her and was always eager to demonstrate the brilliance of his *wunderkind*. It was enough to be a Princess within the family, like Margaret Rose in England, dressed by our mother at Best & Company as the royals dressed their young in velvet-collared tweed woolen coats with matching velvet riding caps.

Indeed, Simone felt sympathy for her cousins, the Hines sisters, Sylvia and Gertrude, who were blissfully unaware that they were born fools, lacking any movie star potential with their pretty but splotched, roly-poly faces and harsh, strident voices. It was so easy to imitate the cultured voices of the women on the radio; she wondered why everyone didn't speak softly like Helen Trent or elegantly like Margo in *The Shadow*, or like my mother who had assimilated that voice without even trying to do so. Neither of her girl cousins, the slightly older Gertrude and the ten-year's older Sylvia, offered her the slightest competition within the family. They were content to accept her superiority as the daughter of the queenly Aunt Lilly; only Sylvia had suggested that Simone was spoiled. When Ida foolishly repeated that observation to my mother, my mother replied, "No child is spoiled by having too much love or attention, or even too many toys. It's what you don't have that spoils you. I was spoiled. You were spoiled. Not my children." Fortunately, Ida did not understand or take this as a reproach to her own indifferent mothering and parsimonious treatment of her daughters.

With my arrival Simone felt under siege by this newborn pretender who everyone praised merely for having two eyes, two ears, a mouth and a small nose, while moving his bowels regularly. It was difficult to find within herself that natural sympathy for the less fortunate when she looked at me.

I was a bald, red-faced and cranky infant, given to short but dangerous asthma attacks that left me gasping for breath as my frantic mother held me in her arms and paraded me around my room, walking in circles for miles in the hope that ceaseless motion would put me to sleep and thus end the attack. For Simone, my appearance was proof of a world gone suddenly and disastrously awry. She studied me carefully during my first months, looking for some practical reason for my being there. I was not the pink-cheeked, golden-haired brother featured in the magazine advertisements, or one of those delightful infants found in the storybook romantic color illustrations of *The Water Babies*. I was no feast for the eyes and, with all my crying and wheezing, no feast for the ears either. Later she would confess to me of how she approached me once in my princely pram, the ebony-lacquered Silver Cross carriage, and peered over the gleaming nickel-plated handles, grabbing the handlebars and bouncing the springy mechanism when my mother's attention had wandered to a shop window. She had hoped to bounce me out of the carriage, so high that I would bounce out of the world. She tried, failed and felt such guilt, she later confessed, adding in her wry fashion, "but not for long." What was I doing there? Why had I come to complicate her perfect life? Why had she been pushed aside by a bundle of human rage, drooling, urinating, wheezing, and defecating rage? I had failed to be beautiful or useful, so what was I doing there, spoiling paradise?

For my grown-up family I was the boy wonder child who would carry their name into the future. A new star had emerged and although I lacked any star quality, I was it. Only Uncle Frank, who came by the house twice a week to pick up and deliver our laundry, understood Simone's pain; her sense of having lost her place in the world as its greatest wonder. He had ground out his perpetual cigarette into the oriental ashtray, picked her up in his large rough hands (holding her by her thin arms) and tossed her high in the air with the ease with which he tossed the heavy bags of laundry into his *Mother's Friend Laundry* truck. As he cried, "Ally Ally Oop!" in their rehearsed circus act, my mother would shout "Stop it, Frank, you'll throw her arms out of their sockets," against the sounds of Simone screaming with joy.

"She just ate lunch," my mother protested fruitlessly, "you'll make her sick from all that excitement," but Frank playfully and lovingly ignored his older sister and kept Simone high above him in her proper place as the smart one, the wonder, the delight of the family deserving of those thrilling flights towards the chandelier that he offered as acts of his undisguised love. I was later to be the recipient of these very same trapeze acts, and I recall them not just for the thrill of being tossed into the air by my loving Uncle, but because they were the only spontaneous acts of love I had ever felt, free from concern for my well-being, simply there to provide undiluted joy.

Protecting the Young

At the time of my birth, murder was in the air. The Lindbergh baby had just been kidnapped, and was soon discovered dead. The unspeakable had happened. And for my family, prosperous beyond the fortunes of our Bronx neighbors, and now living in the largest private house on the block, it was clear to our mother that we would be the targets of any kidnapper operating north of Manhattan and east of New Jersey. We alone among our neighbors had bushes and trees and gardens surrounding our house. Bushes, dangerous bushes, that come nightfall might hide the evil ones who could lurk about ready to seize and kill her beloved offspring. So we were protected. Not with armed guards. None were necessary with my mother, Lillian, on the case.

My father arrived home one evening to discover that the ornamental bushes that surrounded the house had been cut down by my mother, assisted in this radical pruning by our live-in maid, Polish Mary. It was an arduous task, and one my mother refused to explain when my father demanded an explanation. He looked at her smooth hands and saw that they were covered with scratches from the branches.

"Did you go nuts, Lilly? What did you do that for?" he asked.

"I didn't like the way they looked. They needed a haircut," she said when he pressed her for an answer.

He called her a "Bahaymah," Yiddish for a mad cow, and started to rail about the consequences they might face. "We only rent this house; it was not for you to make war on the bushes."

By now the rumor had reached them that the house belonged to a gangster who had purchased a great deal of Bronx property with his prohibition profits, a gangster whose name was disguised by the rental agent but might as well be the notorious Dutch Schultz, who was known to have invested heavily in Bronx real estate. "You don't dig up Dutch Schultz's hedges on a whim," my father protested, speaking the forbidden name to give emphasis to his complaint. But he soon understood what she would not explain, because to speak her fear might make it real, that she wanted a clear view of whatever might secretly creep into our garden and endanger her children—a kidnapper, a wild dog, a hit man searching for the miscreant owner, a peddler offering to sharpen dull knives but actually spreading polio for sport, gypsies on the hunt for beautiful children to maim and turn into crippled beggars, or possibly one of my father's uninvited relatives who might focus their jealous, evil eyes and rapacious hands on her children when she was not there to guard them. If to fear was crazy, then she admitted to being crazy. But to her it was crazy *not to fear* such people and such possibilities.

It did not matter to her what my father thought. It rarely did. My mother went her own way, undisturbed by his rages and his threats that later dwindled into complaints, deep breathing and headshakes, only to be reborn as apologies and gifts. No matter what he said, her children would be watched, and watched again until the Lindbergh kidnapper was captured, tried and executed, the polio epidemic had subsided, the annoying Yellen relatives sent into oblivion, and she could again breathe deeply and report to her sister Ida that all was well. And after that, we would be watched some more because you never knew what threat was waiting around the next corner.

The Wanderer

My father liked nothing better than to have a mission, a quest, to be sent out into the world with an impossible task, proof of his determination to succeed against all odds in pleasing his wife and providing for his children. If a child was ill and the local pharmacy was closed, he would walk the length of the Bronx into Harlem or Washington Heights, crossing the Macomb's Dam Bridge that spanned the Bronx and upper Manhattan to find an all-night drug store and purchase the cough remedy, the Kleenex, and the camphorated oil my mother requested. If she so much as expressed a desire for a particular loaf of seedless rye bread or a special layer cake, he would head for the Grand Concourse, four miles away, and buy the best pastries from Sutter's Bakery, and a half dozen of that treat she adored, the small Charlotte Russe cakes, whipped cream concoctions perched on small circles of lemon sponge cake, topped with cherries, all held together with shiny white cardboard collars, and set upon small paper doilies.

In the course of his travels he would sometimes stop off at Ruschmeyer's, the German ice cream parlor on nearby University Avenue, the main thoroughfare that led to the campus of New York University. This ice cream parlor was famous for its vanilla malteds and strawberry banana splits and he would bring back tightly hand-packed cartons with three of her favorite flavors inside. This spotless, white marble-countered store was later rumored to be a Nazi spy hangout in the years preceding the war, that rumor eventually destroying the reputation of the German Ruschmeyer family, but the business prospered nonetheless, so good was their ice cream that it survived imaginary swastikas and rumors of atrocities plotted in the back room. My father's pride in satisfying my mother's requests was that of a fairy tale suitor sent out on an impossible quest, a Parsifal determined to find and bring home today's particular Holy Grail, all for the reward of her smile and her perfunctory thanks.

My father liked to walk and he liked to lie, and these missions allowed for a combined expression of both preferences. My mother knew he often exaggerated the miles covered in search of her current necessity; he may have found what she needed a block away in a shop on University Avenue and stopped off at the Macombs Junior High School to watch a handball game for an hour or so. But she had learned, as we all would, that Nat's stories were improvisations on reality, improvements on the humdrum nature of life. He liked more than anything else to control his short supply of the truth and not squander it, even among his loved ones.

Years later, when we had all moved to Manhattan, and he was long retired, I was seated in a crosstown bus, looking out the window, when I saw him walking down East 86th Street in Yorkville. I asked him later that evening what he was doing there and he replied, "You must be mistaken. I wasn't there. I was walking down 79th Street to visit the library." It was clearly untrue, but I didn't press him on it. I'd long ago learned that he liked teasing reality whenever possible and keeping his secrets close to his chest—even when there were no secrets to keep—just for the sake of his game.

Prisoners of Good Fortune

What had first drawn my mother to the house on Andrews Avenue—its isolation from its neighbors, its situation as the largest house on the crest of the hilly street, it's separation from those disease-breathing crowds of the Lower East Side—now acted as a threat to our safety. Mother knew that we were alone and conspicuous in our good fortune in the darkest days of the Great Depression.

The family's extraordinary leap into upper middle class comfort, brought about by the prosperity of my father's new sweater business, allowed for a series of Polish housemaids from Pennsylvania; plain, pale, mousy women who would ultimately enter a convent; young women who had taken an unspoken vow of chastity and obedience long before they took the veil. For my mother, they were perfect household helpers. "You didn't have to tell her what to do," my mother said of a new Polish recruit to her sister Ida, this being high praise, followed by the yet higher praise, "She's spotless." They were indeed clean girls, in their plain-collared dresses that looked like uniforms; quiet girls whose first introduction to indoor plumbing and electric lights was in our home. These women freed my mother from other housekeeping tasks, the cleaning and the cooking, the diaper changing and the feeding, while she was on her constant, unrelieved watch. Like my mother, they were all great house cleaners and terrible cooks.

My mother discovered the wonders of Campbell's Tomato and Chicken Noodle Soup cans long before Andy Warhol. This, together with the easy, forgiving ways of steaming hot overcooked spaghetti served with an unheated Del Monte tomato paste direct from the can and topped with farmer's cheese, provided a special treat. She made little effort to improve her culinary skills. These few dishes, together with the fried liver in onions and the familiar boiled meats of her childhood, had completed her weekly menu. A side dish of Del Monte apple sauce, straight from the jar, a shimmering of Jell-O, or a dollop of sour cream on some burned latkes were as far as she would go with her gourmet cooking. If one didn't have the time to stir up a pot of Jell-O or Junket for the children, there were local bakeries with their Danish pastries to complete a dessert. She rarely looked inside *The Way to A Man's Heart*, the Fanny Farmer cookbook which remained unread in the kitchen. A wedding gift from her friend Muriel, its white oilcloth cover illustrating small chefs marching towards a large male heart, it was kept for its intentions rather than its usefulness. It stayed pristine in the breakfast nook, carried from apartment to apartment for her lifetime, just in case. The few simple dishes she had learned from her mother and older sisters in her childhood—the beef flanken boiled into a skein of brown rubbery strings and spiced by a delicious red horseradish, a leathery steak tossed about on a frying pan and smothered in onions, kosher chicken laundered to an incredible tasteless whiteness—completed the family menu. As long as the dishes and the glasses were spotless, what was placed on and in them mattered little if it was fresh, for fresh was always healthy.

Our diet would be varied on a Sunday by kosher corned beef brought in from a restaurant on Burnside Avenue, with a fruit juice drink or a Dr. Brown's cream soda. For all its failures as culinary art, it was a wonderful time for eating, before diet laws and gourmet cooking spoiled the guiltless innocence of the American table. My mother, as one might expect, began to put on weight with all the starchy foods she prepared. Although she would never be fat, she had soon outgrown her model-size clothes, and she was now what was then called "pleasingly plump." Our lunches, the peanut butter and jelly sandwiches on white bread, crusts cut off neatly, were only supplanted by skinless and boneless sardines packed in oil on a bed of iceberg lettuce, varied by a cut-up banana sinking in a sea of sour cream. The kitchen always contained sour cream jars decorated with Walt Disney cartoon characters that served as glasses for the malted milks—shaken in an early, delightfully noisy Waring Blender—all in my mother's desperate effort to fatten up her inexorably skinny children.

The many Polish girls in our life came from one Wisneski family, and all were called Mary. There was Mary Margaret, Mary Alice and

Mary Jean, all with their distinguishing second names left off to make their employer's lives easier, and although many of our neighbors employed a weekly maid, a live-in maid was nearly unheard of, and nobody else employed white help. Perhaps it was her admiration for her first teacher, the Negro woman who had given her that doll, but my mother could not go down to that train station on Jerome Avenue where the desperate black women congregated during the Depression years. The local housewives were looking for cheap labor, the black women hoping for a day's work cleaning houses and doing laundry, and a back and forth of bargaining for wages could be heard for a day's work. That was where her sister Ida found her "schwartzes" and where Uncle Mike hired the young black women for his laundry, but it offended my mother to think of any woman forced to beg and bargain for work at slave wages, particularly those who had been the granddaughters of slaves.

My mother knew instinctively that this was wrong, that these desperate women were obliged to offer themselves up for the cheapest wages and humiliating treatment by people who had learned nothing of charity or decency from their own early poverty. It was not that she paid her Marys much more than the going rate, good help was not to be ruined by excessive wages, but they sat down at table and ate with us, and for their tenure with the family were treated with respect, "respect" being part of the unspoken bargain struck between my mother and her servants. It translated into "I am no better than you are. I am just luckier. Do as I say and some of my good luck may rub off on you." Later, during the war years, when the supply of white labor dried up, and the new generation of Marys having found jobs in war factories, my mother would employ Negro maids, but she was never comfortable with them in that capacity. She had an overwhelming sympathy for people who were trapped by their dark skin in the poverty her fair skin had helped her to escape. When we had a black woman working in the house, my mother worked beside her as a team effort, allegedly to "keep an eye on her," but in truth my mother was eager to show her employee that hard labor was something she could share, and was not despised here. She would learn about their families, their lives, and manage to both patronize them with cast-off clothing and suspiciously out-of-date food, and befriend them with honest practical advice and extra money when needed.

My mother found it necessary to have a young woman on call at all times, never knowing when my next asthma attack might happen. It was at this time that my mother feared that her good fortune was harming her children. She started carrying her mink coat about in a large paper bag to avoid the scrutiny of neighbors, past the castellated Salvation Army Training campus towards University Avenue where she caught a taxi cab, only to put on that coat when she was safely out of the neighborhood, so that no prying, envious eyes might settle on her and wish us harm. On occasion she would take me and Simone on a walk to the small antique shop on University Avenue near the Park Plaza theater, where she indulged her taste for hand-decorated Viennese plates, cut-glass bowls, black modernist Belgian pottery lamps and vases, a hodgepodge of decorations, unified only by her liking them. She shared with my sister a love of beauty and, later on, an easy recognition of what was fine and what was not, what pleased the eye with its craft and beauty, or what was absurdly fancy, that being the worst failure in style, something being *ongepotchket*, the Yiddish for overdone. Years later, when my sister was a renowned interior designer, she would recreate some of my mother's furniture for her clients, fancifully placing a clock in the back of a small regency chair that my mother had purchased years before. But it was in the Bronx on these antique store trips that my small discerning sister developed a love for beautiful objects—the Boch Freres pottery and lamps, the Waterford crystal vases, the Japanese prints and the Viennese bronzes that were offered there. These forays of my mother's into antique shops started a fascination in me for curiosities, for in that very shop on University Avenue there was more than pretty china, there were oddities. I had discovered an object behind a glass dome labeled a stuffed merman, a form of starfish that had been altered to look like a man-fish, complete with the grossest of features, bulging eyes and jagged teeth, something that intrigued me mightily, and disgusted my mother. My mother, observing my fascination with it, and rejecting my request that she buy it for me, declared that it was repulsive, but to me it was as amazing as anything in the Ripley's Believe It or Not cartoon, suggesting that there were wonders that went beyond the limits of the Bronx, wonders worth examining and keeping safe behind glass cases. Only once before had she denied me an object of desire that I seriously craved. There was an elderly "colored" man named Jimmy who did odd jobs about the neighborhood—washed windows, carried out refuse, and shined shoes—in a desperate effort to support his family. During the Depression years he had developed a remarkable skill of making ship models out of old chewing gum, collecting the used gum, moistening it with a pail of water to make it malleable, and shaping it with great precision into a model boat with his pocket knife. He had shown me a schooner he had put together in this fashion, complete with a mast and sail. It was a masterpiece in its detail and proportion and I admired it greatly, running inside the house to ask my mother for the two dollars he asked for it. She came out to inspect the ship, saw its unusual materials, and told Jimmy that she would not purchase it for me. When he left in disappointment, I was given a gentle lecture on avoiding such repositories of germs in the future, bad enough that I played marbles in the streets, and may have put some of those "immies" in my mouth from time to time, but a ship of used chewing gum? Never!

As soon as our lease expired, we would move out of the dangerous house on Andrews Avenue into one of the undistinguished two-family row houses that lined Loring Place, and it was here, with its glass-enclosed sun parlor that faced the street, and its warren of small rooms, that I best remember my early years and my sister Simone.

The Laughing Time

My mother, for all her beauty, was no match for my sister when it came to what was then called personality. And personality was one part wit, one part looks, and two parts laughter. I recall that giggle of Simone's, its sheer exhilaration; a celebration of the foolishness and unpredictability of life, a laugh she could not easily control once it escaped her throat and was set loose in the world. I remember her laughter as my Grandfather Meyer prayed in Hebrew on the High Holy Days, his head jerking up and down from his prayer book to the Almighty above, as she whispered to me wickedly that it looked like Grampa was bobbing for God as if for apples. He glanced darkly at the laughing child who had made this ridiculous connection, which had then set off my own uncontrollable laughter. Simone would then run from the dining room and collapse in a fit of giggles, quickly forgiven by the elders whose first concern was that she was not ill. "It's too much excitement for her," my mother explained without apology.

Simone's laugh would challenge anything that smacked of high seriousness. It could be inspired by the self-important performance of a girl who sang "Trees" in a reedy soprano during school assembly, as my sister buried her face in her hands to keep the laugh from breaking out. It was a laugh that punctured the solemnity of Cousin Gertrude's military instructions as she tried to teach her younger cousin the rules of Mah Jong, rattling off the various hands with their bams, flowers and cracks in her crackling, serious voice, all accompanied by Simone's wild amusement. It was the reckless, forbidden laughter that is only permitted to the supremely self-assured. She even laughed at herself, so difficult for a child to do. I recall her as a nine-year-old singing "The Moon And I" from *The Mikado* as she accompanied herself on the piano, hitting a sour high note, her singing voice a brave but dreadful instrument, and collapsing in laughter at her shrill attempt at Yum Yum's solipsistic ballad.

When I was four I caught the laugh, along with the chicken pox, from my sister. Whenever that laugh started to well up inside her, it began to possess me like a demon and we were soon gasping for air. It ran through us, one to the other until we were doubled over with that inexorable, inappropriate, disrespectful, delightful and childish shout of joy, so powerful, so filled with its release from the lies that people told in their search for importance, shattering the airs they assumed to win respect; that laugh that no disapproving adult look could silence. We shared a lifelong distrust of solemnity, pretentiousness, and other people's lies, often forgiving and forgetting our own along the way.

My mother, for all her admonishments, was also laughing at such times; only she buried it deep in her throat, so that it was forced to come out in the tears of joy that occasionally flowed from her eyes. Somehow, she had connected with our childhood, and allowed herself feelings she could not afford in her own youth. Our laughter awakened the rebel in my mother, if only for a moment, to release her from the role of good mother, good wife, good friend, but never for long; she soon resumed the role, the one that gave her such power in our family.

Despite her early disapproval of me, Simone was curious about me, as she would be curious about everything in life—a painted turtle, a box of fresh, wondrously smelling colored crayons, a new dress, the rooms of the enormous doll house my father had bought for her filled with perfect reproductions of fine English furniture, the lives of movie stars in the fan magazines she devoured. Hers was a curiosity that knew no limits, wandering out to examine a next door neighbor's cat; a painting of Venice reproduced in a magazine that she tore out and pinned to the wallpapered walls with thumb tacks, or a wildflower that found its way to one of the many empty lots that were situated between the castellated apartment buildings of the Bronx. Curiosity was part of her small but powerful arsenal of artistry that would complicate, enrich and define her later life. As part of that curiosity, she was prepared to accept me; if only she could discover some purpose for my existence, and since I was neither decorative nor useful, some possibility of pleasure that could be balanced against my annoying presence. Why the need for this interloper Sherman, if she was as dear and as perfect as our parents professed? She soon suspected that I was our mother's favorite, and indeed I soon was, having greater need of her time and affection, but Simone would forever be her father's girl.

Simone read early. My father would take her out on his long walks; aimless wanderings that could last for hours, usually ending in a return trip with Simone riding high on his narrow shoulders. They would walk along finding animal shapes in the clouds and he would hoot with joy as she made out an elephant in the sky. During these peregrinations he would buy a copy of *The New York Times* and use it as the main prop in her public reading performance. My father, like many men of his generation, was a master of the art of folding newspapers so that they could be read section by section, but for the newspaper performance of my sister he kept it unfolded, spreading it out before him, determined to contrast its enormity with that of his tiny, brilliant daughter. He put the huge paper into her doll-sized hands and, to the delight of passers-by, the infant phenomenon would read the headlines, announcing Roosevelt's plans for the NRA or Hitler's rise to power, while standing on a park bench, her tiny head hidden from view as the words poured forth from behind the huge newspaper with ease and clarity in a soft child's voice. Only the pompom of her woolen cap bouncing up and down as her eyes traversed the pages of the paper betrayed the existence of a small child.

Later, my father would artfully fold the paper into two tri-corner Napoleon hats, one of which he placed over his gray felt fedora, and the other over the bow on my sister's curls; together they would wear them proudly home as he held my sister's hand, until the wind, or a disapproving look from a stranger, made my sister lose hers. He had a great need for praise for his children, praise that had been denied to him for anything but the money he could offer his family; praise for their good looks, their cleverness, and their unmatched charm. But the praise wore off quickly. Too soon the compliments passed into the air, and more were needed to satisfy his hunger for acceptance. Once, a few years later, when it was my turn to accompany him on his walks, he made that newspaper hat and placed it on my head. I tore it off and told him I would not wear it. People would laugh at me. He replied with his customary remark, "Nobody's looking at you." But I knew that my father wanted me to be looked at, that he tempered his great love for us with his uncontrollable desire to tease, to trick, and to make our moods march in lockstep with his own. He never succeeded with me, or with Simone, but he never stopped trying.

As I grew, Simone protested vehemently against my wild ways. It offended her that as a four-year-old I preferred to tear the pages of a book or newspaper rather than study them for clues to the mystery of the world. She was disappointed by my refusal to arrange my wooden alphabet blocks into anything that represented a word or a building; amazed that I preferred to use these blocks as missiles to destroy whatever doll house or castle stood within my reach. From her earliest years she had a natural sense of style and design, and I seemed to lack all of that, adding nothing to a room when I entered it. I was clearly the demon seed that had sprung up in the family to torment her. I would scribble in her books, eat her crayons and rip up her paper dolls, pull the wigs off the heads of her composition dolls and crush the faces of the celluloid ones with my foot. She soon learned that nothing in that house was safe from me, nor were limits being placed on my feral ways by my indulgent, worried mother. My childhood asthma had made me exempt from the ordinary laws of family life; it was larger than the desire to civilize me. Mother would excuse any of my household crimes by claiming that I was cranky, I was overtired; "forgive him, he's still a baby." I was never reproached, only distracted, as quick hands removed dangerous scissors from mine; it was no wonder Simone came to regard the intruder as a source of ceaseless annoyance, with no hope for a better future ahead. It was perhaps her complaints to our father that caused me the most troubling nights.

From time to time, my father would come into my room right before my bedtime, push back my hair from my forehead, and declare in a somber voice, "Sherman, you have a guilty forehead." He then proceeded to tell me exactly what crimes I had committed against my sister, and what I had broken in the course of the day. I was not punished for these but I was astonished and frightened, and for years it seemed to me that he had this great forensic skill to read crime on a guilty forehead. After all, I could look at his face as he told a lie, and watch as his thin lips twitched slightly, a sure giveaway of his embarking on a tall tale that was sailing further and further out to sea away from the harbor of truth. If I could read his lying lips, he could no doubt read my guilty forehead that furrowed up whenever he approached me. But then one morning it struck me that only my sister knew these crimes of mine and I went at her with a vengeance.

And so we fought. Simone was master of the hidden slap and the secret pinch, while I struck out for the belly or the chin, and failing that, kicked ankles. When I hit her she held my tiny wrists in her hands and danced me around the room, teasing me. I cried. She called me "A stupid, ugly baby!" I repeated this in a loud voice as I approached her again in tight-fisted fury while she caught my hands once more and laughed with contempt at my pitiful rage. Mother entered the room to still the commotion and enforce a peace that was more a temporary lull in our battles. When I accused Simone of picking on me, she claimed that I had caused all the trouble by interfering with her toys or messing up her room, even on those occasions when she had entered my room to provoke a fight that might relieve a boring homework assignment. My mother would reiterate her favorite phrase, "No fighting. No hitting. No pinching. And stop this name-calling. You mustn't belittle each other. You are all you have." What a bleak prospect that must have seemed to Simone. If I was all she had, what she had was next to nothing, worse than nothing. We rarely obeyed my mother when it came to the cessation of our fights, but the phrase, repeated time and again, did its intended work. Somehow, she instilled in us this sense of the other as our first and last hope in this dangerous world, and so it remained throughout our life together, until Simone died and I learned the terrible truth of my mother's claim.

We understood that it was our obligation to love one another, no matter how hard the slap, how cruel the insult, how nasty the pinch; forgiveness was the all-purpose answer to the offense. "You must never go to bed angry with one another," my mother intoned. How many times she must have taken her own advice, as she tried to make peace with my tumultuous father. How many times did she recall that he brought her the money she needed for a comfortable life, money that meant safety for her children and herself. She would not allow herself to dwell on his sudden rages after they had subsided. She buried the fact of his violent shouts, and perhaps worst for her, his annoyingly amorous nature.

My mother was cursed and blessed with a literal mindedness that allowed her to live on the surface of life with contentment. It was a lack of imagination, not to be confused with a lack of intelligence or a hard heart. She was as smart as her needs and her life required; as smart as the welfare of her children demanded. Only in her old age did she think about the world beyond family, and then with disapproval for the ways of the warmongers and political hacks, an interest in the world she never showed in her youth. Her taste in literature and films was sentimental and ecumenical; a religious epic about the sorrows and triumphs of a Moses or a Jesus would move her deeply, as were stories of poor mothers obliged to give up their infants to be raised in luxury by the rich; mothers who could only watch them from a distance, tearfully standing in the rain. Hers was a nun's taste in miracles and resurrections, waters parting, the dead raised, renunciations followed by reconciliations; it held out the hope that sometime, somewhere, she would be reunited with her lost brother, sister and mother in a heaven she did not believe in, yet she dared not deny. It was a hope she would never altogether abandon. The hard, bitter past lived in her. It was never far from her present day consciousness. It lived behind her welcoming smile and her love for her children and her generosity towards anyone who needed her. It had bred in her old age patience beyond all human understanding.

I was a poor eater with a small appetite, reflected in my bony physique, and she spoon fed me, slowly, carefully, scraping up whatever gruel I let drip on to my chin and reintroducing it to my open mouth; all this continued into my third year. When she had run out of nursery rhymes and picture books to distract me, she took what she knew about her family and fed it to me with my farina. I learned from her about her life in Europe, her life on the Lower East Side, a world as distant from my own as that of those ancient nursery rhymes she would read to me. These were stories of Cossacks riding into town on horseback accompanied by packs of barking dogs, while the family hid in cellars; tales of that young cousin Bella sold into prostitution by a wicked stepmother; dangerous howling creatures, half wolf, half dog, who wandered the muddy dirt roads of the squalid village main street at dusk; and wrinkled ignorant peasants, their faces as furrowed and cruel as the land they tilled; men and women who regarded the Jews as less than human, who mocked the Jews as creatures with hidden horns and murderous rituals. It was as if she had sprung from a medieval world of evil goblins and rampaging giants into this modern age and, indeed, she had. Although she had left Russia by her third birthday, these memories were passed on to me and my sister as reminders to us that we had found a safe haven in this country, only marred by the ugly, diseased slums, the craziness of kidnappings and race riots and such anti-Semites as Father Coughlin. She warned us about the Irish boys at Holy Spirit Church on Fordham Road who regarded us as "Christ killers" and might toss an ice-ball at innocent Jewish children, but despite such incidents, she assured us that this was a place of refuge, a place where one could do more than survive.

Growing up against the background music of my father's outbursts, I thought it a natural event; this was the norm, it was the father's role to shout, reach for his belt, unbuckle it, grab the belt and wave it around like an enraged rodeo cowboy spinning his lariat, threatening his disobedient children with immediate doom. It was the rage of a man of his time, filled with bluster and angry threats, raised hands, flailing leather belts; a rage permitted by the world of the 1930s in a man of wealth. In our own time, it most closely resembles road rage. But the rage was brought on by one of us trying to pass him without warning—which meant something he saw that set us apart; that might make us reject him and shut him out of our lives. He rarely caught us as we scrambled for safety behind the lock of the bathroom door, aided by our mother who stood between his rage and us. Chances are he didn't want to catch us, but when he did catch one of us because we stumbled in our haste towards safety, or sometimes foolishly stood our ground, we received a smart blow from his strap on our bottoms but never more than one, my mother was always there to intercede and stop him, to his own great relief. Once, having removed his belt in a fury, intending to punish us for a word of disrespect, his pants fell down around his knees and he stood there, shouting, trapped within the trousers, his long underwear, his "gotkis" on view, as Simone, my mother and I laughed as never before. "Crazy lunatic. *Mishigas Nat*. Enough with this temper of yours. Stop now. Stop!" she demanded. And he did as he pulled up his pants in shame.

Since I never managed to know what brought on these rages, what set off this otherwise gentle man's hair-trigger temper, it was like life in old Japan, where the calmest of tea ceremonies could be followed by earthquakes and tidal waves. Anything could bring to the surface the torrents of rage bottled inside him; an unexpected demand for some toy, a disapproving or mocking remark about a relative or a friend, any sign of discontent with our happy, prosperous lives. The one sure thing was that it always came to us as a surprise. What was perfectly acceptable to say on a Monday was a cause of fury on a Tuesday. As we grew, he viewed every sign of disapproval on our part as a criticism of his capacity to provide for us. The most innocent remark became an accusation of failure that he could not tolerate. But since the very same remarks might pass without incident at other times, one could never learn how to predict the next eruption. There was no true barometer to predict a coming storm. And so we pretended that all the fathers of the world exploded with rage for no discernible reason at unexpected times and figured that we would live through it and someday escape from it.

Aided by my mother, we accepted her view that my father was crazy but well meaning, loving us beyond life itself, and driven to these volcanic outbursts by overwork, business worries, and the secret manipulations of his begging, demanding brothers and sisters, the infamous Yellen *schnorers*. She now viewed them as a well-organized group, a trained militia, a trade union of beggars and a choir of mendicants, well-rehearsed in the art of snatching money from my generous father. Yet there was an upside to his rages for our family. Such paternal explosions were always followed by extraordinary gifts. A new fur coat for my mother, toys from FAO Schwarz, and a Baldwin baby grand piano bought at auction for my sister. A sad, apologetic look in my father's large watery green eyes accompanied his attempt to patch over the event with a wet kiss on the cheek and a mournful "I love you, Sherm. I love you, Simone. I'm sorry I frightened you." Irrational punishment would thus be followed by irrational rewards.

And never did my sister or I think that this was extraordinary behavior. It was the world as we knew it. People could be punished for expressing their true feelings and rewarded for suffering the rages of an angry father in silence. His need for affirmation was so great that years later, when reading *King Lear*, I understood Lear's choice of rewarding flattery and punishing candor not as some aberrant act of a mad king but as something my own father might do.

As far as we understood, this was something that all families endured behind closed doors; something one did not discuss; something to be put out of mind as soon as possible. And my mother encouraged us in this. Perhaps she weighed his behavior and found that the good far outweighed the bad. Perhaps she had to accept him as he was, only hoping to modify the unacceptable. She knew that as a married woman with two small children there was no escape from this marriage. Where would she go? Who would take her in? Divorce was unthinkable to her. Yes, Tante Mary was divorced, but that was in Europe, and Tante Mary was ugly, eccentric, childless, self-supporting, and the exception to all rules. Once my mother refused to lease an apartment that offered a fresh paint job and two months free rent, because the superintendent had disclosed the fact that the couple who had occupied it previously had ended their marriage in an angry divorce. Divorce was a sign of weakness, a moral giddiness that she could not accept in herself or others, a sign of being a quitter, a weakling and a failure. It is hard to judge her by the standards of our time. Indeed, it is altogether hard to judge her at all, because all I can remember most days is her loving kindness and the gentle care that she gave to us. Even my father resists judgment. It is far too easy to characterize his outbursts as child abuse, to pin a tail on this donkey and thus win the game. He was so much more loving than cruel, so much more caring than crazy, that he left us with an inextricable knot of good and bad memories, which cannot now be untangled. I can now see the complexity of his humanity, as well as the crazy giant of my childhood.

Fortunately, my father would be away most of the day at work. He never stayed home from work at the George Washington Knit Goods Company, and later at his own Ro-Nat Sportswear. At work he was beloved by the deaf stock girl, Mildred (who groaned with inarticulate pleasure when she saw him), worshipped by his hunchbacked messenger, Jerry, and adored by Dorothy his stammering receptionist, whose hair lip amazed me. Even the Negro employees who worked the stockroom called him "Nat," and he knew the names of their children. They all forgave him his occasional rages, knowing that a raise in salary might soon follow the tantrum. Not only did he employ the unemployable, he paid them good wages and gave them the dignity of work—unusual in that day and age—despite the protests of his partner Max, who complained that the office looked like a charity ward in an asylum. We visited that office on school holidays and the employees treated us as royalty. Their love for my father was unfeigned; he joked with them easily, and I most enjoyed washing my hands in the bathroom with its black, gritty lava soap, the carbolic cleanser that most offices used. Here, unlike home with its soft Turkish towels, were coarse paper towels, all of which spoke of hard work and the grown-up world where such fripperies must be avoided. And so Simone and I would grow up knowing that the most generous and loving person in our life was also the angriest when possessed by his demon rages, but a man of limitless charity and a gut understanding of the suffering of others.

On Saturdays, once a month, my father and mother took us to a matinee at a Broadway theater and, on rare occasions, a touring show that played a small legitimate theater that still existed off the Concourse in the Bronx. My father's ticket broker, employed by him to obtain orchestra tickets for buyers he wished to impress, provided us with the best seats in the house. We saw all the new musicals such as *Rosalinda*, *Song of Norway* and *Connecticut Yankee*, and the family shows devoted to the subject of perky teenaged kids falling in and out of love, from *Life With Father* to *Junior Miss*—the kind of plays that would later become the sitcom on television and leave the theater as a place for the big hits. Thanks to my father's love of theater he wanted us to see it, whether it was appropriate or not. Thus, we saw the early performances of *A Streetcar Named Desire*, *Death of a Salesman* and *The Glass Menagerie* at a time when theater attracted the greatest of actors and the audience was made up of New Yorkers from all the boroughs with a longing for the new, rather than tourists with a passion for the familiar. There were dozens of shows to choose from and the theater programs piled up on the tooled leather Sheridan drum table in our living room.

On Sundays I often accompanied my father to Yankee Stadium. I enjoyed the first game, the excitement of the crowd, the players running about on the field as I tried to keep score in the program and distinguish between Joe DiMaggio and the other players from the grandstand where we sat, but the games in those days went on forever, only to be called by darkness. They felt like triple-headers, and by the end of the afternoon I was asleep, failing to master the art of keeping score properly, only to be awoken and told that the game was over. I knew he wanted me to ask who won, so I did so with feigned interest. He then went over the game play by play, enjoying this chance to act out the excitement he had felt, an excitement I had somehow inexplicably slept through. But these ballgames were a small price to pay for the visits to the Museum of Natural History, where my taste for wonders was fully satisfied by the stuffed whale, the huge elephant, the dinosaur bones, and the tableaux of exhibitions of American Indian life. It was not the gleaming museum of today with huge banners advertising million dollar exhibitions, but a place of dusty dark corners and molting taxidermy which only added to its mystery and wonder of worlds I did not know, worlds I longed to see.

Despite the time out for theater and ballgames and museums, my father's rages developed in me the impatience with him that I carried to the end of his life. I began to understand without a word being spoken that I was a tremendous disappointment to him. His marriage to my beautiful mother and the production of their first child, my clever, charming sister, together with his new, spectacular business success, had lifted his spirits, given him a sense of self-worth that he had never known before. Just looking at his wife and daughter told him that he was no longer the poor, ugly boy with a broom in his hand and an onerous burden to support his brothers and sisters. But with me, this strange, asthmatic, willful boy, scrawny as a chicken, deeply innumerate despite all efforts to teach me the basics of arithmetic, filled with a temper to match his own and showing signs of wasteful and costly talents, the flaws he saw in me made him less certain of his own accomplishments. If a man cannot make a son in his own image, what failings he must have within himself.

Sensing this, I turned away from him and his need for constant affection and affirmation. If I was not the son he wanted, a boy who jumped up and down and cheered during ballgames, a son who could multiply numbers in his head with alacrity, he was not the father I needed, one who protected me with quiet days and truthful statements, but we were father and son, locked together for our lifetimes. As I grew older, he continually annoyed me with the excessive pride he now took in my accomplishments, my college awards, my career awards, and my place in what he considered the great world. Hadn't I spent my honeymoon in Norman Rockwell's Vermont cottage, a friend of that family? Hadn't I become a collaborator and friend of the great composer Richard Rodgers? Didn't I have tea with Cary Grant at his Plaza Hotel apartment? But when he asked about my career and I answered with information about my current work, it never seemed to be enough to satisfy his own need to be filled up with his children's glory. On his deathbed he asked me to tell him about my Tony nomination and my Emmy Awards, and when I indulged him in this he turned to me and asked, "So Sherm, how come you never got an Academy Award like your friend Peter Stone?" It was then that I exploded. "When can I ever do anything to please you? When will it be enough to make you happy?" As soon as the words came out of my mouth he began to weep and I regretted them. This was no way to talk to a dying old man, but there was no way to take it back, and I did not know another way to talk to him without losing myself in the process.

Shortly before he was hospitalized for his undiagnosed final illness, one that was causing him to waste away, one which according to the best medical advice was the result of his geriatric depression—it was in fact a pancreatic cancer that would take his life—he had drifted into a lethargy and depression that resisted any efforts of mine to cheer him up. My mother, now desperately eager to see him smile, called the dreadful Yellen brothers and sisters to tell them of Nat's illness in the hope that they would visit him, but none of them came to his hospital room, although it was unlikely that they could have cheered him. Even his beloved Yankee ballgames, which he watched religiously on the television and which often gave him relief from his demons, failed to calm his agitation and growing despair. Simone and I took him to a round of doctors, geriatric doctors, doctors who specialized in eating disorders, gastroenterologists, helped him out of his clothes, and into them again after the various examinations, forced to take stock of his wasted body. He was now the bag of bones that he had called me once when I was a child, refusing to eat. My sister and I had been worn out taking him to doctors who had no answer for his weight loss and lethargy, other than some form of senile depression. Despite the fact that she was enjoying a great career as a designer, her show house gaining attention in *The New York Times* and in magazines, she was to be the caretaker of our aging parents. I was only there when the burden of getting one of them in and out of taxi cabs on medical visits was more than she could handle alone.

One day, shortly before his death, when I was a man in my forties out on my own family shopping mission—I was going to the supermarket to buy some milk for my young sons—I passed the apartment house where my parents lived and I saw my father standing quietly across the street, leaning against the red brick wall of his apartment building on Third Avenue and 78th Street, a thin, sunken old man, his ashen face held upwards to catch some fugitive rays of the winter sun, lost in his now constant despair. I sensed his isolation and loneliness and for a moment thought of crossing the street to speak with him. I waited for the light to change and started to cross, then turned back and continued on my way towards the supermarket. I didn't wish to hear his litany of complaints once again, his "What's wrong with me, Sherm? What's the matter?" Nor did I feel like taking the time in my busy day to chat him up briefly, answering his inevitable request, "So, what's the good news?" or accept the wet paternal kiss. I knew that upstairs in the apartment my mother was struggling with her own helpless feelings, unable to endure these long weeks of his latest depression. All about their apartment were little notes he had written to himself: *Cheer up, tomorrow is the first day of...*; *Nothing is ever as bad as...*; followed by quotations from Norman Vincent Peale and other popular savants, some long out of date, but still valid currency for my desperate father.

This was the last time I would see my father outside of his hospital bed in Mount Sinai, where soon I would watch him quietly die as the Yankees ballgame on his room's television set droned on. He would eagerly await our arrival, smile brightly, and then fall into his trance. Despite this lethargy, there was always a fellow patient, a roommate in a bed nearby who knew more about my life and my accomplishments than I cared for him to know, having been informed by my father about his renowned son and daughter. I was always being asked if I knew so-and-so, some distant relative of the patient who had made good in Hollywood, and although I usually didn't, I felt obliged to say that yes, I had heard of the man, after which I was treated to a list of his credits. The Yellen relatives—all of whom were alive at that time—never came to see my father after my mother alerted them to his condition, proof to my mother that her early judgment about them was correct; they were takers, *schnorers* and moral miscreants only worthy of her contempt. I came only because it relieved my mother and my sister from attending his deathwatch alone.

And yet the picture of the failing, querulous old man is a false one, or only partially true. He had made a great feast of his retirement, spending his days with his grandchildren, and finding at long last the childhood that had eluded him. I had watched him become the best, the most attentive, the most loving of grandfathers, generous with his time and interest in these marvels that had come into his later life. He would rejoice in my sister's young daughter Mindy, taking her to Nunley's Amusement Park in Long Island where my sister then lived, often losing his way because he was the worst of drivers, but somehow always getting the child home, exhausted and delighted. He would take my sons to Central Park for visits to the zoo and to watch the mechanical clock, and as they grew, accompany them to the Natural History and Metropolitan Museum on a rainy afternoon, as he did their father. He never raised his voice to these children who adored him for his geniality and his generosity. Age had given him a peace, a respite from his demonic temper, for nothing now was demanded of him except what he did best, which was to love. My ten-year-old son Nicholas was devoted to his grandfather, who took such pride in the boy's encyclopedic knowledge of baseball statistics, and made daily visits to the hospital, often alone, after his own long school day. The old man brightened when he saw the boy and they played gin rummy together until my father fell asleep, exhausted but delighted that here was one person who loved him in the most uncomplicated way, someone whom he could freely trust with his love, someone who asked nothing of him other than just being there.

It is now many years later, yet I still reproach myself for not crossing Third Avenue and greeting him on that day when he was still alive. I was in no mood then to waste time on a sick old man who couldn't give you a straight answer about how he felt. By that time, I didn't want to hear the truth about his feelings, even if he was capable of speaking it. At that moment, I had nothing to say to him nor he to me, so why cross the street for an empty greeting? I have done some questionable things in my life, but passing my father by that day remains with me as my most shameful act. I, his son, had made him invisible to myself. Was it the innocent act of a busy man, caught up in his own active life, or was it a form of patricide, for to the elderly to be ignored by a son or daughter is more than a Jewish joke, it is a form of assassination. Whatever it was, it was something for which I still cannot forgive myself decades later. And lately, I dream of my father. He is lost, poor, separated from our family, living in isolated squalor, and when I come upon him by chance in the street I try to reach out to him, but he is beyond helping, and I know there is no remedy for his dreadful situation. This gregarious man is forced to live alone in my dreams, abandoned by all, despising himself, and avoiding me in his shame, uneasy in my presence, while I feel myself overwhelmed by pity and guilt. I ask for his phone number but when I try to call him later to arrange a meeting, the number is not in service. I ask myself was there ever a number? Is he living cut off from everyone? I wake up, relieved that this was just a dream, but in many ways the dream was not that fanciful. Just as he had failed me, I knew that I had failed him.

Looking back, it seems an odd irony of my childhood that my father with his terrible temper was so affectionate, so eager to give and receive love from us, while my mother rarely kissed us and only embraced us to restrain us or take some dangerous object out of our hands. Her fear of spreading some infection lived within her like a succubus, something that she could never lose, implanted in Russia and in the Lower East Side by the deaths in her family, placing these restraints upon her most loving feelings. Perhaps she thought a kiss would betray her great love for us, a hug might remind God that she was too happy and snatch her happiness away by destroying us. So she restrained herself from betraying her love in any physical way.

For all his angry scenes, his pointless lies, his gross exaggerations, I would not have traded my father for any of the fathers of my friends. It was not the gifts that made me prefer my father. It was his true interest in my being happy. My friends' fathers appeared to be gloomy milquetoasts who barely nodded a greeting over their cigarettes and newspapers, totally disengaged from the life of their family. My friends envied me having such generous parents. Where else but at Sherman's house would you be offered some Walnettos—the caramel candy that most of us loved in those days—or money for an ice cream cup when the Good Humor truck could be heard outside. These friends never knew of my father's rages; this was my great secret. Instead, they thought that I was born into a magic toyshop—a world of never-ending painted soldiers, tinker toys, model trains, Lincoln Logs, puzzles and pickup-sticks provided by parents who actually greeted their children's friends by name, asked them how they felt, what they wanted, what they needed, 'take some fruit, have a cookie" parents who offered all with a warm smile and an enthusiastic greeting.

My first best friend, one who remained a friend until his recent death, was Eugene Linnet, a classmate from the first grade at P.S. 26. He was a clever, handsome blond boy, neatly dressed, well-spoken, serious in his pleasures, interested in everything about him, having studious, informed opinions, and he was a great companion to me. Eugene was the chosen Columbus in the class play, where I was a mournful looking Indian in full headdress and tribal regalia. My parents approved of his good manners and the fact that his mother was a schoolteacher and his father a local dentist. The mother, a stout woman who had all the forbidding hauteur of Margaret Dumont, the dowager in the Marx Brothers movies, had set down her rules for neatness and regularity, evidenced by the pride she took in his picture of a perfect orange, shaded in pastels, and sitting for years on an easel in his bedroom, never to be disturbed or supplanted by another foray into art. We rarely played inside his apartment at 1940 Andrews Avenue, and when we did, feared disturbing anything in it. I recall the address because Gene and I waited anxiously throughout 1939 for the year to end so that his address matched the calendar, a most propitious sign for him. It proved not to be, for in that year we were both removed from the prestigious 2B 1 class to the middling 3 class, spared by the neatness of our clothes and the prosperity of our families from sharing a classroom with the 4 class, the children of the seriously poor, who were regarded as seriously stupid for having being born into poverty.

We played marbles in the streets, bought "loosie" cigarettes together from the local candy store, formed a circle of close friends, Marty Moses, Lionel Sherrow, Ronald Di Maria, all of whom regarded my house as a playland. They were all decent in a way that was peculiar to the era. They shared a boy's sense of honor. At Sherman's there were no slipcovers kept on the furniture after summer, no forbidden rooms for children, no bowls of wax fruit collecting dust in the parlor, only fresh fruit offered by the very welcoming Mrs. Yellen, glasses of malted milk whipped up in her blender, and the bland sugar biscuits she proffered in their wax paper packaging, all these in the effort to fatten me up. If we made a mess, my mother, or the Polish maid would clean up after us without complaint.

I was fast becoming a collector, proud of my acquisitions, generous in sharing them with friends under my watchful eyes, but jealously guarding them from theft and abuse. My early collecting obsession began with those lead soldiers my father bought for me; soldiers who still dressed in the uniform of the Great War, wearing removable metal helmets, some standing, some crouched, carrying carbines, wheeling cannons, bearing ambulance stretchers, finely painted and well molded. Sometimes the soldiers were a reward for passing an arithmetic exam, a triumph of willful cheating over my innumerate condition. The huge lead army that I assembled was a great pride of mine, and I watched over it jealously. No General ever guarded his troops as I did, particularly from my school friends who came over to the house to play, hoping to trade some inferior infantry of their own for the well-equipped army that I had assembled. It was no surprise that my friends loved to visit me in my Aladdin's cave.

Shut ins and Shut outs

I n those days I was what was called a "shut in." The childhood asthma which descended on me at six months old, for which there was no cure and little relief, kept me housebound for some of the school year during my early schooling. I soon realized that I was part of a hidden, secret, privileged group for whom the cruel rules of childhood were ignored: the *shut ins*. Our radio entertainers—Uncle Don and The Singing Lady—told stories for *us*, the sad shut ins, and around the afflicted was an aura of sanctity and virtue. Listeners were advised to send a birthday card to Roberta Stoltz in Ann Arbor, Michigan, a shut in laid low by a rheumatic heart, a get-well card to Herbert Frost in Wilton, Connecticut, a victim of polio who was out of his mechanical lung and doing "nicely" on his new crutches. There were the asthmatic boys like me, gasping for air during an attack, the girls with damaged hearts who were forbidden any exercise, the diabetics who carried about oranges to fuel their blood sugar, and the crippled children who dragged their paralyzed legs about in heavy iron braces, a collection of the stricken in a world that might occasionally pity them but could not help them in any practical way and used sentiment as an anodyne for illnesses. Sentiment was there to justify the great worrisome inconvenience that sick children represented. We were holy because the bible taught that suffering was a prelude to holiness, and this is how the world chose to view us, rather than as the unwanted pests that complicated the lives of their struggling parents in hard times.

Although I attended school intermittently and always managed to be promoted into the next grade, I was home too much to master the uncompromising laws of arithmetic or properly diagram a sentence, separating its verbs from its adjectives and its pronouns. It became my sister's job to collect the homework from my teachers, and I made a desultory effort to keep up with the schoolwork of P.S. 26 and avoid the classrooms of the excellent Mrs. Ryan and Miss Connelly, the fierce female offspring of Irish immigrants, and the Mrs. O'Conners who chose teaching over the nunnery and taught the children of the Jewish and Italian immigrants with an iron hand that today would be forbidden, even in the harshest of parochial schools. It was a world in which neatness counted above all, not so distant from the way my parents had been taught to form their letters. As in my parent's day, good handwriting, filled with well-made loops, a properly dotted i, a well-crossed t, and a shapely s, was rewarded with praise and check marks. Perfectly formed upper and lower case letters were a sign that the child was being prepared for the real world, where a neat script was a passport to future success. The presence of a pocket-handkerchief in the shirt of a small boy would win him favor, as my sister's smartly ironed organdy dresses and hair bows won the approval of all.

School, when I attended it, was for me a place of terror and wonders. I was absent so often that despite the best efforts of my mother, when I returned to school the math work was incomprehensible to me. I felt like I was stranded in a foreign country made up of enemy numbers and their evil allies, fractions. I concentrated on my compositions, knowing that all I needed was a subject and I could scribble forth with the best of them about, "What is the meaning of Flag Day?" "Write about George Washington's childhood days." "My home is…" All this could be finessed with the ease of a born storyteller. In this, and only in this, I had inherited my father's gift for spinning a tale. But the math and geography were constant torments, requiring information I had never learned. Fearing that I would be called upon to answer questions on subjects that were of no interest to me, and therefore unstudied, my idea of hell was to be called to the blackboard to solve an arithmetic problem. I knew my addition, but long division arrived during one of my absences from school and refused to go away. Fortunately, I sat in the back of the class, alphabetical order favoring the Y's of the world, and keeping us from the horrors of direct contact with chalk and blackboard. Once, just as I was being called to answer some unfathomable arithmetic problem by Mrs. O'Connor, the bell rang and we were called outside, as in a fire-drill, to watch the funeral procession of the Assistant Principal, whose entourage included a priest brother and several women draped in black veils riding in dark limousines. So this was death? This was what my mother had hidden from us, had guarded more closely than the secret of birth. We could feel none of the grief that was required of us by Mrs. O'Connor, who advised us to take out handkerchiefs should we wish to cry, but had failed to alert us to the fact of the woman's death, expecting us to cease all chatter and put on mournful faces as the slow entourage passed by.

To keep me from falling too far behind in my schoolwork during my absences from school, my mother would cut up squares of shirt cardboard using playing cards as her template, and transform my homework into flashcards so that I might master the mystery of numbers—the uncomfortable 9 by 7 and the unconquerable 8 by 6. But my childhood was mostly unsupervised reading and game playing, musing, drawing, and "making things" out of empty thread spools (the wheels of a cart attached to Uncle Mike's cigar box), and carving bars of Ivory soap into crude animals with a butter knife; decorating tin cans, wielding the sensual rubber lips of the LePage mucilage glue bottle as I pasted pictures I had cut out of magazines on to construction paper, old milk bottles and cartons; ads of the fat-faced Campbell soup children; all the detritus that served as material for childhood invention in those days. Against this were the ever-present radio serials for boys: *Jack Armstrong, The Lone Ranger, I Love a Mystery*, and on Saturdays, *The Children's Hour*.

The instructions for all of my activity, and thus for everything important in my world, could be found in the twelve encyclopedic volumes of *The Home University Book Shelf*—a set that sat lined up in numerical order in my room within a red maple colonial style bookcase. Bound in apple green linen cloth with shiny illustrations replicating the frontispieces pasted to the front covers, with tissue paper guards bound into the books, these twelve, richly illustrated volumes brought to the Bronx and to my narrow world the illustrated worlds of Lucy Fitch Perkins (mistress of drawing children of "many lands"), Edmond Dulac and Howard Pyle, with their European fairy tales and *Treasure Island*, the *Arabian Nights*—volumes that held the secrets of the world beyond the Bronx, the "real world," secrets that I could never learn from my family who thought that "out there" was nothing but danger. For them, the world beyond our world was threatening and off limits. For me, and for my sister Simone, it was the world we wanted to experience, explore and ultimately conquer. In its own way each generation was an émigré, a refugee from the world they hoped to escape from.

Simone was also a devotee of that home library of books and it encouraged in her that love of beauty in objects and in people that later defined her life, and simultaneously narrowed and enlarged it. She rarely read the instructions carefully, yet somehow managed to get enough of what she needed to get along. Indeed, she rarely read anything through to the end. Her mind was so quick, so impatient, and so unsuited for scholarship, but bright enough to retain any information required for her to get by in the world. Years later, on her deathbed, she would tell me that she had spent too much of her time looking and judging the surface of things, reflected in her successful interior design work, her infatuation with beautiful people, her love of fashion and luxury, driving a Bentley car and decorating the mansions of the rich, so that now, dying in her hospital bed, she wished that she had spent more time in pursuit of some deeper truth and performing some larger good in the world. Sitting beside her in her hospital room, I tried to reassure her that she had lived the best life she could, that she was kind, generous, and loving to her friends and to her daughter, Mindy, but she was not so easily convinced. And so the illustrated pages of *The Home University Bookshelf* opened up that mysterious, wondrous world beyond the Bronx, and set the pattern for her future life. In it she found clues to that world of beautiful people and beautiful objects. When Aladdin would enter a cave filled with precious jewels and exquisite objects, she would easily follow him there, warmed by its beauty, certain she could defy the terrible never sleeping dog with its fiery eyes that guarded the treasure and she could return to earth laden with gems. Oddly enough, my father's rages, instead of making us cowards made us fearless. What had we to fear from a fire-breathing dragon or a barking three-eyed watchdog of the underworld, we who had survived Nat Yellen's rages?

Mexicans and Mustard Plasters

Although an early reader, Simone was far too impatient to become a deep reader; she had only to scan a paragraph or glance at a picture to take in the world behind it, entering it with ease, if not in depth. Her mind was too quick, her eye too keen, to stay too long for scholarly studying. In a world that expected little of women other than looking attractive and marrying well, she was more than adequately prepared for her future. There was one favorite volume called *Things to Make and Things to Do"* which carefully diagrammed the carving of a rabbit out of a bar of Ivory soap, a skill I never mastered because my mother never allowed anything but a butter knife for my experiments in sculpture. Simone, armed with nail file and nail scissors, created wonderful small soap animals worthy of an ark. A master of tracing paper, and with her fine eye for color, she replicated many of the illustrations in our books, designing costumes for the puppets she later made of *papier-mâché*, and dressing her room with the decals of flowers and sleeping Mexicans in colorful serapes purchased at the hardware store during a shopping trip with my mother. As the war years approached, the world was suddenly alive with South American songs and Mexican pictures.

During my long afternoons in bed, lying still and listening to the muffled sounds of the horse-drawn delivery of milk, the rattling of the milk bottles, the cry of the "High Cash Clothes" men, the knife sharpeners with their whirling blades, the bells of the ice cream vendors and the truck-borne carousels, what I heard most, and with longing, were the penetrating cries of the wild, healthy children playing in the streets, all filtered through the closed windows of my bedroom and in between the terrible ministrations that followed my latest asthma attack. My sister saw my suffering and tried to relieve it by reading to me and distracting me from the terrible treatments that descended upon my frail body to cure the attack. She understood now that she was fortunate. For all the privileges of the sick, I had to endure the suffering that came with those prerogatives. In her effort to entertain and distract me while I was home resting from my attacks, we would sit for hours beside the windup Victrola, listening to Gilbert & Sullivan recordings, only stopping to change the needle from time to time, or put on some of the Crosby recordings Simone had started to favor.

But there was no way to avoid for long the prescribed treatments I was obliged to endure. Fiery mustard plasters made of torn sheets containing a thick yellow mustard, mixed from a mustard powder bought at the A&P, were placed against my thin, bony chest, as steam mixed with camphorated oil puffed vigorously and ceaselessly from a vaporizer near my bed to open the passages of my mucous-stuffed, wheezing bronchial tubes, followed by tablespoons of foul-tasting cherry syrups. These were but a few of the remedies that were tried and failed to reduce the severity or the duration of the asthma attacks. All this was recommended by Dr. Herbert Jackson, our Mississippi-born pediatrician who came to the Bronx in his chauffeur-driven Packard in response to my mother's panicky calls. It was clear to me, even as a small boy, that for all his cheerful, booming greeting, "How's our boy? How ya doin', Sherman?" his real interest was looking upon my mother, the beautiful Lillian, and that my attacks were his excuse to feast his randy eyes upon her. He was blustery, good looking in the manner of FDR, and spoke in a warm Georgia accent despite his years of practice on Park Avenue. Thanks to Dr. Jackson, mother gave up any effort at keeping a kosher home. The good doctor prescribed fortifying breakfasts of bacon, and the kosher habit of centuries was tossed away in the name of fattening up the sickly, skinny child with some forbidden food. My mother's ultimate religion, I would learn, was the religion of childhood, the one she had missed, the one she was determined *we* should have, and the good doctor was her high priest. She was not altogether innocent of his amorous ways, for although he never crossed the line she had drawn, she believed that he was carrying on with his nurse. After a visit to his office in Manhattan, she returned home and reported to her sister Ida that the poor woman, Nurse Peggy, was wildly in love with the doctor, and she had seen him brush against the adoring woman as a patient's record chart exchanged hands.

These asthma attacks not only kept me from school, they allowed me the freedom that children rarely have. Everything that I found worth learning I learned as I daydreamed in my bed, read my picture books, and played in my own home. I soon started to draw on the shirt cardboards that my mother provided when I ran out of drawing paper. Thanks to these early drawings, I won the respect of my sister, since I easily surpassed her efforts and those of her friends at draftsmanship. Although she could trace a picture, sketch a fashion for one of her movie stars, she was still limited to imitating the profiles in the "Draw Me" ads in the newspaper, ads meant to entice the reader into subscribing to a mail-order art course and part with precious money during the Depression by holding out a career as a commercial artist. I could replicate these faces with dispatch, and I had learned all by myself the art of shading, creating volume and perspective, from my *Home University Bookshelf*. It was clear that at last there was something about me that could be pointed to and looked upon with pride.

I had graduated from the spoke-and-wheel construction of my tinker toy sets and was soon making model airplanes out of fragile balsa wood and rubber bands. The art to this was cutting out the pattern provided by secretly using a razor blade I had stolen from my father's medicine cabinet, pasting a skin of tissue paper over the fragile glued frame, twisting a rubber band over the propeller and preparing it for flight, and not removing a finger in the process.

My father admired my building skills but he both pitied and deeply resented my illness and the talents it perfected. I was now declared by one and all "artistic," a word that could only lead to my ultimate doom. Artists were famous for starving and dying young, and although he would never worry my mother with his concerns, he thought my asthmatic cough might well be the precursor of my early death. He was equally concerned when Simone showed that highly refined and precocious taste in what was beautiful. It appeared that we had leapt over the ordinary world where one was obliged to live by hard work and soft lies, a world where all the conventional judgments were accepted into a new world where we could only know rejection and suffering and a pitiful demise. My mother celebrated our useless skills; indeed, she encouraged them. What was the point of all this success which she and my father had achieved if her extraordinary children would be obliged to live ordinary lives? Let cousins Gertrude and Sylvia take commercial courses, learn stenography and typewriting, and prepare for the routine business of surviving in the world, taking orders from others, content with a weekly paycheck and a weekend movie. Her Simone and Sherman would leap over the commonplace and live fascinating lives that would cover them with glory, or if not glory, pleasure. The pleasure she took in our childhood denied to us the ordinary lessons that children need to get by. We casually tossed our cast-off clothing on the floor, assuming that someone would always pick them up, hang them in closets, or place them in laundry bags without judgment or complaint.

In our world the everyday, the commonplace stuff of life, would, as if by magic, take care of itself. Meals would appear by themselves, dishes would be washed by others and money would always be there for our use. Of course it never dawned on us, until years later at camp or in college, that others did not live in a universe where all the nasty necessities of life were taken care of by unseen hands. We were the shoemakers who had unseen elves do our work as we slept. Only on the maid's day off did we help out by doing the dinner dishes. Simone washed, I dried, and we both broke more china and glassware than we put away as we distractedly laughed and chatted about our day. While the Dr. Phils of our world and other child psychologists might see this as the road to our ruin, instead it was possibly our making. By having few household demands placed upon us, other than to pursue our talents and our studies, it made us less demanding of others, more tolerant of the strange ways that other people live their lives. We were undoubtedly slobs, but we were not prigs or judges. If there was a motto, an escutcheon that could have covered those days, it was what my mother so often said: "Live and Let Live." That may seem today the most conventional of statements, but in the early 1930s it was a radical view of life and one which my mother subscribed to in most circumstances, while others stood in judgment of the world.

The Secret of Sherman and Simone

My sister and I shared one secret; it was unspoken, but a certainty to both of us. We knew we were imposters, fully formed human adults trapped in children's bodies, obliged to pretend that we were children to satisfy the grownups of our world. We were spies on the adult world. We reported to no one but each other. At times the pretense of being children was easy. She loved her doll house as I loved playing marbles on the street corner with my friends. But despite these concessions to childhood, we saw everything, understood everything, we loved irony, complexity and irreverence, and refused to be taken in by the straight and narrow beliefs of our family and our world. We longed to get out of this childhood disguise but we understood that we had to serve our time in the prison of our child's bodies before we could do so. We did not know what would happen to us once we grew up and our bodies finally conformed to our idea of who we were, but we knew we were going to live lives that would take us far from this world of 1810 Loring Place in the Bronx of the 1930s.

I rarely thought of myself as a child even then, and when I revealed that fact to Simone, afraid that she would call me "nuts," she admitted that she felt exactly as I did. We were both pretending to be children to satisfy the expectations of our family and the larger world. We agreed that we were changelings, the true story of our births, our secret parentage would be revealed to us once we grew up and took our rightful places in the world. We were clearly delusional, but happy in our delusions, knowing that there would one day be a revelation that would explain it all. It was sufficient to keep us going disguised as small children, content to play marbles, cut out paper dolls, and quarrel like children.

My mother's desire to forge an even greater solidarity between us prompted her to buy brother and sister clothes at Best & Company—identical Peter Pan collars with big button-on short pants for the boy and button-on skirt for the girl. Fortunately, we only wore these for photographs and on birthdays; otherwise I was allowed the joys of corduroy knickers and Simone the pleasure of crisp cotton outfits that matched her doll's clothes.

My Parents and Me

I now commanded most of my mother's attention and concern. I would call out imperiously from my sick bed, "Bring me some paper and something to lean on," which minutes later produced a tray, colored craft paper, blunt children's scissors, and crayons or water colors and brushes. While my precocious artistry delighted my mother, it continued to dismay my father. I was not the perfect boy he so desperately wanted—sturdy, athletic and shrewd. Yes, I was growing up good-looking—the fat red baby had evolved into a tall, thin boy with a well-shaped head, a small, straight nose and large brown eyes like my mother's family, my looks spoiled only by the pencil-thin arms and the chicken chest of the asthmatic, my ribs pushed out of shape by the hours of wheezing and coughing. The Horowitz and Busch clan, my maternal grandparents, provided me with wavy brown hair, dark observant eyes, and a ready smile, but my father could derive no joy from me as he did from the perky prettiness and easy brightness of my sister. Worst of all, it was clear that like my mother I had no head for numbers. I would not prosper in his business or any business. I could be shy, cut off from strangers, unwilling to accommodate them with a smile, incapable of reciting an amusing story or telling the simplest of jokes, and clearly annoyed when my private thoughts were intruded upon by a call to dinner or homework. If I did survive my childhood illness, how would I live as a grownup in that hard world, the only world he knew? It placed a greater burden on him to earn more, to surpass the limits of his salesmanship, so that this child—lacking in all the important skills of survival, skills that he had mastered in his lower East Side childhood—might be kept from penury by the dozens and dozens of sweater sets he sold daily.

How many thousands of sweaters would he be obliged to sell to keep his children from the dire poverty that surely awaited them? How despairing it must have been for him to have such a son and such a daughter. He knew we were spoiled—Aunt Ida and others had warned him about that—but what was the purpose of all his work if he could not spoil us? He remained determined to give us the toys and the childhood he had foregone. He, who had been forced from childhood to work ceaselessly to keep food on the table for his large, ever growing family of brothers and sisters, now saw no relief in sight, no future businessman, no heir to take up the burden of the business, no one to discuss the madness of buyers, the fights with the woolen mill, nobody to teach the art of flattery and bribery that went into the making of a great salesman. He must go on meeting the dependency of everyone in his world; that mixed blessing which brought him few signs of love and expressions of gratitude, and kept him constantly uneasy, always on the tip of rage, lest he fail us. He must smile more, sell more, give away nothing of his real feelings, and never let up in his efforts to earn more, while suffering his fear of failing us. The more he gave to us, the more we would need from him, and if he took any comfort in that, it was because of this that we must love him. Clearly the demands would never let up, and to live his life as a "success" meant he must satisfy the ever growing needs of those around him.

He worried because I had great difficulty falling asleep, and I would often wake in the night, fearful of some shadowy figure I saw emerging from my bedroom closet. My father would lie down beside me and take my hand in his, trying to reassure me that there were no demons in the closet, but I knew better than to believe him. After all, I had a sometimes demon beside me.

In my father's view, Simone had a better chance than I did for a happy future. Given her good looks and quick mind she might make an early marriage to the son of some titan of the garment business with a good rating in Dun & Bradstreet, a prosperous hotelier, or even a physician. But that would make demands on him as well It would mean that she would have to be gowned by Bergdorf Goodman, sent to the finest summer camps, and educated at a good university in a four-year course of home economics. Marrying well did not come cheap, even in the late Depression. And the girl showed a rebellious spirit that was troubling. She did not readily obey orders. Like her mother, she did not often contradict his commands, but like her mother she largely ignored them and rarely, if ever, paid attention to his opinions. Moreover, her eyes were already settled on a world beyond the safety of the Bronx. She grabbed the *Life Magazine* as soon as he brought it home on a Friday night and pored over the photographs of film stars, millionaires in their large modern homes, and a world of theater actors, new plays, and debutantes at fashionable parties, depicting a world unknown in our small, family-centered world. Manhattan and Hollywood—the anti-Bronx—were fixed in her outward gaze.

Toyland and Teepees

As time passed and my father's rages grew more frequent and more violent, the gifts he brought home to us were more and more remarkable. There was the great wooden fortress from FAO Schwarz which accommodated my new army of finely-painted lead French foreign legionnaires and their white-robed Algerian horsemen. This gift was topped by a magnificent large scale European model train that traveled at high speed through a toy Tyrolean Alps dotted with elegantly fashioned train stations. Ingeniously painted passengers in bowler hats and smart traveling clothes, circa 1913, inhabited both the stations and the trains. These painted passengers and the uniformed conductors who served them were enjoying the elegant metal dining car with its tiny plates of gourmet dinners, while others slept in luxurious sleeping cars. The auctioneer who sold it to him claimed that it was a special 2 gauge Marklin set made in Austria for the children of the Astor family twenty years before.

At that same auction he bid on and won the shiny black baby grand Baldwin piano for my sister, which came with a piano bench containing manuscripts of songs written by Cole Porter, songs that remained in that bench for years until my mother read the lyrics and discovered that they were privately published lyrics, and banished them to the trash bin for their salaciousness. New, modern toys came from FAO Schwarz. A red metal biplane on a hard metal rod, controlled by an electrical box with a rubber rudder to navigate its wide airborne journey as it dove and swooped dangerously around the living room, barely missing the Capo-di-Monte bowl of white porcelain fruit and the cut crystal flower vase, always empty of flowers because of my asthma. American Indian costumes—feathered headdresses, buckskin trousers and beaded moccasins—would appear in lockstep with his rages. Others in my family might pretend to be Jews but I knew for a fact from the very first trip to the Museum of Natural History that I was a changeling, an

American Indian boy, and that a mistake had been made in placing me far from my bright world of pueblos and mesas, here in the outer reaches of the West Bronx.

Tribal affiliation was unimportant. Hopi, Apache, Iroquois, Sioux, Mohegan and Lakota, were all acceptable, as I read about them in cloth covered booklets published by the museum. Still, I favored the Hopi with their pueblos and pottery and the Prince Valiant haircuts their children enjoyed. To my young mind, their pueblos were similar to the apartment buildings in the Bronx, only lacking elevators. Once established that I was a young brave, it became the main source of play between my sister and me. Using a broom handle in a bucket to support my blanket and sheet above my head, I would sit beneath my makeshift tepee and impersonate a young brave who had just brought back a slain deer in triumph for the delectation of his tribe.

Many years later when I was in my early forties recovering from tuberculosis in Arizona, in the company of my supportive doctor cousin I climbed to a remote pre-Columbian Indian pueblo, sat down for a moment to catch my breath, spit blood into my handkerchief, and knew with a remarkable certainty that this was not the end, but that I would be cured and the illness would never recur. I sat there inside a mud-walled room feeling a calm and a freedom from care that I had not felt in years, since my faux-Indian childhood. I had attached a powerful magic to my Indian fantasy, one that was started under those quilted Bronx bedcovers and, indeed, I did recover as I knew I would, assisted by a new course of medicine. But in my mind, the cure was in that moment when my Indian boy fantasy met my adult reality in that ancient relic of a pueblo.

In my early years, Simone would enter my room, pounce upon me as I sat under my wigwam, and together we would scream with delight. "You're my prisoner, Chief Poopskylovebump," she cried out, using a name of her own invention, a name so ridiculous in its blending of scatology with affection that I laughed so hard I thought I would die of joy and wet my pajamas. In those lost days, God was clearly revealed in laughter. We called those extraordinary moments of bliss—those out of body experiences of joy—"supreme exaltation," an expression my sister plucked out of a child's book on Parsifal and the Holy Grail that described the feelings the crusader had when he was filled with the ecstasy of his holy mission. We laughed so much that a glass of water was kept nearby on the nightstand in order to relieve the hiccoughs that invariably followed the holy fit, with my mother rushing into my room holding my ears and chanting, "Sip the water slowly, Sherman. Try to stop laughing and start sipping," until the hiccoughs subsided.

We were joined, not just by blood, but by our common sense of the inexorable silliness of life; laughter was something so wonderful that it armed us against the everyday injustices of childhood, the rages of my father, the betrayal of friends, the threats of bullies, and the harshness of teachers.

Time always took us by surprise. Children have no sense of days passing. It was our outgrown clothes rather than our changed condition that informed us that we were growing older, and suddenly my toy soldiers lost their power to amuse and made way for my stamp collection. America had become stamp crazy, thanks to the fact that FDR collected stamps, and the growing awareness that the world was facing greater danger with the rise of Hitler. Stamps were geography and history combined, mostly commemorating European colonialism; the worse the colonial oppressor, the more beautiful the stamps that were issued. In addition, there were valuable first day issues to collect. Every child of my generation believed that they might come across the "Inverted Jenny," the upside-down World War I biplane stamp printed and quickly withdrawn by the Post Office, the possession of which would make one rich and famous. This billion to one shot seemed very possible to my friends and to me. Not being in control of our lives, we placed enormous trust in our luck, and despite the evidence that no valuable stamp crossed our paths, we continued to hope. At first my collection was a jumble of cancelled stamps purchased cheaply in wax paper envelopes to be pasted into a large red album, matching the cancelled stamps with their plumed helmeted kings against those pictured in the album, all pasted down with small gummy tabs that were delicious to the tongue. Soon I was collecting first day issues, blocks of commemorative stamps bearing important numbers, stamps that had to be preserved in large clear envelopes. And I attended school more frequently.

My sister's reputation as a "delight" had preceded me in school, and I could sense the disappointment of teachers when I failed to live up to her past performances. Simone could easily charm her teachers. My father's rages had made her an expert in dealing with the angry moods of an irate teacher who demanded unflagging obedience. She had learned to tune out the noise of adult anger and threats and enter her own world of daydreams. Throughout her life she was often distracted by random thoughts that were at odds with what was going on in the moment, but she was a master of the quick recovery, and her charm came to her rescue when she was criticized for not paying attention. Often, looking good saved her, which meant a great deal in those public school days. Being well dressed with a lace handkerchief pinned to her blouse pocket, smart hair ribbons and bows decorating her dark curls, was a sign to the teacher that she was cut from a different cloth than the other children in P.S. 26, some of whom arrived at school in the worn-out clothes of older children, or clothes donated by the Salvation Army. Simone was a favorite of her teachers and of her classmates, easily appointed monitor when the teacher left the room to pee. She exercised her authority with a regal fairness, unusual in the temporary wardens of this educational prison.

Only once did my mother's impoverished past betray her in her choice of outfits for her children. Knowing how quickly children outgrew their expensive woolen winter coats, my mother purchased one for my sister in the boy's department of Best & Company on Fifth Avenue, leaving my sister at home and taking only her size with her. It was a gray and green wool plaid with a dark green velvet collar which came with a matching hunting cap with earflaps that snapped tightly under the chin. When Simone wore the coat to school one day, she hung it up in the classroom wardrobe in the rear, never realizing that her classmate, the combative Robert Markowitz, owned another coat, similar to hers in all ways. At the end of day when she put the coat on prior to leaving school, Robert accused her of taking his coat and attempted to rip it from her hands. Their quarrel brought the teacher into the fray. The teacher took command of the coat, examined it carefully, and concluded that it was a boy's coat, since it buttoned on the left, as boy's coats did in those days, as opposed to buttoning on the right, which was the proper fastening for the feminine world. This was news to my sister. When Robert's own coat was located, under a pile of other coats that had fallen to the closet floor, and it proved to be the identical twin to her own, it was clear to Simone that my mother had pulled a fast one, and my sister's shame and fury knew no limits. The mother whom she had trusted with her life had clearly given Simone a coat destined for her younger brother in an effort to gain the maximum use from the coat. Simone announced that she would not wear it again, put her foot down, stamped hard, and my mother relegated the coat to a storage closet where it awaited my eventual growth.

The Joys and the Toys

My sister and her best friend Sandra Alberts—the genial, gleaming "Sandy"—would spend the rainy afternoons gossiping about their classmates, exchanging news of movie stars and their latest loves, and carefully coloring the cut-out costume books which featured these movie stars in their exaggerated Hollywood fashions; Ginger and Joan in draped evening gowns with large orchid corsages that could be folded over the cutout figures whose only permanent wardrobe was discreet silk underwear. With the blunt safety scissors provided by my ever-cautious mother, they cut out the perforated form of the movie star and attached the gowns with little fold back tabs, carefully marked with dashes that guided the scissor as I watched in wonder as to how this pointless exercise could so entertain them.

We were a family that filled our hours making art. We found the smell of Crayola crayons in all their myriad colors intoxicating. I had a set of colored chalks and I would draw on a slate blackboard attached to a small desk, complete with wooden hammer and colored pegs to be hammered into the holes beside the blackboard. Sometimes my sister and her friends would play with their Dionne quintuplet dolls, nestled in a cradle for the tiny five, each one bearing on their tiny garments a heart shaped gold pin, which distinguished Marie from Emily and Emily from Yvonne, Annette and Cecile. There was a Sonja Henie ice-skating doll with small white kid skates, as soft as the finest gloves, and later Snow White and all of her dwarfs in felt caps and jackets with changing sweater sets for all, crocheted by my cousin Bella, the former Minsk prostitute whose fascinating story I unveiled in my earlier memoir *Cousin Bella: The Whore of Minsk*. Bella thought herself a seamstress equal to Tante Mary, although her work was infused with love and missing stitches.

The Telltale Tinsel

I t was Christmas 1937, when a present to my sister of a pair of
Shirley Temple dolls nearly tore our family apart. Although both
my parents had come from observant Orthodox Jewish families,
Christmas offered them an opportunity to worship their children's
childhood with a room filled with gifts, a devotional that they could
not resist and one that we, the children, anticipated with the greatest
pleasure. And in our pleasure, our parents found their own. One
Christmas when I was five and Simone was nearing nine, my father
presented her with a pair of Shirley Temple dolls, each with a different
splendid gown. One wore the polka dot organdy of her film *Heidi*, and
an identical Shirley sported a sailor outfit that celebrated "The Good
Ship Lollipop." Truth is, the second doll—a lesser Shirley in every
way—was meant for my breaking.

At five, I was famous for giving my sister's doll a ready smash with
my toy hammer from my miniature toolset when provoked by one of
her nine-year-old wisecracks, and as a preventative to this and the
mayhem that would follow, I was given one such doll to destroy if I
wished to do so, and warned by my father that the other one was
sacrosanct. We were also gifted with new easels and poster paints, a
black metal coin bank that registered each deposit with a cheerful ring,
a small desk with a peg board for hammering in colored pegs, sets of
pastels in fine blond wooden boxes, and, for Simone, a dressing table
with an organdy skirt where she could house her collection of glass
ballerinas, fancy perfume bottles, and movie star photographs. She was
a particular fan of the handsome Tyrone Power and the undaunted
Errol Flynn, and their pictures were scattered about her room, clipped
from movie magazines, saved from the tops of Dixie Cups, or in eight-
by-ten glossy prints ordered from the studios by postcard, postcards
that she also used to obtain samples of her Lady Esther face powder.

This was the year that mother had taken us into Manhattan to see the department stores windows and to buy us new clothes for the coming school season. As always, she wore a plain cloth coat out of the house so that none of the neighbors might see her in her new mink jacket, which was kept in the large paper bag she carried by its wooden handle. Once safely out of the neighborhood, riding down University Avenue in the taxi which would take us to Manhattan, beyond the gaze of the old women who sat on fold-up chairs against the brick buildings, drinking in the winter sun, my mother would slip out of the cloth coat, place it in the paper bag and put on the warm fur jacket, a process reversed on the journey home. Arriving in Manhattan, she was tempted and tested by the beauty of the Christmas trees, flaunting their artificial snow and tinsel, dressed in small angel lights. It was a test she failed. On the way home in the taxi, she stopped the cab and bought a small four-foot fir tree from a street vendor, who wrapped it in burlap at her request so that it could not be seen by anyone as she took it into the house.

That Christmas Eve she set the small three-foot tree inside a stand she had hastily purchased at the Woolworths on Jerome Avenue, where she had also bought a package of silver tinsel and a dozen red and green glass balls, set it up in the living room and placed our gifts below. It was our first, our training tree. We knew that we had passed some watershed in our family history. We had accepted Christmas as a part of our life and, although we knew few Christians and those we knew we looked upon with great suspicion, we felt we had joined the greater world, and we did so with no remorse, no looking back. This was perfectly consistent with the candles my mother lit for the beloved dead, for the visits to the Synagogue on High Holidays. She clearly felt that the celebration of Christmas took nothing away from her as a Jew; it merely added a holiday that would give joy to her children. Theologians might argue with that, but my mother feared less the wrath of God than she did the disappointment of her children. That she kept her Christmas celebration from the rest of her family showed that she did not court their disapproval—she enjoyed her status as family saint—yet she would even risk that for her children.

Christmas morning came with its great tearing open of packages, all recorded by a small, brown metal 8 millimeter Revere movie camera that my father cranked up and pointed at us, its whirring noise marking the journey of the film as it captured our Christmas in the joyful faces of his children. These were moments of enormous happiness. Greed, if you are not told it is greed, can be a delight for any child. It was often said in those hard times that you could not buy happiness, but in my family it *was* possible to do so, at least on Christmas morning. In childhood, as opposed to architecture, less is not more, more is more and much more is much more. Into this scene of torn foil wrappings and shrieks of surprised delight from Simone and me ("Look what I got, Sherman. Daddy, how did you know I wanted that?"), came the ringing of our outside doorbell.

Mother knew at once that it was her sister Ida, accompanied by her younger daughter Gertrude, standing outside our door. Although a year older than my sister, Gertie was a girl with a sad, pretty moon face who uttered an endless stream of inanities fed to her by her small-minded but kindly mother. She was the small price one paid for living near the worshipful family. All attempts to include Gertie in Simone's play were doomed to failure. Simone loved her as she loved all that was familiar in our world, but the love could not change the fact that Gertie was a bore. Moreover, Gertie was genial but jealous in an open, innocent fashion. Worst of all, she was always unimaginative. She wanted Simone to live by whatever rules of the game they played, for which my sister had little patience and no time for her complaining older cousin. Ida, never conceding defeat in her effort to forge a bond between her own daughter and Lilly's, had brought Gertie over to play with my sister once again, this being a school holiday. It had been arranged on the telephone days before and forgotten by my mother in the excitement of getting the children's gifts wrapped and the tree set up for Christmas. My mother knew that Ida had a great deal to say on all subjects but she had no conversation. She spoke in a series of judgments, leaping from one to another without pausing to reflect on anything like evidence for what she said. So-and-so was no good, such-and-such was truly bad, this was cheap and nice, that was too fancy and expensive.

Unlike my mother, who rarely judged and often sought excuses for the inexcusable, particularly if it was the behavior of her children or a luxury toy that they wanted, Ida had fixed ideas about the world, where there was only one way to do anything, the right way, and she knew it. She would not act on her various prejudices, but she lived a life that was rigidly confined by them. In her mind Jews were good people, smart people, and all others were bad and had "goyishe kops." The *goyim* drank, cheated, lied, raped, robbed, killed, and were bound for hell, even though her religion provided no evidence for hell. God loved the Jews, but lately he napped a lot, particularly now with the European world spinning out of control, something that Aunt Ida for all her piety could not avoid facing. How she could have adhered to such beliefs in light of what was then happening to the Jews of Europe defies all understanding, but she did, and summed them all up—Hitler, the Pope, Mussolini and Stalin—as crazy *goyim*.

Ida admired my mother with an almost religious fervor. Lilly could do no wrong, even when she did wrong, as she clearly did when she refused to take Ida's advice about the proper way to rear children. Ida's view was to deny children everything they wanted so they would not expect much from life and, therefore, never be disappointed. Ida claimed that any fool knew that life was just waiting to trick you and cheat you and it was never too early for children to learn that. She adhered to the strictest views of what made a good Jew. It was not so much attending synagogue, but refusing to imitate the crazy *goyim* in their holidays and habits. She was prepared to make a few small exceptions out of love for her sister. She could forgive the fact that we Yellen children hung up our stockings on Christmas Eve by calling it our American Chanukah. She preferred not to notice the absence of Chanukah candles, and she knew that these stockings were filled with small toys, jacks, marbles, tiny paper umbrellas rather than dreidels, but she indulged this as something she could tolerate in her beautiful younger sister, "the American."

My mother did not respect Ida for her old fashioned ways, but she honored her right to hold them, and knew that her sister would be shocked and repelled by the Christmas tree, with all that it represented of blasphemy and "conversion." It would be a mote in the eye of Ida's unforgiving Hebrew God, and in this time of growing anti-Semitism in Europe and in America, a sign that her beautiful baby sister had gone over to the enemy.

Knowing that Ida was outside our door, insistently ringing the doorbell, and that she would not go away if it remained unanswered, my mother panicked. It was the only time I ever saw her do so. She, who preferred to move slowly, easily gliding from calm to calm, looked startled, drained, as if a demon was calling to her beyond our front door. I had never seen her at such a loss before. She lifted the tree with its stand and rushed towards the bathroom, dropping tinsel, scattering pine needles, and shattering glass balls as the flying fir tree made its way toward a safe hiding place. When Ida and Gertrude entered that room, the tree was nowhere to be seen, but all was soon discovered. It was not just the incriminating trail of tinsel and the gleaming shards of broken colored glass on the Kerman carpet, it was the two Shirley Temple dolls still cradled in their cardboard and tissue paper packaging that the wide-eyed Gertrude spied, prompting her to let out a hungry animal's howl of dismay. She was a stranger in paradise, stuck in the wrong part of the family, the part that forbade everything that was fun, everything that was beautiful, everything that mattered. Her cries were inconsolable. My parents looked at her and then turned to us. "Give her one of the dolls," my father told Simone.

My sister chose the doll in the modest polka dot day dress and turned it over to her anguished cousin. A few of my Moroccan soldiers were thrown in with the gift, despite my protests that Gertie wasn't a boy and wouldn't know what to do with them. To add further insult to my sense of possession, my new box of crayons and my Uncle Sam metal bank were offered up to the howling Gertie until she finally stopped crying, a smile of triumph on her thin bow lips. Gertrude now enjoyed her first American Chanukah, an orphan's wide-eyed Christmas to which she responded with groveling gratitude, causing my sister and me real dismay for this hideous act of generosity imposed upon us.

Many years later, that doll continued to be a cause of family strife. Gertrude never played with it. It was far too precious to be taken from its box. Her daughter, who was what was then called a tomboy, found it far too girly to deal with, so it passed on to her older sister Sylvia's daughter, Carol who saw little of interest in that doll. By this time, Sylvia was rich, a matron in Manhasset, while Gertrude's husband was employed by Sylvia's husband and ill paid for his labors. There was a new interest in Shirley Temple, sparked by the television show she hosted in the fifties, and the value of the original dolls had reached the four-figure stage. Sylvia prepared to sell it to an interested collector. Gertrude, hearing about this, insisted that the doll was hers and if anyone should profit from its pristine condition, it was she, herself. My father, who had given the doll to Gertrude, declared the judgment of Solomon. They should sell it and give the proceeds to charity, but failing that, they should divide the proceeds between them and put an end to the dumb quarrel over an old doll. They heeded Uncle Nat's advice, knowing that he might be crazy but he was usually fair.

A Grab Bag of Relatives

My mother's younger brother Ally had abandoned the ways of a shoplifter and become a successful shopkeeper. No doubt his experience as the former had aided his success as the latter. He had become the owner of a small department store in Pulaski, New York, a town famous for its long, deep white winters and taciturn dairy farmers. Albert's Department Store was the only retail dry goods and hardware store for thirty miles, serving all the rural small towns in the area. He proudly told my parents that customers came to his store from as far as Oswego, and a few Canadians had come there as well. It was both the five and dime and Macy's of the rural Northern town where he had settled. He sold rough country clothes, long johns and plaid flannel work shirts, farm implements, seed, feed, canned goods, tall boots and children's shoes, as well as gallons of gasoline and kerosene for stoves. He learned to buy the goods that people used up quickly or outgrew: cheap boots that would give out in a year or two; clothing with no excess cloth in the seams to let out as one fattened up or pass on if one died. Al prospered quickly, remaining one step ahead of the farmer customers who came to his store for supplies, but feeling a true affinity for these flinty Germans and Poles who had settled there. He always sent us Christmas gifts of itchy woolen mittens, clumsy rubber boots with metal latches, ugly plaid woolen hats with oversized earflaps, earmuffs that hurt your ears because they were never made to stretch over a child's head, and from time to time, a crate with a live chicken, one of which my mother kept briefly in the bathtub of the maid's room before taking it to the butcher for slaughtering.

We saw little of the upstate relatives in our youth—they only came to New York for family weddings and a yearly trip to the Radio City Music Hall—and what we saw of them was rare, excitedly anticipated, but not always welcomed by my parents. Al and his wife Ida arrived for a visit bringing with them badly wrapped gifts from their small department store. His Ida was always distinguished as "Ida from Pulaski" since our family was overrun with Idas, including two Aunts and a Cousin Ida (whom I have renamed Cousin Bella for the sake of clarity). The Pulaski couple had so easily absorbed the manners and beliefs of their rural customers, one would never suspect that they were raised on the Lower East Side or that they were Jews who shared the liberal culture and social ideals that my parents espoused in the thirties. Uncle Al took great pride in the fact that his Ida had worked as an operator for Bell Telephone before they married, since Bell did not hire Jewish women, and she passed with ease for a Protestant. With her snub nose and straw-colored hair she could easily be a farm woman, sporting a particular kind of rural homeliness that camouflaged her origins. Their outlandishly upstate opinions, offered without being solicited, were considered insane and cruel to my progressive parents. Al and his Ida had become Americans by absorbing the local prejudices of their small town; they had assimilated all the ignorance of their customers and they were proud of their new found bigotry that established their bone fides in their new world.

Uncle Al was now a registered Republican, a fact that my mother treated as a dirty secret; it was an affront to her lifelong passion for FDR and Eleanor, her hatred for the KKK and their lynchings in the South, and her concern about the turmoil in Europe. Everything was personal to my mother. She saw the hatred in the world outside as a distant but real danger to her family. But Uncle Al felt exempt from the troubles in the world in his far North refuge. There was no world that mattered to him outside of the one he had conquered in that upstate village where he lived and prospered, amassing wealth coin by coin, dollar by dollar. Unlike his brother Frankie who scraped by at manual jobs and cared about the lot of the poor, knowing he would always be one, Al had a head for business and money, aided by his malleable conscience. Al had once offered to set Frankie up in a small business upstate but Frankie refused to leave the city and family he loved. "Poor Frankie," as he was often called, slaved away delivering and collecting laundry for "Mother's Friend Laundry"—a business owned by Ida's husband Mike and some of Mike's former gangster friends from the Lower East Side.

Mike had enjoyed an adolescent notoriety as "Little Jeff," a member of a Jewish gang of shoplifters, shakedown artists, and pickpockets. He had resigned from the gang as a condition for marrying my mother's sister, the implacably honest and mercilessly plain Aunt Ida, but his connections had provided him with this laundry business, which included servicing the linens of several bars, hospitals and diners, whose tablecloths, sheets and napkins were picked up weekly and whose profits were shared by the mob.

The fact that Uncle Mike scraped by earning barely enough to pay for his cheap cigars and food for the table, and that they did not prosper despite the possession of a storefront and a delivery truck, together with the fact that they ate the cheapest, boniest of sardines packed in a thick, glutinous tomato sauce and not Granadaisa Skinless and Boneless packed in rich olive oil, that their walls (like Ida's costume jewelry) were decorated with plaster bas-reliefs of black women with huge lips and large brass earrings; all this was proof to my parents that he was merely the front for unnamed criminals and that his real job was laundering gangster money for which he got a small commission and the opportunity to *shtup* Rose Walker, one of the middle-aged "colored" laundresses who worked at "Mother's Friend" for years.

Al would have higher aspirations than anyone in my mother's family. He would soon change his name from Horowitz to Harwitt and, together with his wife Ida, raise two black Scotty dogs, Blackie and Mackie, whom they loved as if they were their children during the years before they had children, and whose photos were sent to us every Christmas as a greeting card. When their children finally arrived, Al and his Ida immediately put down those healthy, once beloved dogs, something that shocked my mother, who could not abide dogs but hated cruelty more. Al would someday send his personable son Mark and his lanky, awkward daughter Joan to the best New England preparatory schools. He would live to see his son become a successful surgeon and his daughter a banker, before she was hideously murdered in San Francisco. My mother had fallen out with her brother and his wife years before when, after my father died, they failed to send a condolence card, a sin so great that even for her—a woman who had nurtured him and could forgive him nearly anything—was unforgivable.

Uncle Frank had married his girlfriend Sue, a small, pretty woman with an aquiline nose and brightly dyed red hair; a generous, kind-hearted woman with a ready smile; a woman who had few ambitions beyond keeping food on the table and pleasing her husband's relatives. My mother liked her for her cheerfulness and good nature, but Sue's easy contentment troubled her. She thought Sue was bad for Frank, a man who needed a stronger motor to move him forward in the world. Mother complained to my father that Sue did nothing to encourage her husband to find better work. His deliveryman job was hard on his back and harder still when bills had to be met.

It was enough for Frank and Sue to get by on his small salary and to enjoy their lives and their two small children, Serena and Jeffrey. Both the children were smart and attractive, but like everyone in that family, they lived in the shadow of my mother and father, king and queen of the family, whose prosperity and generosity was the beacon that drew the others to them. It was Jeff who would inherit all my toys, the fabled train set, my stamp collection, all given away by my mother in one of her infamous house cleanings, and sold by Jeff in the flea markets that became his occupation. I would later call her Aladdin's mother who gave away the magic lamp, but I had already gone on to new pleasures by the time my younger cousin received my old ones. What Simone and I both recognized was that Uncle Frank was a man of high spirits who took pleasure in the moment, something we rarely saw in our own parents who lived for our future triumphs. In the company of Frank, we were expected only to enjoy the pleasure of being alive and to enjoy the splendid here and now. He shared with my mother a kind heart and a loving nature, but he lacked her steely ambition and considered himself a failure, while for me and Simone, he was the most successful adult in our family, the only one who seemed to enjoy life for its own sake, who did not view his life as an endless obligation to grow rich in order to be safe. Frank, alone, was safe in his own skin. He could not teach us joy, but we could easily see it in his sweet, noisy, loving kindness, and we honored him for it.

The Tooth of Walter Knipe

One spring evening in the late thirties, my father announced that he had invited Walter Knipe to have dinner with us in our new Bronx apartment at 1810 Loring Place. It was a spacious eight-room flat with long corridors that allowed for more privacy than usual; our children's bedrooms were at the far end of the apartment. This invitation to a stranger, albeit a rich one who owned the Pennsylvania woolen factory where my father's sweaters were manufactured, was an unheard of event, unprecedented in our family saga. Although we had occasional Passover dinners with my mother's family, we had never had a stranger to our house, and most certainly no stranger of the mythical reputation of Walter Knipe, a Main Line Philadelphian. Despite their different backgrounds, Knipe and my father had become fast business friends. Knipe, who had an ancestor who was allegedly a "signer" of the Declaration of Independence, was a simple man, or so my father told my mother when she was disconcerted by the news of his invitation. "How could I refuse him?" my father protested when my mother claimed she could not entertain the man; they were unprepared for such an event. Knipe had expressed an interest in meeting my father's wife and children after seeing their photographs on my father's office desk. After years of asking, "How are the beautiful wife and children? When can I meet them?" there was no delaying the invitation. For once my mother acquiesced and preparations for the arrival of Walter Knipe began.

Polish Mary took out the Rosenthal China, laundered the Belgian lace tablecloth, polished the best Gorham silver, waxed the mahogany table, vacuumed the carpet, washed and starched the cotton curtains, all in preparation for the royal visit. The never used dining room table was now set for the event, days in advance. We, who only dined in the Dutch breakfast nook, were going to have dinner in a room which was only used to run through or hide in on some rainy day stuck in the apartment. My sister and I were scrubbed, combed and dressed in our best. An expensive ribbed roast beef was purchased and prepared. For once and only once, the cookbook "The Way to a Man's Heart" was consulted and, if not followed slavishly, used in an advisory capacity. Potatoes were mashed. A chocolate layer cake was bought at Sutter's. Spanish olives were offered in place of our usual half sour pickles. The Harveys Bristol Cream Sherry that my parents favored was purchased, together with the twelve-year-old Johnny Walker Scotch Whisky which a gentile of Knipe's heritage and habits would certainly favor.

Knipe arrived with a huge bouquet of red roses for my mother, a tin of Louis Sherry candy for my father, two large Steiff stuffed animals for my sister and me, and the largest smile, which revealed the biggest set of teeth Simone and I had ever seen. It was only slightly short of the wolf's smile in *Little Red Riding Hood*. Polish Mary helped him out of his blonde cashmere velvet-collared coat and hung it in the recently organized hall closet. He was a genial man with a thin moustache and a bad case of dandruff that settled like granulated sugar on the shoulders of his dark suit. He had a kind voice, nervous hands, and watery blue eyes, a sure sign of a *shikker*—a congenital drinker—to my mother. Conversation was halting but punctuated by hearty laughs issuing from Walter Knipe as my father regaled him with some jokes and stories. Then great silences would descend upon us as Knipe looked at us, grinning toothily, and we stared back, amazed by those heroic teeth and that booming voice. Knipe's glass was filled and filled again during the silences. My father told another joke. Knipe laughed and turned to us with his stranger's questions in his Main Line accent. After we had delivered up the requested information about our ages, our schooling, our grades, and our talents, he asked to see my drawings and hear Simone play the piano. She began to play her showpiece, her "Für Elise," and what she lacked in technique she made up for in self-assurance—a wrong note was easily incorporated into the melody without backtracking or apologizing. Walter Knipe greatly admired her playing, requested an encore, and she gave him the identical piece a second time. Finally, after an interminable hour, the meal began.

Other than the fact that the meal was delayed by forty minutes due to various kitchen catastrophes, starting with an oven that someone forgot to light, the dinner went off without incident. The meal began with a consume provided by the all-purpose Campbell Chicken Soup which for once arrived at the table steaming hot with little sprigs of parsley floating on top. The roast beef, though overdone, was edible, not always the case with my mother's cooking of meats. A large bottle of ketchup was placed beside the mandatory red horseradish. These two stalwarts were the emergency troops that stood by waiting to conceal, if not rescue, my mother's culinary disasters. To our amazement, Knipe never reached for that ketchup bottle and he asked for seconds.

"Would you like some blood?" my mother asked him ladle in hand. "Yes," he replied. I will have some of the essence, dear Lillian, some of the essence." It was clear that Walter Knipe was hugely enjoying his meal, although he seemed somewhat distracted as he stared at my mother. Perhaps he wondered how such a genial but funny looking fellow as my father had captured this prize, or perhaps he was just a bit drunk on the fourth glass of aged single malt Scotch, but he reached into the olive tray, grabbed a large black pitted olive, bit down hard into it quickly and let out a startled cry as his front tooth cracked before our eyes—the olive had contained a dreaded pit—and the tooth landed in the gravy boat, where it promptly sank. This left a great gaping hole in his wide mouth, as all of us stared, stunned by the enormity of the missing tooth and the disaster that had no remedy. No dentist could be trusted other than one who practiced in Manhattan, and none were open at that hour.

Knipe collected his broken tooth from the dish, wiped it off in his napkin and placed the fragment in his pocket handkerchief. He turned to my mother and said, "Sorry to cause such trouble, Lilly. Think nothing of it. I never much liked that tooth, anyway. That meal... Delicious. Delicious." But, of course, she did think about it. In the future, olives would always be served with the warning, "Remember poor Walter Knipe," with the same solemnity that Americans were enjoined to "remember the Maine" during and after the Spanish American War. Knipe, we knew, was a true gentleman, and we respected his lack of complaint, his ability to carry on in the face of that lost tooth. Alas, when, in the early 1950s, woolen mills began closing in the North, migrating to cheaper labor in the South, and later moving out of the country altogether, and when, ultimately, synthetics such as Orlon dominated the field, Knipe closed his large Philadelphia woolen mill, putting an end to the Knipe Empire with a resounding bankruptcy. We heard that he had had a run of bad luck with stocks and bonds and, finally, had gone broke. To my father's great relief, he learned that Walter Knipe had found a job as a zoo keeper in the small animal house of the Philadelphia Zoo. Walter Knipe called once and told my father that he was happier in this work than as a woolen czar. But forever after Walter Knipe was the man who had lost that great early American tooth and acted with grace in the face of such a disaster, a model for us all, and a lesson that *goyim* could be human too.

Library Days

My health improved and as I approached adolescence, my asthma subsided and then disappeared. I now attended school regularly, and my friendships with Eugene Linett and Marty Moses, Lionel Sherrow and Ronald DiMaria flourished. We were pals, friends in so far as the petty jealousies and shifting alliances of youth allowed, each genial in his own way, and we knew we were smart as paint. If we were not a true gang, we were buddies who played together after school, secretly smoked loosies—the single penny cigarettes sold by Mr. Katz in his candy story near Sedgwick Avenue—talked about girls endlessly, and tried to learn everything we could learn about the mysterious mechanics of sex, the what went where and the who does what of it. Our instructors in such matters were rumors, dirty jokes, a pornographic flip page book, our own experiments with masturbation (which left the experimental phase and entered the habitual), and a sex manual published in the early twenties called "Modern Marriage." We formed cabals against each other, fought, reunited, and laughed together at the movies we attended every Saturday afternoon at the Park Plaza movie palace on University Avenue. What was wonderful about these friends is that they could accept you in all your embarrassments.

One Saturday, Tante Mary arrived on the very afternoon that I had planned to join my friends at a matinee at the Park Plaza. When she learned where I was going she said she would go with me; she had not seen a movie in ages, and she would enjoy my company. As we approached the theater I saw my friends standing on line. I watched as the Tante headed directly to the box office to buy our tickets, avoiding the line, an unforgivable sin in those days. Her natural authority was such that no ticket booth clerk or theater usher could stop her. We entered the darkened theater together; she reached for my hand to make certain I was beside her, and I prayed that nobody inside that theater had seen us. But my friends, knowing their own shame of odd parents and crazy aunts, pretended that they had not seen me being led about by the blustery, strange looking woman and never asked a question about her afterwards.

In those days there was no such thing as a good movie or a bad movie. There were just movies, the chance to sit in the dark and watch the wonders of the world take you away for an hour or two. These wonders were not so much the travelogues that were popular in those days, but the range of emotions, the grand feelings on screen, the *Four Feathers* with their tales of friendship, betrayal, sacrifice and redemption. In life, nothing was ever resolved; in film there was a pattern, a design that we could not find outside that theater, where one day only led to the next, unless illness or accident intervened.

As much as I loved movies, I loved books more, books being stories that unfolded for you alone, drawing you inside and not releasing you from their grip until you had come to the last page, and sometimes, if the book was wonderful, filled with comic twists and brave goings on, not even then. Books then had nothing to do with literature. I was devoted to the boy's novels of Leo Edwards—the *Jerry Todd* and *Poppy Ott* stories that were published in cheap red bindings by Grosset & Dunlap and sold for fifty cents in the local Womwrath's Book Store. These were stories of life in Tutter, Illinois, an imaginary small town where clever boys could get into delightful scrapes, solve mysteries, start businesses, form deep friendships, and always prevail over the bullies and the wise guys, books pattered on Huck Finn and Tom Sawyer, but addressed to the boys of the twenties and thirties with morals wagging from them like puppy tails. Since the Bronx of my childhood was a self-contained village, with its Main Street, its University Avenue with its small shopkeepers, its schools and its playgrounds, its friends and its bullies, it was not difficult to project oneself into that small town world. I seemed to have missed most of the class trips to the Metropolitan Museum, but my passion for fine art was satisfied by a large book of art reproductions, the big ones of the day, "Blue Boy," "Pinky" "The Laughing Cavalier," a domestic Vermeer, a Canaletto scene of Venice, and the Van Gogh sunflowers. I forced my mind to walk in and out of these pictures, constructing stories of the people depicted; even the flowers had a tale to tell, because art to me held no abstract pleasures. Art had to hold a narrative to be great in my mind because nothing was better than a good story.

Early in my reading years I would go to the small public library on Webster Avenue and once a week take out two books; one from a series of books written and illustrated by Lucy Fitch Perkins, books that told tales of the young twins of the world—Dutch, Japanese, Irish, French, American Revolutionary, Chinese, Belgian, Spartan, and "pickaninny"—until the world and most of its historical times were covered by these books, calibrated to the different ages of child readers. The strange and wonderful ways of these foreign children, and how they met the challenge of growing up in strange places with strange customs, was infinitely fascinating to me. In that world, marvelously illustrated by the gloriously gifted Perkins, people had customs and they wore costumes, they had ceremonies, traditions, and obligations. In my world they just had habits and wore clothes. My world was filled with men in hats, ties, and suits, women in feathered hats, dresses, coats, and high heeled shoes, all very dull. In the thirties and forties people dressed to conceal, to be part of the crowd, but in these books people dressed to distinguish themselves and carry on some tradition. Once a week I borrowed one of these "twin" books, together with one by Maud and Miska Petersham which told the *Story of ---*, covering such subjects as ships, forests and minerals, in which I had little interest, but felt an obligation to read so that I could someday make my way in the world. These books and my never-ending passion for the lore of American Indians formed my childhood education.

My daily diet of reading started with *Famous Funnies* comics, which offered the misadventures of the cave man Alley Oop, Nancy and Sluggo, a pair of mischievous kids who were the bane of their aunt Fritzi Ritz, *Gasoline Alley*, and other early comic characters. As the thirties ended, the humorous funnies continued but their power to amuse diminished as superheroes entered our world; Superman, Batman, Captain America, Sub-Mariner and Wonder Woman arrived to keep the planet on its axis and to fight evil. My sister read Nancy Drew mysteries, formed girls clubs with Sandy Alberts and Lorraine Derene devoted to the worship of movie stars, and then gave in to a newly acquired taste for adult romantic novels, bodice busters like the *Black Rose* and *Captain From Castile* which topped the bestseller lists, copies of which could be borrowed from Womwrath's on University Avenue for a quarter a week. Simone and I had both begun to read the adult books of our time, not fine literature, but the potboilers that made their way to the best seller lists—mostly historical novels that satisfied our curiosity about other times and places, which my mother in her innocence brought to us from the pay lending library in the greeting card and stationary store on University Place. She had no idea that these books would introduce us to sex and its throbbing wonders, but they did. And so we read and entered worlds larger but in many ways smaller than life in the West Bronx, because those books dealt only with great deeds and grand emotions, while the life we knew was about the small stuff that kept you going.

That great mess of reading, combined with our growing observations about how the real world worked, began to shape the people we were, and the people we would become. All this was accompanied by the sounds of swing music, the big bands, the Dorsey Brothers and Benny Goodman, Ella Fitzgerald, and Artie Shaw. Simone loved their music from the first time she heard it. It was part of that larger world of easy voices celebrating feelings one didn't speak of in the Bronx; of bodies in motion, of bandstands and dancers that our parents, devoted to the operetta music of Jeanette and Nelson could not understand. This music welcomed us into a new world of sound, a sound filled with energy and longing. This was not the music for the old women who sat on fold-up wooden chairs in front of the apartment houses catching fugitive rays of winter sun; it was the music of youth, the music of summer, and we delighted in being young and warm.

The Patterson Summer

In the summers we always went to Long Beach, Long Island, a comfortable resort community on the Atlantic Ocean dominated by the ruin of a great 1920s hotel, The Nassau. It was located on the boardwalk, where you could find rows of arcades with ski-ball parlors and pinball machines, together with apartments and small Spanish style beach houses that were let to city people for the summer. The Nassau was once a palatial hotel where the famous Vernon and Irene Castle danced the fox trot and the two-step. In honor of the dancers, it was originally called "Castle by the Sea," and it had become a resort favored by middle-class Jews from the outer boroughs. During the war years, it was a place where soldiers and sailors congregated, and where one could spy the fat rubber rings of used condoms under the boardwalk, together with the lost sand pails and rusting shovels abandoned by children. It was there, under that boardwalk, that I was always obliged to change my wet bathing suit by my fretful mother, who held up a towel as I scrambled out of the wet wooly suit into a fresh dry one, she feeling relieved that I would now not catch a chill, I feeling exposed and humiliated. Then I would play for hours with my sister, building our sand castles, as my mother worked her needle into a printed table cloth, its design made up of tiny printed blue x's to be filled in by various colored cotton threads. She never completed one, and didn't particularly like needlework, but she did not enjoy cards, as most of the other mother's did, and this was her way to deal with the boredom of the beach. Needlework was so undemanding that it would not prevent her from watching over us. A year before a boatload of Catholic orphans had been taken out on a charity cruise and the boat had capsized and sunk in the Atlantic nearby. The small bodies of the orphans had washed up on the beach for weeks, each one in different states of decay, and my mother was fearful that we might encounter one as we splashed about on the shore. Suddenly, Long Beach was no longer spotless. So for once, she decided against a summer rental there, and what followed was our summer at Belle Harbor among the *goyim*.

Belle Harbor was a quiet, affluent beach colony on the Atlantic in Queens, one that my mother had stumbled upon by chance when she answered a summer rental ad in *The New York Times*. In those sultry summer days before air-conditioning, my parents sought a cool retreat near the ocean, a distance from the heat of the Bronx in summer, a place with a spotless beach, hot, soft sands that burned your feet, and an easy hour train ride from the city. The plan was that my father would come for weekends, while we would have the pleasures of the beach all week.

My mother took the Long Island Railroad to the advertised address in Belle Harbor. The rental price was not cheap. If it was, she would have suspected it of hidden faults. But she liked the clean summer cottage she saw there. She sniffed it carefully for mildew and cat odors, and finding it free of both, and spotless, she rented it at once. She loved the quiet neighborhood and the sight of small children playing safely on wide tree-lined sidewalks, riding three wheelers and selling lemonade and painted seashells from fold-up bridge tables near pretty stucco Spanish style summer houses. With the help of my Uncle Frank's laundry truck, she moved us in for the summer one night during the following week. Two large camp trunks packed with our own towels and bedding (no strangers could be trusted there) and an assortment of shirts, shorts, and bathing suits for the children, were brought to the rental house. My father stayed on in the city to work at his business during the week, planning to visit later on weekends, and my sister and I settled into the cottage.

We went to the beach daily, and my sister quickly made friends with a wizened little girl of her own age who was the daughter of Robert Porter Patterson, Sr., a renowned Civil Court Justice who would become Undersecretary of War under Roosevelt and whose family owned a large summer house on our street. The two girls were soon close buddies, united by their passion for Tyrone Power. They traded pictures of their hero, some obtained free from the wax paper underside of Dixie Cup tops, others from the studio that employed the star. Soon they enlisted me into their new business of collecting sea shells and decorating the backs of the shells with sunbursts and flowers, to be sold as ashtrays outside our houses on the Patterson's leatherette bridge table. Our friendship with the local children flourished. These were not the rough Catholic boys that roamed Fordham Road, but young boys in clean buttoned up short pants who admired my toy soldier collections and my indefatigable digging in the sand to create castles and moats, bulwarks against the tides. The girls were drawn to Simone's encyclopedic knowledge of movie stars and their mates, the troubles of Tyrone and his Annabella, the rocky romance of Errol and Olivia, after the dashing Flynn divorced his Lili Damita, and she was a font of information about the dicey marriage of Joan Crawford and Douglas Fairbanks, Jr. These were my mother's first gentile neighbors. And they appeared to be so accepting of us, the summer renters. Whatever uneasiness she may have felt by not seeing a Jewish face or hearing New York voices that trailed into Yiddish, her fears were put to rest after a few days. All might have proceeded well, a long and happy summer of seashells and sunburn, a summer without incident if not for the visit of Maryasha, our Tante Mary.

You may recall that Tante Mary Horowitz was the aunt who made it possible for my mother and her sisters and brothers to emigrate to America. A stout, energetic woman with a full chin that fell in graduated rolls of flesh over her high collared shirt waist, large arms with generous hanging flags of waving flesh, she did not let the New World get the better of her. She would make no accommodations to its styles. Like Mae West, who she somewhat resembled, she had found her style early and had no intention of abandoning it because of new fashions. She was a walking advertisement for 1910, twenty years later in the late thirties. She had salted away some money from her excellent dressmaking business and that gave her a special confidence. And she knew her own value. Customers arrived with photographs of dresses they wanted her to make, ripped from magazines, and she reproduced them down to the smallest button and flower. For this she demanded that she be paid at once or they would not see the new dress or the stylish suit. No pleas of "I'll pay you in a few days but I must have it now for my son's wedding" would soften her heart. She had no weakness for anyone but my mother. Tante Mary dressed for summer in her large Lillian Russell style wide-brimmed felt hats with huge ostrich feathers, a yellow and white Lynx collared merino wool coat, and a tiger-eye amber clasped leather handbag, looking much as she did when she greeted my mother at her ship when it arrived in New York. At that time, she took them into her own tenement apartment above her shop, and helped them to resettle, finding night watchman work for her soldier brother, whose only skill was to look large and stern. She even found him work as a welder repairing the Brooklyn Bridge, but that job did not last long since he feared heights. Tante Mary was the one who helped pay for the sanatoria when the children became ill, and covered the cost of their funerals when they died. Childless, and unwilling to risk another failed marriage, she regarded her brother's children as her own. The gratitude my mother felt towards her was immeasurable, and she welcomed this bossy, difficult woman into her life without complaint.

My mother understood gratitude; it was for her the primary virtue, and Tante Mary was the person in her life who seemed fully deserving of it. That the woman did not bother to call on the telephone, or even drop a postcard before appearing at our door did not upset my mother. It was the price one paid for having such a caring relative. Even the fact that she woke the sleeping babies with her rough, loud voice when she entered the apartment, and that she was in this country for forty years yet refused to learn a word of English, none of this mattered to my mother. Tante Mary bypassed all judgment. She was the one, the only one, who had been there for them when it counted, getting them out of Russia, looking after them when my grandmother died, and my mother was content to speak Yiddish with her for a whole afternoon, a sacrifice to one who, like my mother, considered Yiddish the language of death and desolation.

Our tranquil summer in the Belle Harbor cottage, miraculously free from my father's tantrums and my asthma attacks was suddenly and irrevocably shattered when Uncle Frank arrived with our laundry and delivered Tante Mary to our doorstep. He announced that she had missed seeing Libby and the children and wanted to see for herself that all was well. Moreover, she had decided to visit for a week and enjoy the company of her family and dip a toe in the sea, the latter being something she hadn't done since her disastrous honeymoon in Odessa with that rascal husband she later divorced.

Her first public appearance in Belle Harbor was in full Tante Mary regalia. Under her coat, she wore her dark greenish-black silk dress with the enormous "dressmaker" pockets, her summer style. After greeting my mother, the Tante decided to take a walk to the ocean, and thus passed the front of our house where Simone and the Patterson girl were selling their painted sea-shells. Tante Mary approached my sister, planted a blustery kiss on her cheek, and examined the painted shells carefully, snapping open the amber clasp of her handbag and removing some silver coins to pay for the shells which she placed inside her handbag, flashing a gold toothed smile at Simone's friend and questioning the startled child in her voluble Yiddish. Just as she was doing so, the girl's father, the portly Judge Patterson appeared. He wished the strange woman a very good morning. Was she lost? Could he be of assistance? Tante Mary looked confused. She replied in Yiddish, smiling, as her gold front tooth caught the bright ocean sun. Tante Mary pointed to Simone, hugged her and indicated in a rush of Yiddish and sign language that she was a part of our family. Horrified, the good Judge took his daughter by the hand and rescued her from the immigrant woman's corrupting presence. A note was delivered by their maid later that afternoon in which the Judge's wife explained that the forthcoming birthday party for Ellen Sue to which we had been invited guests had been cancelled, requesting that we stay at home the following day.

My mother guessed the real reason for the aborted invitation and watched with Simone as a large group of children bearing gifts entered the Patterson house for that birthday party. She told Simone that it was just as well, one of the children looked like she had a bad cold. Later that week, when my mother came upon the Judge walking down the street, she boldly asked him about the party. She wondered aloud if the invitation was rescinded because he had discovered that we were Jewish. The Judge lashed out at her. It was not that we were Jews, it was that we were liars, he claimed. He accused her of deception. She must have known this town was restricted, yet she chose to sneak herself and her brood into it under cover of darkness. He claimed that my mother's beauty and my sister's charm had "fooled" them into believing that we were nice people, good people. Tante Mary's arrival unmasked us as city Jews who had no place here in this town; surely we could find someplace where we would be welcomed, where we belonged, like Coney Island or Brighton Beach? My mother replied that one didn't have to go to Germany to find an anti-Semite. She turned around and reentered the house, angry with herself for speaking with this man, who must be put out of her mind at once. The Pattersons, like the abominable Yellens, would no longer exist for us.

When my father heard of this on his first trip to the beach house he was enraged, but my mother cautioned him to keep his temper. This was America and this bigot was a Judge. She had told him what she thought, and that was enough. My father soon blamed her for this entire Belle Harbor business. Any fool could see that there wasn't a Jewish face for miles about in Belle Harbor. How could she be so misguided as to think that we would be welcomed in such an alien place?

The last of our Marys had returned to Pittsburgh for the summer, and with no replacement at hand, my mother hired the sister of a woman who worked in Uncle Mike's laundry, a black woman named Cora who claimed to have had experience caring for children, and who admired my sister and me as "God's own beautiful wonders," something my mother couldn't dispute. Moreover, she did not drink or smoke and asked only to be given every other Sunday off so she could attend her Harlem church. Unlike the Marys who wore housedresses, Cora came with a gray uniform, something my mother would never ask a servant to wear, but it nevertheless delighted her, and enhanced our prestige among our neighbors until, ultimately, we were exposed as Jews.

All went well until I decided that it was time for me to ride my bicycle without its training wheels. I was seven and feared that it was unmanly to be riding on a two-wheeler tricked out like a tricycle. Simone and I determined to surprise my mother by my riding unassisted on the two-wheeled vehicle as she returned from the market. My sister walked with me to the bicycle store where she purchased, for a quarter, two rubber blocks to be affixed to the pedals, making it easier for me to reach the pedals and ride. The training wheels were removed and, with Cora traveling uneasily behind us and

Simone holding on to the handlebars to improve my balance, I began my wobbly progress down the street. At first, all went well. I was shaky, but I managed to stay upright and traveled half a block, passing the Good Humor truck. Delighted by my new prowess as king of the world, I insisted that Simone let go and let me steer by myself. She did. I rode along filled with so much pride that I did not see the broken Coca Cola bottle that lay in the path before me. I hit the broken glass and fell off the bike, my face landing in a pile of jagged green glass shards. One of the larger shards pierced my upper lip and an unstoppable torrent of blood spurted from it.

Simone rushed to me and cried out for help from Cora to carry me home. But Cora decided that what I needed was less of Cora's help and more of God's. She was, we now discovered, a "Holy Roller, a member of an Evangelical Sect that obliged her to respond to life's traumas with violent shaking and prayers, followed by a speaking in tongues and a rolling about on the ground as the Holy Spirit moved through her. It was the sight of Cora rolling on the sidewalk, shouting for God's mercy, speaking in tongues, that greeted my mother as she returned from her marketing. I lay in a stupor, my face covered in blood. She lifted my head and surveyed the damage to my upper lip. Years of practice with her brother Ally had made her an expert on injuries, and she decided that this one could not be patched up at home with witch hazel and a Band-Aid, but needed a hospital to do the job.

It was the first time I ever saw my mother frightened in an emergency. Usually calm and comforting during the worst of my asthma attacks, she now looked scared. My upper lip was torn in half and hung down exposing the inner gum. She looked around for help, but this was a strange town, and she hardly knew where the hospital was located. She turned to Simone and told her to hold my head as she entered the street and flagged down a passing car. The auto happened to be a large white Packard touring car with whitewall tires and matching white leather upholstery. The driver was our nemesis, Judge Patterson, wearing his white linen summer suit. My mother stood in the path of the car, forcing him to a screeching halt. The Judge looked horrified as he realized that this demanding woman intended to convey her bleeding Jewish child inside his spotless automobile, but before he could protest my mother opened the back passenger door, had me inside, my sister beside me, as my mother gave orders to the startled Judge, changing him from a bigoted Jurist to chauffeur in her new voice, one that was born to command and would tolerate no opposition from a fool. According to my mother, my blood gushed from my cut lip and splattered the white upholstery and the Judge's impeccable Brooks Brothers linen suit.

I was taken to the hospital and treated by a doctor at once. Head wounds at best are terrible but this one was a bloody horror. After the shards of glass were removed, a "clamp" was placed on my upper lip in the hope that the deeply ripped flesh would eventually grow together, held in place by this metal vise since stitches would not do the job. If they did, the doctor warned, I would likely be disfigured. I would have to wear the clamp for weeks as the skin grew together. With me clamped and chastened, my mother called a cab and we returned home where my mother found Cora still rolling on the sidewalk, lost in communion with her Lord. My mother knelt down beside her and spoke firmly to her, telling her that she would have to leave our family. She gave her carfare to the city and an extra twenty dollars, and Cora disappeared from our lives forever. This accident was duly reported to Sister Ida in the morning telephone conversation, and Ida in turn passed the news on to Tante Mary and Uncle Frank.

The rest of the summer was uneventful. The Patterson children never came round, never acknowledged our presence on the beach or as they bicycled past us on the streets. They did not taunt us as dirty Jews; they did far worse. They pretended that we did not exist. We did not know that in Europe at that very moment, Jews were suffering far worse than this social humiliation, or if my parents knew, they refused to pass this information on to us. It was one of the dirty secrets best kept from the children. My mother had closed the book on Europe years before, and she, like so many immigrants, refused to confront the horror that was transpiring there, seeing it only as an extension of those infrequent but dangerous Cossack raids that had marred her early childhood, not as a well-planned genocide.

It would be after the war, when the first photographs of the murdered bodies piled up in the camps and the tales of the crematoria were told, that my mother finally allowed herself to confront the unspeakable. It was the first time I ever heard her curse. Someone had mentioned the death camps and she muttered, "Those goddamned bastards, may they burn forever in the fires of Hell." But until that time, she had so narrowed her world in her personal struggle to survive and prosper, that she allowed little of the larger world to enter into her life or ours. History, alas, was not spotless.

A digression—one that illustrates this part of my mother's psyche and the way she had narrowed her world into a small but manageable size. Years later, in 1963, my mother was coming over to my apartment on East End Avenue in Manhattan to see our newborn son, Nicholas, who was suffering from a cold. I had just learned of the Kennedy assassination and my wife Joan and I were stricken by the news. When my mother arrived I told her to sit down, I had some horrible news to convey. She sank into the sofa and looked up at me, expecting the worst. "The President is dead," I told her. "He was assassinated while riding in an open car in Texas." She took a moment to absorb the information, shaking her head sadly. "That's terrible," she replied, "but how's the baby?"

Back in Belle Harbor the summer dragged on. Simone and I turned to each other in our loneliness and ostracism and became closer. We failed to sell our painted seashells to any of the neighboring adults, now that it was known that we had come to Belle Harbor disguised as ordinary Americans. We were alone daily on the beach, building our sand castles as my mother watched us vigilantly, looking up from her cross stitch needlework, knowing now that in Belle Harbor, a vicious Cossack could be disguised as a Judge and that the fascists were not all in Berlin.

Sylvia's Complaint

I don't know how summer camp came into our lives, but in the late thirties and early forties it became my parent's solution to summer holidays and the city pools that bred polio and ringworm. And it was after a summer at camp that my father had the most memorable of his rages.

When Simone was thirteen she was sent to camp Truda in Maine, an expensive girls camp whose campers came from Riverside Drive or West End Avenue in Manhattan, the daughters of rich lawyers and doctors who resided in comfortable, large, art deco apartments. At camp she proved to be immensely popular among her fellow campers, and she returned from that summer determined to get my family to leave the Bronx and resettle in Manhattan where she could continue to see the friends she had made at summer camp. Simone was primed and ready to leave the Bronx for a larger, more glamorous world than the one we inhabited; a world of soft gray woolen wall-to-wall carpets, gray velvet sofas, abstract paintings, and private High Schools; a world with girls who carried nicknames like Bunny and Bubbles and who wore camel hair coats, smoked gold-tipped Dunhill cigarettes with parental approval, dated college boys and band drummers, and looked with disdain upon any girl from the Bronx or Brooklyn.

She worked steadily upon our parents, extolling the advantages of Manhattan life, the ease and convenience of it all, how everything and everyone in the city was better than in the narrow, provincial Bronx. I would be near the Natural History Museum and could spend days looking at the dioramas of the animals and the Indian tribes I loved. Mother could buy better hats than the one's she purchased at Lillum's, the local hat shop on University Avenue, Daddy would be closer to his office, and didn't they both complain that you couldn't get a decent corned beef sandwich or a sour pickle in our neighborhood? Manhattan had so many delis, it had Chock full o'Nuts for date nut bread sandwiches, and Longchamps and The Tip Toe Inn for roast beef dinners, not to mention the automats which were everywhere with their inexpensive roast beef au jus. Living in Manhattan, my mother would no longer be obliged to carry her mink coat out of the Bronx in a bag, but wear it proudly among her fur coated peers. I could be closer to the High School of Music & Art which I had hopes of attending, and there were so many private schools in Manhattan for her to go to should they decide to let her join Bubbles and Phyllis at Ethical Culture. Her pleas were largely ignored as a passing fancy which would soon disappear as she began public High School and found new friends there. But the remembrance of that summer at camp and telephone calls to and from girls with such glamorous exchanges as RIverside, LEhigh and BUtterfield—even the PEnnsylvania exchange had a Stork Club glamour that was irresistible to her—suggested wonders that our TRemont exchange, shared by candy stores and delis, could not evoke.

Simone had now visited their Riverside Drive and Central Park West apartments with the views of the park and the Hudson, and she had been astonished by what she saw there. The modern paintings, the muted colors, the crystal chandeliers, all of it spoke to her of a way of life that was far removed from the way people lived in the Bronx. She had fallen in love with that luxury wed to gentility, the Bach and Mozart on the phonograph, and the wine in crystal decanters on the marble-topped art deco highboy. Unless she could get her parents to leave the Bronx that love would go unrequited and her future would be forever spoiled. Surprisingly, less than three years later, when she was offered the chance to live that way, she declined. Larry Tisch, the son of a hotel millionaire, and later one of the richest men in America, the future owner of CBS, had met her during our Easter holiday stay at "The Laurel in the Pines," his family's hotel in Lakewood. Within a week he asked her to marry him, presenting her with a large diamond engagement ring, which she refused. She had flirted with him—that was only polite—but he did not attract her. She was only seventeen and she would not marry him, a decision that astonished my father, but earned my mother's grudging respect. Her Simone was not born to compromise with life as *she* had done. And if this rich young man could fall in love with her daughter so easily, others more attractive to her would follow. Her daughter's eye for beauty could not be bartered for wealth in her search for the good life. She would meet her Harris at college, years later, a good looking young navy vet; they would marry and he would enter my father's business, becoming the "number smart" son my father never had, and after some time in the suburbs, they would settle in Manhattan where she would enjoy a great career as an interior designer until her death.

Thanks to Cousin Sylvia, Ida's oldest daughter, Simone's infatuation with the Manhattan life of wealthy Jews brought down the wrath of my father as never seen by us before, and delayed the move into Manhattan by a few years.

It began innocently enough. Sylvia came to the house to introduce her fiancé, an affable, heavy-set soldier named Freddy Greenberg. She saw my thirteen-year-old sister dressed in a fashionable silk peasant blouse, with its matching embroidered skirt, and the 18 karat gold bangles and charm bracelets that dangled from her wrists. Simone was a fashion plate in expensive clothes, all flowing silk and embroidery, the kind that was featured in Vogue and bought at Bergdorf's. Simone's voice was in transition; it was newly refined. She had picked up bits and pieces of the Park Avenue accent of her friend, Phyllis, which mingled comfortably with her Bronx earthiness and made her seem older, more stylish, more sophisticated than she had any right to be. Only my mother was permitted to break the common mold to her nieces who idolized her and envied the role my sister played, as daughter of the royal and rich Uncle Nat and Aunt Lil.

Sylvia listened to Simone's tales of Phyllis and Bubbles Yudah, her Park Avenue summer-camp friends who went to private schools and attended coming out balls for the cream of Jewish society. Sylvia heard her express the wish to move to Manhattan where her new friends lived. The city was filled with museums and skating rinks, Radio City, and other wonders. Sylvia protested that the Bronx was good enough for all of them. It had everything one needed. Simone replied, "What's here in the Bronx? The zoo? The Hall of Fame? You go there once and it's enough for forever. The people in Manhattan speak about art and theater and they know the best people and the best places."

"Who needs those snobs?" Sylvia interrupted, dismissing her younger cousin's argument for a change of venue.

"I do!" my sister stated. "They know how to live."

Sylvia waited around to report the conversation to my father when he arrived home from work, announcing that "Simone wants to move to Manhattan. She wants to hang around with those snobs on West End Avenue. She thinks herself too good for me and Gertie, and too good for the Bronx. Uncle Nat, watch out. Though she may not say it, she even thinks she's too good for you and Aunt Lil. She's ashamed of us! A snob, ashamed of being a Jew!"

Bingo! On her very first try, Sylvia ignited the volcano. Yes, he wanted us to prosper, to flourish, to reach high in the world, but not at the expense of denying himself and my mother. The world Simone longed to enter would surely threaten his standing. In the Bronx, he was *the* rich man who could bid and win the honor of holding the Torah in the small shul that Rabbi Bleiberg made out of his wretched house. If he, Nat Yellen, was obliged to live in Manhattan among men richer than he was, he would lose this hard won distinction and the respect of the world that he cherished.

For Sylvia, her inciting of her uncle's anger was a small act of revenge for having to worship at the altar of Nat and Lilly and their spoiled rotten children. This claim of Sylvia's—that Simone was a snob—was enough for him to listen carefully as Simone spoke in her own defense, his anger rising as he found evidence of the charge in her every word. Here was his daughter, given everything that money could buy, discontented and miserable despite all the love and all the luxury she had received, now turning away from him and her own kind, towards rich, snobbish strangers.

Suddenly, there was a vast explosion of rage in which he parroted Sylvia's words and shouted that the Bronx was good enough for my sister, that she was a goddamned snob, a discontent; she was all that Sylvia said she was, and he would not tolerate this in his daughter. He blamed my mother for this. She was no longer shopping at Klein's or Orbach's, but was now buying Simone's clothes at Bergdorf Goodman. Who bought there but snobs? His own shouts fed his escalating rage. He kept stoking the fires of his own anger, shouting "Snob! Snob!

Snob!" in ever rising fury. Soon he was red faced and screaming at my sister at the top of his lungs. She answered him in a clear, quiet, infuriating voice. "I hate it here. I want to move to Manhattan and live like other people live. I don't belong here. It's boring here and it's ugly!" He took the palm of his hand and struck her hard across her cheek, his fingernail scratching her chin, sending her reeling backwards against the wall, weeping and terrified. My mother hurled herself in front of Simone and stood between them, her own face filled with hatred and rage. She told him that she would leave him forever if he ever hit one of her children again.

"Where do you plan to go?" he asked her sharply.

"I'm going nowhere. It's *you* who'll get out, you crazy fool. I'll pack your bags. There's a war on. I can always get a job somewhere. Go back to your rotten family in Brooklyn; those *schnorers* will take you in—for a price!"

He raised his hand as if to strike her. She did not recoil. Rather than placate his rage with, "Nat, that's enough!" she stood up to him and defied him to strike her.

"Go ahead. Do it. But it won't make you happy, unless my leaving you makes you happy."

Using both his hands he raised them to his head, covered his face, slapping his own face violently with both hands as he began to weep.

The only other time I would see him weep was on the day of my Bar Mitzvah, when he learned that the IRS was going to investigate him for tax evasion, and that his accountant was planning to blackmail him for some fancy bookkeeping for which the accountant himself was responsible unless he paid up. He survived that audit and that ordeal, but I don't think it was as threatening to him as my mother's warning that night.

He knew that she considered divorce a sign of weakness, but now, for the first time, she thought it a greater weakness to stay with him. He also knew that his transgression was so great that she might truly send him packing. After all, she owned half his business for tax purposes, and she knew that neither she nor her children would ever starve. She was still a good-looking woman. The few extra pounds were no impediment to her attractiveness; she saw that in the looks of so many men. Even with two children, there could be another husband in her future, but there was no such calculation in her threat. His rages and the violence had to end. He began to search for a way to apologize, but she would hear none of it until she had her full say.

"Nat, I will not allow you to hurt my children again. Never! Never! Never! Never again! You want to be crazy? Go ahead, be crazy, Mister Crazy! But be crazy by yourself. Without us!" Her face was now a terrible grimace, her mouth was square with rage, her lower lip pulled down. Tears flowed down her cheeks. She was outraged, defiant, and merciless.

The threat silenced him at once. My mother went to the refrigerator and chipped off some ice, wrapped it in a clean dishtowel and applied it to my sister's bright red chin. My father looked at us and began to weep, great gulping sobs provoked by his guilt and the threat of abandonment. The sound increased, as if he was trying to swallow all the air in the room in his shame. Nobody attempted to comfort him. We stood there and looked at him, transfixed by what we saw and heard. And although he would rage against us from time to time in the future, he never struck either of us again. He had lost the power to punish us, and he knew it. For years my mother had endured his rages, knowing there was no place for her to go if she left him. But that day, he had crossed a line and so had she.

"If Simone wants to move to Manhattan, what was wrong with that?" my mother queried later in a calmer time. Hadn't they wanted to leave the Lower East Side and make a new life in the Bronx? Hadn't her parents wanted to leave Russia, and his father leave England? He was now frightened. His love for my mother was so great it forced a discipline on him that nothing else could have done. He never dared risk her wrath again. She had tamed my father with that one threat, and although he continued to shout and rage throughout his lifetime, all it took was a stern look from his Lillian, followed by a "Calm down, Nat," to silence him. Later, his demons would turn inward, and a paralyzing depression would again descend on his life. He would turn to my mother, my sister, myself, and ask, "Why? Why is this happening to me?" as if he was a victim of a terrible accident. By 1946, his depression had become so profound that he willingly volunteered for a course of shock treatments, suggested by his doctor. I can recall taking him to the doctor who administered the therapy and returning home with him, a silent ghost of my father seated beside me in the taxicab. But that was later. For the rest of the time we lived in that Bronx apartment, until we left for Manhattan in 1948, he was quiet, loving, and obedient to every look my mother gave him.

The New World

It was the year 1939. I was seven and Simone was eleven. The great New York World's Fair opened and it changed the course of our lives. My parents had been reluctant to take us; their fear of dangerous crowds breeding polio and other ills was greater than their wish to take us to the much heralded "World of Tomorrow." We both longed to see the pavilions with their giveaway sample products, the pickle pins and elongated Lincoln pennies, the Trylon and Perisphere—that great white ball and tapered tower, shaped like nothing the world had ever seen. Most of all, it was a white city, a Shangri-La, only a nickel subway ride away to experience the future in Corona Park, Queens. The greatest event of our lifetime was taking place and our parents stubbornly refused to let us go.

We spent weeks whining, wheedling, complaining, and assuring our parents that it was necessary for the success of our future lives to see the Fair. You could not grow up and become anything without having seen the Fair. They refused. Mother feared that exposing us to crowds might bring down the dreaded disease. My father was eager to see the Fair for himself, but he would not contradict her on a matter of such import. And then, much to our amazement, my mother relented and agreed to take us. She had read in the *World-Telegram* that exposure to the wonders of the Fair was an absolute necessity for one's children, that it was the chance of a lifetime, and having missed it one would regret that lost opportunity to one's dying day. And so we went to that Fair and, to my mother's chagrin, my father had invited *his* father, "Little Grampa" to meet us there. It appeared that the old man had lifted his eyes from his pinochle game long enough to set his sights on the Fair.

We were to meet at the Corona Gate but the old man failed to appear. My father worried that his father was lost; the old man rarely left his Lower East Side neighborhood and when he did it was to travel a familiar path to Brooklyn or the Bronx to visit his children. For all the

signs and publicity leading to the Fair it was very possible that Little
Grampa was lost in Queens. Worried, my father insisted upon staying
by the gate to wait for his father, urging my mother to go on alone with
us and begin our day.

The great white city with its vision of "tomorrow" was our visit to
Oz. The play of water fountains against the white buildings, the
lagoons and avenues of trees were only a small part of its charms. That
it was fundamentally a way to publicize and stimulate commerce in a
world struggling out of a Depression and on the brink of war meant
nothing to us. So what if motor car makers and chewing gum
millionaires were behind the great sights? So what if the world of
tomorrow in miniature as viewed from moving seats or the parachute
jump were basically commercial events, there to sell by astonishment.
They were wonderful in all senses of the word "wonder," as was the
Aquacade with its precision swimmers, the Indian alligator wrestlers,
the puppets who performed Don Giovanni, and the futuristic Trylon
and Perisphere, the symbols of the fair which we purchased as
souvenirs in various forms—plates, pencil sharpeners, ashtrays. Freed
from Little Grampa ambling behind us slowly, we raced through the
fair, mother abandoning her languorous stride as she excitedly
experienced the Fair through our eyes. It was as if she needed us to
translate "fun" into her life; fun being a language she had failed to
master as a child, but one her children knew instinctively. And for one
day, this day, we brought her into that world, our world. The fair was
too clean, too spotless to represent a threat for her, and the sights too
thrilling to resist. For Simone, the sight of the modern style found in
the pavilions made its mark. She now knew that there were many ways
to see beauty in the world; that everything did not lead to the drab past,
that there was a palpable, gleaming future. Far beyond the various
rides, the Fair advanced the notion that there was a tomorrow; that we
were not locked into the drab today of our lives. I loved the carnival
aspect of it, but the crowds from all over the country and abroad, the
variety of faces, sizes, costumes, and languages fascinated me. Each
foreign pavilion allowed a glimpse into the larger world, from the
Balinese dancers to the glass blowers and automatic washing machines.
It was not the purity of the Fair, but its very impurity, its crass

commerce of automatic milking machines and pickle pins cheek by jowl with abstract art and sensuous modernism that delighted us. Today, looking back, one sees men in suits and ties and Stetson hats, women in summer dresses; polite, ordinary people, but I saw mainly the faces of strangers, faces to be read, to be enjoyed for what one found in them—a longing for pleasure and a world at peace—and I wanted to be a part of the world where such faces could be found.

At the end of the day, as fireworks lit up the night, giving a wondrous glow to the Trylon and Perisphere, we found my father sitting by the Corona Gate with Little Grampa. He had found the old man waiting by the wrong gate, playing pinochle with another old man, not a bit concerned that he was not found or was missing the Fair. He could not be lost, because wherever he was it was where he wanted to be. They had seen a bit of the Fair and my father had taken the old man out for a hot dog. We discovered that they had attended the very same performance of the Aquacade that we had seen, but we had not noticed them, nor they us. So they decided to wait by the gate for our return. We were hours late, flushed with excitement and determined to return. We never did. That world was soon lost in war, the Fair closed, and our lives, magically touched by another world, were just about to begin.

Havana Nights

In 1941, when I was nine years old my father took me on a short flight from Miami to pre-revolutionary Cuba. He wanted to gamble and I was his excuse to do so when he told my mother, 'Sherman really should see Havana. It's such a beautiful city… and we boys should spend some time alone together." She did not discourage this plan—although she knew he would lose a few hundred dollars in the casino—because my father was often depressed (what today we call bi-polar) and when he was on an upswing she encouraged him to enjoy his life—preferably without her. We stayed at the old Hotel Nacional, a very beautiful Spanish colonial hotel, where he would gamble in the casino. We took in the nightclub show at the Villa Rosa but, usually, after a day of sight-seeing, shopping at the Woolworths in the El Prado, or visiting the Moro Castle and the turquoise sea, I would go to bed early. Or, at least, I was *supposed* to. But I was a very adventurous and curious nine-year-old and would sometimes sneak out of my hotel room and wander the nearby plazas and streets of Havana by night and stay out for a few hours exploring those streets, returning to the hotel well before my father came back from the roulette tables. I don't think of myself as having been a particularly fearless child, but my curiosity served as a replacement for courage. I never felt safer—or happier—than in those busy, cheerful night streets. The music, the laughter, the smells of deliciously spicy food cooking in carts by vendors, the guava empanadas, the delicious black bean burgers in a creamy lime sauce, the tame wandering street dogs, and most of all the people I encountered in the streets made it magical for me. The "nice painted ladies" hanging out the windows or sitting on iron railed balconies blew kisses and praised me in Spanish, shouting down "chico guapo" at me. Everyone was protective, but not overbearing. And I had developed a precocious liking for Cuban coffee, filled with chickory. Coffee that could be bought piping hot from street stalls.

One early evening I saw a street performance that astonished and thrilled me. A young woman in bright-green satin trousers appeared on stilts, the trousers extending over the stilts giving her the longest legs in the world. She was soon joined by her partner, a young man wearing ten-foot-long yellow satin trousers; both had on blouses with ruffled multi-colored sleeves—as they moved it was like looking at a rainbow in motion. The guitarist struck up a tango and to my amazement they began to dance the tango on stilts, complete with back bends and those sharp, fancy flamenco turns with arched aristocratic arms. True, this may not have been the most graceful tango ever danced, but it was surely the one danced highest in the air, and with such precision and artistry—artistry made all the better by my fear that they would topple from their stilts before the dance ended. They didn't. And then I noticed the straw hat that was placed before them by a gnarled old woman who acted as their assistant. Some of the people in the streets tossed coins into the hat in appreciation of the dance. I only had a five-dollar bill that I had lifted from my father's jacket pocket— guiltlessly, knowing that he was losing far more in the hotel casino at that moment—and feeling the freedom that only generosity can bring, I tossed it into the hat. The two dancers bowed to me from on high and as the music struck up again they encircled me snapping their fingers, urging me to follow them in the steps they were taking—the Cuban rhumba. Fortunately, the only Latin dance I knew was the rhumba. Simone, in her desperation to practice the rhumba and lacking a partner nearby, had taught me the basics steps of that dance which was then so popular in the United States. Knowing that her kid brother was not the creature of grace that she was—indeed, she sneered a superior "klutz!" at me as she broke the dance down to its geometric patterns, the gist of which was a box step accomplished with a bit of wiggling of one's rear end. I liked the box but I was not enthusiastic about setting my backside into motion. And so I did my best in that Cuban street and I was amazed when cheers and applause greeted me. I knew that the crowd's acclaim was given for effort rather than accomplishment, but I was ready to accept it. The old woman who held the hat offered me my five dollars back, a gesture of enormous generosity which I refused. If it was possible to be deeply embarrassed, ashamed of my clumsiness, and yet proud and thrilled by my accomplishment, those were the only feelings that I recall.

Looking back on those Havana nights now, from the vantage point of the Twenty-first Century, I can confidently state that nobody robbed or assaulted me—in fact, I was often treated to a free meal from a cart—and nobody thought it peculiar that a child should be out alone at night wandering the streets or joining an act of stilted flamenco dancers. I felt at home. Indeed, among these easygoing, all accepting people, I felt that I had come home. No, I didn't see the Batista repression that led to the Castro revolution, or the American gangster-run casinos—though I was later to learn that my brother-in-law's uncle was an associate of Meyer Lansky, who ran the rackets in Cuba. I was too young and I probably would not have recognized the poverty and the oppression among the warm and welcoming people I met on my night wanderings. Night did not fall on that city. It got up, grabbed a guitar, and the people danced. Stray cats, like stray children, were treated with kindness. Bowls filled with milk were left out in the street for the strays. It was there in Havana that I first came to love the Hispanic people and the Spanish colonial architecture that still exists in the city—even more beautiful when seen by gaslight. What we call progress, in the form of modern hotels and Bauhaus-inspired skyscrapers, had not yet arrived to destroy the past, even during the Castro years as a result of the fifty year embargo. Havana may now be crumbling and needs to be spruced up and restored, but the past is still alive there. I was fortunate enough to see Hemingway's beloved Havana, and although I was too young to read his books, later I would understand his love for Cuba and that city. If I live long enough—and my health allows—I would like to go back and see if I can recapture the sense of freedom and wonder that my nine-year-old self first felt in that city so long ago.

A Skinny Boy's
Guide to Survival

For many years I have had a dream of myself as a small boy with my foot caught under a railway track, arrested by fear and unable to free myself as my older sister Simone stood by screaming for me to run as the train came roaring towards me. Doomed. I would wake up, my heart beating wildly, just before the train came close enough to kill me. It was like a silent movie, *The Perils of Little Sherman*, one that was not the main feature of my life but a serial that I would be obliged to return to the following week to see how it all came out. Only when I returned to that dream theater, I got the same chapter of the serial, caught in a loop, and never learned how it came out.

Even in my psychotherapy, some sixty years ago, I was unwilling to discuss this dream with my analyst, even though he was privy to every sexual fantasy I ever had since I reached puberty at twelve, and they were as lurid as any adolescent boy could conjure up: sex with a pneumatic blond beauty on the beach (that universal Fellini-like fantasy shared by many boys), sex with a lascivious brunette teacher on a desk top in High School, sex on the stairs with a Rita Hayworth redhead, sex with maids, sex with aristocratic ladies in grand limousines, sex with, sex and, sex on… Well, you get the gist of it. Sex.

I thought I had figured it out for myself, and that it didn't need a public airing. The killer train was to my overly psychoanalyzed mind the symbol of my father bearing down upon me, capable of killing me in his inexorable rage, and I was incapable of moving out of the path of his anger; an anger that paralyzed my will and would kill me unless I woke up. Strangely, I was not the one screaming. It was my sister Simone whose cries I heard. Since she had often, in life, cried out "Run, Sherman, run," as my father chased me through the long apartment hallway screaming, "You ungrateful little bastard," or "You fucking brat," wielding his belt like a lariat, the dream fit in perfectly with that reality, but it did not stand alone as true. As I matured I learned to be suspicious of anything that required too much interpretation, and would hang a sign in my own mind: "Beware of symbols."

Joan and I made a pact early in our marriage never to discuss our dreams. She agreed with me that reality is difficult enough to comprehend, but dreams are a yawn to everyone but the dreamer; the more fascinating the dream is to the dreamer, the harder it is to listen to, except perhaps for a therapist who has to be paid a great deal of money to endure the tedium of someone else's dreams and nightmares.

So I tucked that train bearing down on me into the discard dream pile of my youth, until a letter from a stranger arrived the other day. As I opened the envelope, pictures of myself as a young boy, and those of my sister dressed for a portrait in her graduation from Junior High School, fell out on to my desk, together with a typed letter on a plain piece of paper. It read:

> Dear Sherman,
>
> My first remembrance of you was walking along the railway tracks in Long Beach with Simone, my brother Martin Brussell and myself. What guided that misdeed I don't remember but the inevitable did happen, and a train came chugging towards us. Simone, Martin, and I ran to the other side and you were left standing on the track. Simone, your ever watchful little mother, screaming hysterically RUN! You chose to wait, then finally run, so that childhood foolishness ended on a happy note.

Everything that I had suppressed as reality came back to me as I read this letter from a self-described eighty-five-year-old stranger who had been a witness to my childhood misadventure. Clearly on that day, during the summer holidays that we spent at a nearby resort, four children decided to disobey our elders and walk along the railroad tracks in Long Beach, Long Island. As a train approached the others ran but I was too frightened to move, my feet frozen with fear, trapped on the track, and yet the train passed by without injuring me in any way. Had I found my legs and my courage? Possibly. Or had instinct forced me to move from the track to safety? Was my foot caught under the narrow metal rail, and did my sister pull it out from its trap before the train came towards my foot? I'll never know. Nor did Ms. Lebow, my new correspondent and long ago witness to this near catastrophe.

This was not an adventure to be reported to either mother or father; mother would become crazed with worry, and never let us out of her sight all summer, and my father would be crazed with anger, feeling that such dangerous, disobedient stupidity demanded the harshest punishment. And since Simone was in charge of me, and unwilling to take the blame for that illicit adventure, she kept it our secret; a secret that was never to be discussed between us, never relived, a secret given a somber burial until it was disinterred when I received the letter from Irene Lebow.

That letter made me question how many of my childhood fears were fantasies or the result of actual events. I had no trouble sorting out the true from the imagined when they dealt with my father. If he told a story I knew it was untrue, so that even when he professed his great affection for us I doubted that hyperbolic reality, while at the same time knowing that he loved us. He gave new meaning to what would later be called cognitive dissonance. But looking back to that time I imagine that we kept silent about that near tragic event not to spare ourselves from punishment or a stern lecture but to spare our mother. We knew that we were the center of her life, and that her discovery of the misadventure would worry her more than ever about our vulnerability, and our future capacity for dangerous mischief. My childhood asthma and Simone's flirtations with nearly everyone who crossed her path were both considered life threatening maladies—trouble enough without adding this to them.

It was not me that day, but little Martin Brussell who would die a few years later of some childhood illness that was too horrible to be discussed in front of the children. He would attend Camp Robin Hood at Lake Winnipesaukee in New Hampshire with me the following year, my first time away from home. Forever smiling the smile of the genial fat boy, he found a perfect companion in me, skinny, sulking and precociously acerbic. His parents being wealthy and convivial and knowing all the right restaurants, theater brokers, and summer camps, they convinced my parents that the long established camp Robin Hood in New Hampshire would be ideal for both boys. It would help Martin to lose weight and it would no doubt add some needed flesh to my all too protruding bones. And to make matters better, there was Camp Truda in nearby Maine, an all-girls camp for well-to-do Jewish girls like Simone, so that a visit to one meant an easy visit to all.

Nothing about a summer at camp appealed to me until I was advised by the avuncular head counselor who arrived at our apartment with slides and a sales pitch that the camp was on Lake Winnipesaukee. Was there ever a word that better conjured up the lost world of the American Indian? I would be able to spend a summer at a place that had for centuries been the home of an Algonquin warrior tribe. I longed to paddle a birch bark canoe through a lake thick with water lilies, just as the smiling boys in the photographs provided by the camp were doing. I wanted to hike through a dense forest whose only sound was birdsong, and experience the crunch of moss covered bramble underfoot as I stalked the wilderness in my camp-required moccasins hunting my elusive lost Indian self. I was desperate to peel the birch bark from a tree and construct a miniature canoe from it in arts and crafts or write a letter home on it. And I wanted to wear the various tee shirts and ponchos that my mother had been obliged to purchase with the Camp Robin Hood logo and a cloth name tag neatly sewn into everything Camp Robin Hood by one of the Polish Marys.

Since I had never lived apart from my family, I never experienced homesickness, and that separation from family held no terrors; the loss of my sister and my mother's company was more than compensated for by the loss of my father's temper for two long summer months.

I was then, and remained for many years, the skinniest child on the block, wherever that block might be at that time. At eight going on nine, I weighed no more than sixty pounds, and I was quite tall for my age. All this was brought back to me in the photographs that Irene Lebow had enclosed in her letter.

There was no road towards fattening me up, no amount of malted milkshakes or pot roast with mashed potatoes could put on a pound, and no visits to Dr. Jackson, whose best effort was the prescription of a daily dose of cod liver oil—one I refused to accept as I held my mouth locked tightly shut until my guileful mother tricked me into opening it by telling me some family story—but none of it made any difference in the weight gaining arena. To my mother who associated such skinniness with the wasting away of her own mother, brother and sister from tuberculosis, looking at me must have been a torment. The photograph of me and her brother Martin that came with the recollection of Irene Lebow, sent as proof of our past connection, reminded me of all that and more as I sat reading it in my office in my now plump old age.

It also reminded me that a few days spent in the camp told me that I was doomed. The owner and head counselor who had visited our apartment with a slide show of activities had taken one look at me and the art work of mine which my mother proudly presented to him as proof of my genius, and edited his sales pitch down from team sports to such activities as arts and crafts, campfire songs, and Gilbert and Sullivan style theatricals. Somehow the rigorous day filled with sports was eliminated from the home sales pitch. He left us with a long list of the special Robin Hood shorts, tee shirts, ponchos, baseball caps, sheets, blankets and pillow (mine being made of rubber to ward off the asthma attack that might come from feathers), all of which could be, indeed had to be, obtained at a special store, and once acquired each item of clothing or bedding sewn to small cloth nametags, particularly important in matters of the white socks with the green trim that Camp Robin Hood required.

Since I was not without athletic skills—I could hurl one of those pink rubber balls that we kids called Spaldeens against the point of a stoop and run like hellfire in a game with my school friends—I thought I could adapt to the games at Robin Hood. But the first day of activities showed me that I was lost on the formal green sward of a baseball field unable to gauge the distance between any approaching ball and me. My hand-eye coordination wasn't suited to team sports, and I was far too slight for football, more fit to be a goalpost than a player.

I was, however, a whiz-bang at Ping-Pong since I had years of practice playing table tennis in our sun parlor, but Ping-Pong was a rainy day activity and it never rained at Camp Robin Hood. So I was assigned to that dreaded place in the outfield, right field, where counselor and teammates exiled the weak and the uncoordinated; last chosen, first to leave the field when the whistle was blown. For me that whistle was less a sign that the activity had ended than it was an all-clear after an air raid. Those promised arts and crafts activities took place only on rainy days, and to my despair, it seemed never to rain on Lake Winnipesaukee.

Being best friends with Martin the cheerful fat boy did little for my reputation in my bunk house, where the bunk houses were considered camp teams and my lack of athletic prowess was regarded as a blot on the reputation of "Friar Tuck," the name of our house inscribed on a rustic looking sign, since all the houses took their names from the Robin Hood legend. One of the camp wits renamed our house Try or Fuck, and I did try at first to fit in. Failing that, I attempted to demonstrate a serious interest in sports by oiling my new leather outfielder's glove and hurling my baseball endlessly into the center of the glove to achieve that perfect Babe Ruth leather cavity, but I could not get the hang of it. I knew all the rules of the game and the arcane methods of keeping score from my Sundays with my father at Yankee Stadium, but I could not catch a ball with that glove, hit one with a bat, or if by chance I was hit by the ball when up at bat, make it through the bases to a home run.

The counselor was a kind enough fellow, probably accustomed to getting one like me every year, and knowing that it was his job to return me alive to my parents. He did his best to keep me out of harm's way. Thus left field, which came along with the nickname "punk." Verbal abuse by my bunkmates was permitted, possibly encouraged as an aid to better performance, and as a guide to reality, meaning that I should entertain no false illusions about myself, but any life-threatening act of physical violence would be stopped. My bed was "frenched," with the sheets pulled tight in such a way that one could not enter it fully, almost as much as poor Martin's sheets were, but I shrugged it off with a remark to the culprit, "What's with you? If you're practicing to become a housemaid you gotta do better than that," while tears welled in Martin's eyes every time he tried to enter his bed, only to find that it was impossible to do so, or if possible, that it contained the remains of a dead frog.

The camp, like all camps, was the breeding ground for ruthless competition. It was bunk against bunk, green against red in color war, a constant summer of us against them. And if, like me, you were the weakest link in the "us," every day you prayed for rain like a farmer in the dustbowl; a rain that refused to come.

And I was insulted. In those gentler days of the 1930s, "punk" or "piss face" sufficed among my bunkmates, since "sissy" would not fit a kid as brazenly outspoken and feisty as me. I may have been inept at team sports, but it was clear to most of my bunkmates that I was fearless, that I would fight back and lose, but that I would not accept insult without retaliation. I had heard Martin cry when he was called "fatty" or "pig face" by the other boys, and when we walked together we were mocked for the extremes of our size, often to the chant of "fat and skinny ran a race, fat fell down and broke his face," but I soldiered on, refusing to cry, or abandon him, offering the best insult I could dig up in my deep store of insults—a collection developed in my home-front battles with my sister—in return for any insult addressed at me, and also at Martin. The fact was that I was protective of him because he lacked what I knew I had—a will of iron, forged at home in the foundry of my father's rages and those everyday fights with Simone. Beyond that I knew that I was not half as nice as my mother thought I was, that my sister had it right when she called me a "little stinker" and that I had a mean streak too, but unlike the other boys in the bunk I was unwilling to share my meanness with my bunkmates like candy from home; rather I hoarded my nastiness, kept it well hidden, comforted by the knowledge that it was there to be called upon when the opportunity presented itself, but that chance grew more unlikely with each passing day.

I suspected that befriending Martin, as I had, was not a show of character, loyalty or virtue, but a refusal to join in another team sport— bullying—in which I had little interest. Like Martin, I was an outsider, but unlike Martin who grieved about his status, I was an outsider who took some pleasure in it. Being set apart did not make me feel inferior; it made me feel more like me—the boy who saw everything, and more. Looking at others, trying to figure them out (as they said in those days) was my natural sport, my true talent. Drawing pictures was just a hobby; observing, even as a boy, was my true avocation.

Nevertheless, while others collected specimens of leaves and stones during the nature walks, I collected grievances, hurts, and abuse, and my bunkmate Alvin Barkin was the prize grievance in my collection. I had stored him away starting from the time we arrived at camp, made a study of his cruelty, and while despising him for it, admired its expertise. Kids are mostly amateurs in the dark arts, and when a real professional faces us, even in his cruelty it was hard not to admire the ease of his expertise. No bunkmate was more active in declaring me a punk than Alvin Barkin, the freckle-faced kid who occupied the top half of the double-decker bunk that we shared. Because my name was Sherman and he was of little wit and less imagination, he chose to mock me by calling me "Worm-man," suggesting a spineless creature that could easily be crushed underfoot.

To make matters worse, Alvin was the best athlete in our cabin, recognized and admired by all for the length of his throw, the speed of his running, gifts that in a normal boy might breed generosity and confidence. But Alvin was not a normal boy. He had a talent for cruelty that I had never before seen. My father could lose all control over himself in a rage, but he was by nature a kind man. Kill one in a rage? Possibly. But he was never one to humiliate another human being. I once watched Alvin catch a living frog and tear its front legs off and watch it struggle to crawl back into the brush on its belly, then have him turn to me and say, "You're next, punk."

He would spit exuberantly as I passed by barefooted, as his well-aimed saliva formed a little puddle of hatred just short of my toes. And to make matters worse, he was rich with gifts from home that added to his popularity. By camp standards rich meant that a boy received weekly parcels of dark brown salamis mottled with fat, boxes of Oreo cookies, and money for buying Cokes for himself and others in the canteen, and lots of hair tonic to keep the head sleek. My mother did not trust the post office with food, fearing that it might be held for weeks in some filthy way station in New Hampshire, so instead she would send me five dollars from time to time, money I hid deep inside the fingers of my baseball mitt, feeling that this was the last place that anybody would look for it. I shared my hiding place with no one, not even the loyal Martin whom I felt would betray me under the torture that was sure to come to him before the summer ended. It was 1941, and even as children we had all heard horror stories about the cruelty of the Nazis in Europe, and here we were, Martin and me, two Jews living among the nine-year-old Wehrmacht, with no hope of surviving this camp.

Alvin's cruelty accelerated with each passing week. He would hang his spectacularly freckled face over the side of the bunk, looking down at me, and whisper, "Asleep yet, Worm-man?" When I failed to reply to his questions, he would aim his spit into my moccasin with the skill of a WWII bombardier, shouting as he did "bombs away" so that I would be obliged to wash out the inner sole before I could use the moccasin again. And of course, his humiliation of me was no secret to my other bunkmates. They saw that I was fair game and that there was strength in numbers, and that our counselors, some of whom were no more than sixteen or seventeen themselves, would turn a blind eye to torture as long as it ended short of death. So "Worm-man" I became at the beginning of July, and I had nothing to look forward to but further horrors and humiliations from mid-July through the end of August.

Once, a group of boys spurred on by Alvin, finding that our counselor was distracted as we swam, held my head down under water just long enough to make me believe that I was drowning, and released me just in time as the counselor's eyes returned to the campers as they finished baptizing me and began their swim in the lake.

Reader, hold on tight. Sherman the Worm Man not only survived that day, but it gets really good for anyone but Quakers and child psychologists. No, it was not a letter home to my parents, describing my torture and the torment of Martin that brought me salvation by their arrival to take me home. One or two of the other boys in different bunks did manage a rescue by a parent who heeded their tear-stained letter home, but that was not Sherman's way. I saw in their departure the ultimate disgrace, the admission of a failure that would brand a boy for life, and I would have none of that. Yes, I longed for salvation but not the humiliation of leaving camp a failure in my own mind, something that would mark me for life with a word far worse than punk, "quitter." It would be blind luck, and my own innately mean spirit sharpened by years of fights with Simone that got me through those weeks at Camp Robin Hood alive.

One day I watched my friend Martin Brussell being viciously insulted by Alvin who in the brief absence of the counselor had set up a makeshift dart board with a cruel cartoon marked "Martin as Porky Pig," and invited others to hit Marty the pig on his snout with a rubber ball, darts being denied to boys under twelve. I saw the tears in Martin's eyes, and I rushed towards the paper target to tear it down, but before I could do so, Alvin hurled the ball at Martin himself, hitting him smack in the center of his forehead. I rushed at Alvin who tackled me with ease and sat on top of me as the game continued with one boy keeping score for the others on the number of bullseye hits that landed on Marty's snout, until the counselor returned, the target ripped down by him, as he turned to all of us and called us "Little Jerkoffs." I half suspected that he found the teasing of the fat boy funny, but I had no proof of that, so I forced myself to pretend that our counselor was a good fellow who just happened to be off somewhere every time something awful happened to Martin or to me. But I knew that there was no hope of rescue from counselor or parents. If I were to survive, I would have to do it alone.

Part of the camp experience was learning to clean up after oneself, so that each bunk house had cleanup duty daily prior to an inspection by the Head Counselor, who gave grades for the tightness of the bedding, the neatness of the bunk, and the tidiness of the grounds surrounding each bunk. All the campers in Friar Tuck, including Martin, hated the KP cleanup duty, but to me it meant freedom from the playing fields in the hot July sun, freedom to think up all kinds of revenge, none of which seemed to have a practical application but provided a temporary salve over my wounds, and I would often volunteer to pick up the scraps of chewing gum paper. Everyone was obliged by camp rules to take their turn, unless some sporting event intervened and the best of the athletes, like Alvin, were pardoned from their turn that day. If it was, as on that fateful day, a time when Robin Hood was playing Silverlake, another boys camp, Alvin would be excused from this chore automatically.

My counselor, a strapping fellow named Buddy, announced that Alvin would be excused from his weekly turn at KP that day so that he could play in the baseball competition. He asked for a volunteer to take Alvin's place, staring at me, and I refused to raise my hand.

On any other day I would have welcomed the chance to escape the heat and the humiliation of the playing fields, although today my job was to be seated in the stands with other campers cheering on our team, but today I refused to volunteer. If I was to be the designated cleaner-upper, I would have to be appointed as such. I wanted—indeed I craved—an act of injustice, not a self-inflicted chore that day; certainly not one that would save Alvin from the tedium of cleanup. I was now collecting all these injustices with the precision with which I had collected my postage stamps, so that one day... one day... but suspecting that the famous one day might never come. Still, as with the stamp collection, one had to be ready for the possibility that the famous upside down flying Jenny stamp, removed from circulation and thus worth thousands, might pop up in a wax paper bag of stamps bought at the five and dime. If I was unlucky enough to find myself in Camp Robin Hood, hundreds of miles from home and safety, sent there by my unwitting parents who had been sold a bill of goods by a cunning Head Counselor, I figured that I would never be lucky enough to extract a bit of golden vengeance from the common ore of my everyday humiliation. But there was nothing to keep me from hoping. And I was a creature then, as I am today, of unreasonable optimism.

It was by chance July 14th, Bastille Day, when it happened. There was a small French Jewish refugee boy in another bunk named Pierre Solomon who, despite his size, was the best tennis player in the camp, tennis being the only sport that interested me. He announced to one and all that this was his national holiday, and a fuss about it was made during dining hall when a small French flag was put on top of a cupcake to honor that lost country of Pierre's and Pierre sang "La Marseillaise" in a piping, tiny voice. It was my good fortune to play in a doubles game with him from time to time which meant that for once I was on a winning team, but no friendship evolved from that tennis partnership, given the competition among the bunks, and the fact that even an exiled French refugee boy does not want to make friends with a known victim who is commonly known as "Sherm the Worm."

And so I found myself alone doing KP duty on Bastille Day, collecting scraps of paper and other detritus in a canvas sack, and using a pole with a long nail on it to get to the hard to reach spots that were under the bunk house, the houses being raised off the ground on foot high concrete cornerstones so that they would not flood during the rainy season that followed the close of summer camp.

I liked that pole. Alone, I would brandish it like a lance and aim it at the imaginary heart of Alvin Barkin. For, although others had followed his lead, it was Alvin the ringleader, Alvin the tyrant, Alvin the tormentor, upon whom all my hatred was focused. For a while I was able to convince myself that I hated him for his cruelty to my good-natured friend, Martin, but I knew in my own boy's heart that I hated him exclusively for all he had done to me; for the myriad humiliations he had made me suffer; for all the Sherm the Worms I had endured; for all the mockery of me on some playing field; for all the conspiracies he had initiated to torment me every day.

Moreover, I hated him for his freckles, I hated him for his slicked back hair, I hated him for his athletic prowess, but most of all I hated him for his unrelenting cruelty towards me, something I had never before experienced, for although I had suffered through my childhood with my father's volcanic rage, I had never before felt a victim, trapped in a world from which there was no escape, except, perhaps in that dream of entrapment at the railway, but by the time I had arrived at camp I had already discounted the reality of that day. Here there was no mother or sister to open the bathroom door and urge me to lock it and hide inside until the paternal storm had passed. Here I was living in the open with a cruelty that was not brought on by my father's rage, a thunderstorm of anger that coexisted with his love, but a cruelty that was ordinary, and if I understood the word then, it was banal. I had not forgotten then, nor would I ever forget the feeling of dying that I had experienced as Alvin and his cohorts held my head under water, but even that felt like part of the everyday camp program.

Having finished collecting and bagging all the scraps of paper, wads of hard chewing gum, and bits of string and rope from parcels sent by parents, the cellophane wrapping from salamis, and envelopes that had made it out to the lawn, I began to probe under the bunk house with my pole. I felt something heavier than paper under that house, and it took me a few tries to spear it but what emerged on the end of that stick was a pair of boy's underpants clinging to the nail. I tossed it down beside me and saw that it was smeared with human excrement. I read the name tag on the underpants and it read Alvin Barkin.

I began to fish desperately under that house with my pole, hauling in ten pairs of boy's underpants and one pair of shorts, all covered in shit and bearing the name of Alvin Barkin. I knew then for the first time that there was a just God. I carefully collected the treasure into a pile and raced into the bunk where I found Alvin's cloth duffle bag. Each of the soiled underpants was dropped by pole into that duffle bag, which I carried into the nearby woods, and rapidly digging a small declivity in the earth, I placed my treasure inside it, and covered it over with brush. No Algonquin brave could ever have concealed the presence of his treasure as carefully and skillfully as I did that day. I had finally found a use for my Indian studies, gleaned from all those lithographed pamphlets from the museum.

Alvin and my bunkmates returned in triumph from the playing field a few hours later. I could not restrain my smile. He looked me over suspiciously and asked why I was smiling, covering his inquiry if my parents were finally going to take me home with his signature smirk. To Alvin's amazement, and that of Martin, I stated that I was very happy to be at Camp Robin Hood, and never happier than I was that day, having made an amazing discovery. I offered to share that discovery with Alvin if he would share his next salami with Martin and me.

Martin looked at me as if I had finally gone all the way over into lunacy, the final result of all the torment that I had endured. Here I was virtually demanding half of the spectacular salami from my tormentor, a sure sign that I was totally, irrevocably lost. But there was just a hint of fear in Alvin's eye. He tried to dismiss the tone of my voice as meaningless braggadocio on the part of a convicted weakling, and I knew I had to exercise all my self-control to keep from revealing to one and all what I had found. But I had at an early aged mastered the art of holding back, learning never to betray my private thoughts to a father who might find them a provocation for a shout or a beating. I knew the power of silence. I had learned it from my mother who was a master of silences, using them to conceal all that she did not wish the world or her children to know, so that she could create a narrative of her life for herself and for her children that was one of triumph rather than defeat at the hands of a merciless world.

Now, it was not the world but little Sherman who could be merciless, and I waited for the right moment—the perfect moment for me to exact my revenge—and feared that it would never come since Alvin's schedule of sports activities kept him away from the house and lined up with all our bunkmates on various excursions, away from me. But I held out for a few more days until that longed for rain arrived, and we were all sent to the main cabin for arts and crafts activities.

Alvin was weaving a lariat out of leather strips that wrapped around nails set on a spool, while I began to prepare an Indian key chain for my father, incising a tomahawk design with an electric wood-burning needle. I kept sneaking glances towards him as he worked on his lariat, noticing that, for all his athletic prowess, his fingers were clumsy and he was making a mess of his lariat. I walked confidently towards him and asked if he needed some help. His reply, "Go back to your hole, worm," was as nasty as I had expected, as nasty as I desired, because I knew that I needed a fresh provocation to exact my full revenge. For unlike the old saying that revenge is best served cold, boys need it hot, steaming, fiery, to extract the full pleasure that can be found in it. If this was to be my first scalp, I wanted it steaming and bloody.

I did not move away from him as he expected. Instead, I stood over him as he worked seated at the bench on his bungled lariat and I told him in a quiet voice, louder than a whisper, but softer than a shout, of my discovery under the bunk. I advised him that I had hidden it carefully and that I would produce it whenever it was necessary for me to do so. The price of my silence would be his ending the persecution of Martin, and his treating me with courtesy, although the word was not courtesy. I believe I said that he must now regard me as his master. He asked to go outside with me, and as we stood there in the rain together I thought that he might kill me to cover up his crime, but instead he told me that he had a bad bowel condition, that he was under treatment from a doctor, and that he was afraid that he might die from it. It was a plea for mercy, and true tears fell from Alvin's beady eyes.

I am ashamed to say—no, make that proud to say—that I showed him no mercy. If he was sick I didn't care, or as Buddy would say, "give a flying fuck." I understood that his cruelty didn't emanate from his sick bowels, it came from his sick heart, and I knew that I could not allow myself to feel the smallest amount of sympathy, let alone pity, for him. I told him that I was ready to expose him at any time I chose to do so, that I would even contrive to fly one of his shitty underpants from the camp flagpole, the tall one with the brass eagle atop it, the one we were obliged to salute every morning at reveille. His only hope for surviving the summer was to do everything I ordered him to do. It took but a moment for me to turn from victim to tyrant, and although I enjoyed neither role, if I had to choose, tyrant would do nicely.

One evening after dinner at the dining hall there was no planned activity. My bunkmates were bored. Someone asked, "What can we do before lights out?" It was then that I made my first and only suggestion for an activity, proposing that we all use the light to count Alvin's freckles.

Alvin's freckles were commonly recognized as a forbidden subject. Once, a boy had fondly and jokingly called him freckle-face and he had slugged him. My suggestion appeared to one and all a suicide note, to be followed by my immediate death by Alvin. They waited for Alvin to rise to the event and, if not kill me, maim me in a way that would forever silence me from making such a lunatic suggestion. Perhaps he would simply pull my tongue out of my mouth and leave me mute forever, which, short of killing me on the spot, must have seemed the only possible punishment for my suggestion. When no one in the house rose to the challenge, I further suggested that Alvin begin by counting those on his left cheek, and when he got tired, I would complete the tally. I nodded to Alvin, a signal that he begin or face the consequences. I offered him the tin mirror that came with our camp gear and he began the countdown. When he reached thirty of the small brown spots that covered his face, I relieved him of his task, and began my count, only stopping when I arrived at fifty.

Alvin placed a brotherly arm around my shoulder and, turning to the amazed spectators in Friar Tuck, congratulated me on my great sense of humor. They nodded, stunned. And when the inevitable salami arrived later that week, it was to Martin and me that the first slices were offered. I could tell that the others were not happy with Alvin's inexplicable change of heart, particularly when someone decided that Martin and I had lived too long without a dose of bullying, and Alvin was quick to stand between us and tell the other to let it go. It was evident that he did not like us, yet he had chosen for some incomprehensible reason to be our protector. It was no surprise then that at the end of the summer Alvin Barkin was awarded not only the all-around camper award, but "best character" award.

I wish there was a moral to this boyhood story, one that ends with the fact that every Alvin Barkin shits, but we all know that is not true. Every Alvin Barkin does not. More often than not he goes on terrorizing the weak and the innocent merrily through his life. As soon as summer camp was over, I would forsake my role as blackmailing bully and freckle counter, and I would forgo the obligatory winter camp reunion, knowing that I would never return to Camp Robin Hood. Well named, because that camp had robbed me of my small store of innocence, teaching me that sometimes the only way to survive is to take on the tactics of the enemy. I know nothing about Barkin's future. Did he die of his bowel disorder as he thought he might? All I knew was that sweet Martin Brussell would die a few years later, and my parents would not let me attend the funeral because they feared that death, like polio, might be catching. And thanks to that summer at camp, I discovered that there are worse traps in life than having a foot caught in a railway tie as a train comes rushing towards you.

The Tomato Sauce Railway

A t the time of my eighth birthday, I believed that I loved my father because he spoke so often of his love for me, and my understanding of love was that being told one was loved meant that one automatically loved in return. This birthday was to be celebrated at home, where birthdays in the 1930s were always celebrated, and it promised the usual cream cake from Sutter's bakery, a select group of school friends, and noisemakers. In January of 1940, a month before my February birthday, my father, the principal noisemaker in my life, had asked me what special gift I wanted for that birthday, and I told him that I had set my heart on a Lionel train set called the Cloverdale Railway. I had seen it during an exploratory trip to Macy's toy department with my mother. I had admired the well-made tin cars with their glass windows, the railway station with its ticket booth and miniature train schedule sign with arrivals and departures, and the railway cars large enough to show the finely painted details of the passenger cabins yet small enough to fit a boy's hand.

Most of all I admired the layout of the track; just enough for a kid to put together and handle with ease. Better still, the controls were clearly marked and appeared to be simple to use once one got the hang of it, and when it came to machinery that hang of it was often out of my reach. My father must have been much relieved that I had not asked for a set of oil paints or a larger easel, hoping that I was now entering the authentic boyhood years, and would put the child artist behind me to become the boy railway engineer.

During a demonstration at the store, the model train was running in overlapping circles and cunning figure eights on a special table that was covered with a green felt cloth that bulged with mountains and dipped into valleys. I was instructed by a salesman in a threadbare pinstriped suit on how to connect the tracks—"Snap, lock, snap, lock" he repeated while demonstrating—and how to use the controls to get the trains to move forward, to back up, to switch tracks, to crisscross on the elevated rails with other trains below, and to enter into a miniature tunnel built into a small mountain, and finally to arrive at the toy station to discharge and take on the patiently waiting tin passengers on their metal stands, some reading tin newspapers, others carrying briefcases, all of them men in suits and slouch hats, at a time when a working woman was an object of pity, rather than a model to be replicated in a toy train set. The salesman claimed that a boy as smart as I appeared to be could run this set as easily as he might a windup toy train. Little did he know that I had often overwound wind-up toys, and many a tin duck or monkey beating a drum had refused to waddle across the floor or make a noise because of my heavy hand, doomed to remain forever inert.

Best of all for my mother was the salesman's claim that there wasn't an electric shock in the American made Lionel set; no tricky foreign wiring to send an unwary boy reeling across the living room, hair shot upright, with burning brow and incinerated eyelashes, as if struck by lightning, his mind blown out like an over-loaded fuse. This was something the salesman confided to my mother, something that could easily happen with some popular German made sets like the more elaborate Marklins sold at FAO Schwarz, so treacherous that they were as dangerous as giving a small boy a loaded pistol. He whispered that German electric trains ran on another current and required the services of an electrical engineer to divest them of their power to electrocute a boy.

I was certain that my mother had conveyed all this information to my father, and that I would receive the Cloverdale Railway in its brightly colored yellow cardboard box which showed the engine puffing steam while traversing a bucolic landscape as it went around a bend on its way to the idyllic if generic town of Cloverdale thanks to the Lionel Train Company.

The day before my birthday a large polished dark wooden box arrived, easily the size of a steamer trunk, fastened by three-inch leather straps; a box large enough for a seven-year-old boy to hide in, if need be. Given my father's volcanic temper I had come to inspect any new piece of furniture or object that came into the house for its possibilities as a place of refuge. The English mahogany dining room table could easily keep a boy hidden if the long applique tablecloth was on it. And the baby grand piano had an underside that could accommodate my small crouching body if I placed myself away from the pedals with the piano bench concealing the dark recess of the underside and the scarlet velvet piano scarf (with its fancy monogramed Y in gold threads) hanging low, so with a perfect configuration of the planets with the household furniture, I could easily outfox a rampaging father.

Five minutes after this box appeared, it was followed by a trio of heavy boxes all carried into the hallway by a deliveryman who kept returning to his truck, which was parked in the street below, for yet another box. The large boxes filled the long narrow entrance hallway to the apartment. My father gave the man five dollars for his backbreaking labors and promised more if he would open the boxes for us.

"I know I'm a day early," my father said to me, "but Sherm, I want to give you time to set it up for your birthday so that you can enjoy it tomorrow." I disliked the way he abbreviated my name, and he almost always included that "Sherm" in any remarks he made to me, as if he needed to use it as a memory aid to remind him of who I was. Otherwise, I was called "son." He was either unnamed or called "Daddy" by us—his choice, being the one favored by Little Orphan Annie for the bald but loving Warbucks who had adopted her.

The deliveryman used a box cutter to release the leather binding straps, and soon all the boxes were pried opened, revealing the sawdust packing and the bright flashes of metal hidden within. My father tipped him seven more dollars, probably more than the man's daily salary, and the man left, backing up out of the apartment as if he were departing royalty.

"Be careful of splinters!" my mother cautioned.

"They don't make boxes with splinters where this comes from," my father protested with some pride, and indeed these were no rough wood fruit-cases from Florida, but finely crafted boxes that clearly started life as the treasure chests of millionaires. "It's Swedish," he said proudly, as if nothing could compare with a Swedish train set.

As I opened the first box, reaching deep into the fine sawdust packing, my hand emerged with a model train so large that it fell back out of my hand into the box, and I knew at once that it required both my hands to hold it horizontally to study it. I saw that the steam locomotive was marked "Mitropa—Prussian T." Streaming across the body of the locomotive was the painted blue and white banner of the Scandinavian-Swiss Express, pursued by multiple painted lines that were supposed to suggest its great speed. My mother reached inside and came up with the instruction book, clearly marked Marklin—the dreaded boy killer that the Macy's salesman had warned us about.

"This is no Swedish train set," my mother declared, her voice sharp with annoyance which quickly transformed into an accusation. "It's German."

Since the arrival of Hitler on the scene in 1932, the year of my birth, she had considered all German toys to be dangerous for a Jewish child to play with; the more charming or well-made the toy, the more dangerous, and that included the Steiff stuffed animals that my sister once collected, now replaced by a menagerie of wounded glass animals and chipped, one-armed ballerinas.

"They just named it after a Swedish train to avoid tipping off anyone who might boycott a German product," she asserted. "They do this to sneak it into American homes."

Having virtually condemned the train set as a Nazi spy, she flipped through the pages of the instruction booklet and denounced the booklet declaring, "This isn't written in Swedish. It's German."

"Since when can you tell the difference?" my father asked. His last retort was always a declaration that she, an ignorant woman, knew nothing about that of which she spoke. Nevertheless, he knew at once that he had made a monumental error and it would take a monumental lie to patch it over. His hope at that moment was to tell her it was a great bargain, a train set worth hundreds, maybe thousands, which he had purchased for a fraction of its value, and she would see that if she only opened her eyes to the beauty of this gift.

My father first tried to reassure her that this set was several years old, dating from a time before the Nazi rise to power, and he was relieved to show her the roman numerals MCMXXIV on the booklet that indicated that it was produced in 1924. She said nothing at the moment, allowing me and my father to fish inside the boxes for more and more trains, to be removed like precious shards of pottery from an archeological dig, each dusted off and placed in a row on the carpet, each car more beautiful than the one that preceded it, and all of them adding to my terror of their magnificence.

With their artfully inserted passengers dining in the elegant dining car, handsomely robed families sleeping in their berths, others playing cards in the lounge, it was a world of privileged travel and travelers, painted in exquisite detail. There could be no doubt that this was a work of art, a tribute to German craftsmanship, something even my mother could not deny. It was beautiful. *Es war sehr shön.*

Ingrate that I was, I hated these trains. This was not the Cloverdale railway that I wanted. This was something large and alien, speaking a language of old world luxury that I did not understand, yet I knew better than to betray my disappointment in front of my proud, smiling father, knowing the price to be paid when I might least suspect it. Ingratitude, I had learned time and again, was not a fault but a punishable sin requiring the most drastic remedy to my father.

Rummaging through another box we found the precision engineered railway tracks, gleaming tubes of steel and hard rubber, some crisscrossed, others curving to the left or right as parenthesis, some straight, but all requiring intricate connections, the piecing together as difficult as a jig-saw puzzle of clouds that had no picture to clue the player. Nor was there a guide in the top of any box for the assembly of the tracks other than a picture of a smiling German boy of about my age (seven or eight), in short lederhosen pants, white shirt open at the collar with neatly rolled-up sleeves, blonde hair, and a smile of unimpeachable satisfaction. No boy could fake such a smile — at least I couldn't — and I wondered if the secret of putting together this set came with him at birth, just as the secrets of flight belonged to the inheritance of birds. But his joy held no reassurance for me; it only made me feel more desperate and inadequate.

As we reached deeper and deeper inside we discovered only more tracks but no clue to the mystery of assembly. The miniature mountains and trees, the chalet-style station house and the sheep and goats needed no translation. They were the scenic wonders that this magnificent railway was supposed to pass as it made its way from Sweden to

Switzerland or vice versa, and these, I figured I could invest with a life of their own, using them as toys or models for a drawing of the alps if I could only dispose of this deadly juggernaut of German train making.

In yet another box we discovered the inert electric heart of the set, the transformer, half the size of the box itself, a matte black metal finish with a dozen knobs and levers of shining nickel silver on the front, all marked in German and with more wiring on the back, most of those wires wrapped in twisted black silk in the European manner, with plugs color coded to fit into some other electrical device that apparently made the whole model railway run. Dangling from all of these were the covered plugs, awaiting their insertion into an outlet.

It was now that my mother spoke up, braving my father's wrath, unable to hide her anger behind her serious frown and tight lips, those signs of anger only seen when she discussed my father's family, the atrocious Yellen *schnorers*.

"Send it back," she commanded. "Get rid of it before it kills someone." I knew who that someone was. Me. She looked at the box and then at my father with disgust, and then placed a hand on my shoulder, further identifying the "someone" who was certain to die as a result of his gift, if he had somehow missed her point.

"Don't be a fool, Lilly," he responded. "This is the best train set in the world, made for a prince. He's gonna love it when he sets it up."

"Who told you that?" she asked. She was, of course, referring to the unlikelihood of my ever loving this enemy set, but he chose to understand her as referring to its alleged value.

"The auctioneer at the Astor Auction told me. Nice man. Jewish, lives in an attached house in Bay Ridge." Ah, the details of the lie were beginning to lay the foundation for the train sets appearance in our house.

"I knew you were looking for a train set for Sherm and I happened to pass by this auction house on Sixth Avenue. You know the one next to Kean's Chop House? You liked those French crystal lamps they had in the window a while ago, remember? Well, in that very window, tagged for the auction that very day, was the finest train set in the world. It had been made special for one of the John Jacob Astor kids, or a Rockefeller boy, possibly a Rajah's son, they couldn't swear to which one, but it came from the home of someone with millions, someone who would only have the best for his child, and I wanted my son to have it. Why should he have less than the best? Is he worth less to us than some Astor? Some Rockefeller? Some Indian princeling?"

He had now performed a small miracle, changing the subject so that it was about my value to her, and not about the train set that lay on the floor before us. He concluded with a dramatic declaration, "Well, he is worth it to me!" as he turned away towards the now empty boxes with the trains, the stations, the signal towers, all lying helter-skelter on the hallway floor, as he carefully brushed any sawdust that clung to any of the metal.

"He is the best!" he declared, "so he should have the best." To my father we were now one and the same: me, Sherman, and the Marklin Swedish-Swiss Express. "Not only does it make wonderful train noises, but smoke comes out of the engine in puffs like a real train!"

"If it doesn't first come out of his ears after it burns out his brain!" my mother stated, now adding a question to which there was no answer.

"And who's going to put it all together?"

"Why Sherm will. Can't you see he loves it? Do you think he's not as smart as some Swiss or, okay, German kid? Of course he can put it together. Just give the boy a chance. Don't sell him short."

"Nat," she protested, "my son is not going to be killed because you made some crazy purchase at an auction. I will not allow him to plug this into any outlet in our apartment. Who knows if it's even the right current?"

"It's perfectly safe," he declared. "Do you think the John Jacob Astors would have put their son's life in danger over a train set?"

"It hardly looks as if it's been used," my mother replied, implying that the only reason my father was able to buy this set at such a low cost was because the Astors had feared for their own son's life and quickly disposed of it at auction once they discovered its deadly possibilities.

"If you think it's so safe, you do it! Go, go, plug it in."

It was a challenge my sister Simone and I watched with fascination. Would we see our father go up in smoke if he plugged in the transformer? Without a moment's hesitation my father rose to my mother's challenge, took the plug and inserted into an empty outlet in the dining room. He turned on the switch and it began to hum, that Germanic industrial hum with an imaginary umlaut over it.

"See," he declared. "It's perfectly safe, so now will you let the boy put it together. Can't you see he's longing to do so?"

It had to be clear to my father, a very smart man, that I was not longing to do any such thing; that all I was longing for was for this behemoth to go away and never be seen by me again. I looked at my sister who stood nearby, holding up one of the station platform figures, and probably thinking of a way to use them in her glass figurine collection, but we both understood what was coming. My father was a sports liar. By this we understood that he told his lies not *about* sports but *as* a sport. In this he was an accomplished amateur, never becoming a professional prevaricator, which meant telling a lie that had criminal consequences. He had years of practice as the sales half of his small but prosperous company. It was evident that the train set was what *he* wanted—only the best would make up for his lost childhood—and he had purchased it without a thought as to whether or not it was something I might desire.

Some of my father's lies were so hard hitting that they made it out of the park and scored a winning run, too powerful to be disbelieved. But today's lie was a bunt, designed to get to first base safely without striking out, knowing that the odds of a homer in this case were impossible. I knew that I, too, was a liar, pretending to be a little boy whose only need was a train set, when all I truly wanted was to be left to myself to draw my pictures and get through my burdensome childhood alive and unharmed.

The following day was a Saturday. My father worked on Saturdays, so I would be alone with the train set. I was to be given my chance to show my mettle as a boy by putting the train set together with all the time that it required.

Polish Mary, herself a hater of all things German since the Nazi armies had recently invaded her parents' homeland, was nevertheless excited by the prospect of the train tooting its way through the apartment. She set the large felt table top protector on the dining table that served for those few family dinners in which relatives attended, as my mother stood guard over me, determined that no matter what I managed to accomplish in the way of joining those tracks, I would never insert that transformer plug into any electrical outlet and die the hideous death that the Macy's salesman had predicted for any boy using a Marklin train set. My father's survival of the plug-in meant nothing to her. Who knew if he felt a shock? He would never dare to show it! And that shock might be fatal to her small boy. Nevertheless, I worked feverishly to put the set together.

Needless to say I got nowhere with the tracks. It was long division with fractions all over again, only instead of those confounding numbers that refused to obey the calculations of my innumerate brain, there were these cruel bits of steel track that refused to connect, to add up or divide but led only to dead ends where any self-respecting model train would careen over into an abyss off the table.

When my father returned home from work that evening, dinner was set up in the Dutch style breakfast nook off the kitchen, and his one look of disgust at the jumble of trains and tracks on the dining table informed me that a single misstep or a show of disappointment and the earth might soon open up to swallow me.

A loving son might have leapt up and kissed his father on his cheek, thanking him profusely as the man who made his wildest dreams of a model train set come true. But I felt shame for my inadequacy, my absence of feeling (other than distrust) and I hated him for the shame I was forced to feel and refused to say anything about the set no matter how often he might ask me if I was enjoying the putting of it together. I buried my face in a book as he questioned me.

It was as if all I wanted was a rowboat to cross a small pond, and my father with his grandiosity provided a steamship for me to navigate the Atlantic. He looked at me, appealing for some word of appreciation and I knew enough about ingratitude at that age to try to say something, but no words came forth, until I dragged a "nice" from the depths of my voice, and he knew that I not only disapproved of this grand gift, but of his foolishness in buying it for me.

Even at eight I knew enough about the world outside to feel guilt for my ingratitude. Every day the radio spoke of the starving millions during this Great Depression, and my father had more than once reminded me that I was among the fortunate few who had three meals a day, a nice place to live, clean clothes to wear to school, and enough toys to stock a toy shop. He might have also included the best of doctors who came when my asthma attacks reached the danger point; doctors who pulled me back from the brink of death with their camphorated oils oozing from vaporizers. But he did not wish to recall, any more than I did, that illness that so often threatened my life.

Once, when my breathing had stopped during a particularly violent attack and it appeared that I was choking on my own breathing, he had called for an ambulance and I was given the oxygen that brought me back to life. So I owed my life to him in more ways than one, yet I felt no debt of gratitude.

It was clear to me that as much as he loved and needed my love, he much preferred my sister Simone. Hay fever, vanity and carsickness were her only maladies, and these were easy enough for the family to deal with, not the challenge that my gasping asthma attacks presented. I was the son he had wanted to carry on all he had accomplished. But it was clear to him early on that Simone was born to ascend to great heights in a world of fixed social conventions—good daughter, good student, beauty queen, "smart as a whip," and witty as a child could be—while I would face an uncertain future with my tricky little mind full of secret, seditious thoughts and the skinny, treacherous sickly body that held them. And yet he loved me as best he could. There were times when his round, bulging Boston Terrier eyes gazed on me with such affection that I longed to return his feeling, but I could not succeed at that. For all my imperfections I was a handsome child, something he had not been as a boy, and my good looks were something to take pride in, even if my accomplishments seemed few enough. I was unaware at that time that I had replicated the lack of affection that he had been shown by his parents as a child, an affection he could not find in my mother, his wife, so I wrapped his past into his future in the ingratitude that had marked his life.

Today I can see that for all his failings he deserved better from me, but deserve is a word with little meaning in the real world, and has no connection to the lives of children. I could see in his frequent smiles at me, in his exaggerated kiss on my cheek which left it wet and red, in his nod of approval as my mother presented him with a drawing I had made that day, and the pat on my head that was a little too forceful, how much he wanted to gain my affection through praise, but how all his best efforts ended in failure. So he told himself that I loved him, and since he was the super-salesman who could convince the toughest customer of the value of his merchandise, for a few fleeting moments he bought the goods that were Sherm's affection.

He would walk miles on a Sunday to find an open drugstore to buy some medication my mother needed to help relieve an asthma attack of mine. From time to time he would take me for a walk in a nearby park, sit beside me on a bench, and play his favorite game of spotting animal shapes in the clouds, a simple game favored by parents in the thirties. When I found an angel or, better, a hippo cloud he made an exaggerated laugh of approval, a guffaw worthy of a very big joke. At least I had the imagination that was required in a salesman if nothing else. But when we played the hand-slapping game so popular at that time between children and their parents; the one in which the two participants hold out one hand and the first one to slap the hand of the other won, the loser hand having failed to spot the quick movement of his opponent's free hand. There was a special harshness to his winning slap, a sting that might leave another bright red mark on the back of my hand, but one that was sure to fade by the time we reached home and my mother's watchful gaze.

Sons, according to books and movies, were born to look up at their father's with unflagging admiration, as Mickey Rooney looked upon his father, Judge Hardy. They could be mischievous, but good at math and at games, get into trouble through their high spirits. They might tease reality but never scrutinize and question the world they lived in. His Sherman, however, looked at him with a piercing and unseemly scrutiny. He knew that I knew all that I was not supposed to know, and that I knew it without having to be told, a knowledge I could not articulate but one which was clearly apparent in my demeanor. His desperate need for my approval and affection made it that much harder for me to approve and show affection, desperation forces a deaf ear in a child to its crying need. My years of watching my family covered everything that mattered in our family. His strained relations with my mother, his unfulfilled sexual longings for her as he reached for her hand and she eluded his grip, brushing a strand of hair out of her eyes. I knew nothing of sex but I was aware of its absence.

More than that, he easily saw through my disguise of a pretend child, and recognized that confusing conundrum. Here was a child who could not add, subtract, divide, or multiply, a child with a scrawl rather than a fine elliptical handwriting, a child who had little interest in sports yet sat quietly and uncomplainingly through the double headers he cheered at Yankee Stadium, a child who was given everything but never asked for anything, and carried inside him the curse of the critic, the eye of someone who evaluates all he sees; a small, skinny, human scale constantly weighing the good from the bad, the truth from the lies, not always fairly, but always secretly figuring out the worth of all that he witnessed. And since I was silent about expressing my thoughts and feelings, I was one more mystery that he could not fathom. Little did I understand then that it was my failure to respond to his love—that rejection that began with his parents, continued with my mother, and ended with me—that often culminated in his rage.

My father's rages were as formal as a ballet and as extravagant as a volcano. Although when I think back on them, it was a Wild West rodeo. They were always preceded by the rumble of ingratitude, the failure of someone, usually me, to appreciate what was offered by him, building step by step towards the inevitable explosion, ending in that fiery show of flames, sparks and smoke, that sent the witnesses fleeing from its path. The fire raged, the lava flowed, cities were destroyed in its path, and when it finally cooled, the volcano wept with shame and begged a pardon that was only granted because the sobs of repentance were almost more appalling than the deed itself.

"What's that you said? I didn't hear you. You what? Why you little bastard, do you know I would have given my right arm for this when I was your age." And so it began. My father had given away so many of his right arms when my age and I, knowing that he was left handed, was bold enough to remind him of that fact. My mother, if around, began to place her body between us, aware of what was to follow. To her credit, or perhaps pride, she never asked me to apologize. No "say you're sorry to Daddy" came from her. I suspect that she took a certain pride in my unwillingness to bend before his threats, but she certainly wanted to shield me from harm. For some children these would have been traumas, but for me, looking back, they were lessons in courage, for it was during these paternal rages that I learned to deal with my own fears, and to practice the art of standing up for what I believed.

Harm came in the form of his leather belt, or as it was called in those days, his "strap." Screaming with rage, his normal baritone voice rising to a soprano, as if his anger emasculated him, exclaiming over and over on my bastardry and ingratitude, he began to chase me around the apartment. I was small but speedy and in this family rodeo, more often than not, I eluded the crazy cowboy's strap, but when it landed, as it did from time to time, it could leave a mark as dark as a brand on my back, or arm, but never on my face which he missed by chance or design. I usually found refuge as my mother distracted him, calling him "Crazy Nat" as my sister pointed the way to the bathroom that had the lock on its door. Simone would toss in a *Colliers* or *Life Magazine* so that I could sit out the volcano on the toilet seat and read my way through the lava flow. Soon, there was a gentle knocking on the door by my mother, announcing the "all clear" and I went into my room. A half hour later my father would arrive with his pleas for forgiveness. I said nothing. "It's not good to go to bed angry," he advised. "I'm not angry," I would say, unwilling to give him the satisfaction of my anger, although I am certain it seethed within me, but for me to be angry meant that I was like him, and even at seven I knew that I would not be him, I would be myself, whatever that was. Sometimes he wept and that, as I said, was worse than anything. I had no idea about the notion of dignity, but I felt it lacking in him and it seemed to me something my mother had, something that Uncle Frankie for all his hijinks had, and it existed in everyone I admired. Looking backwards, I realize how little he wanted, how little he needed, the simple recognition of his desire to please us, to be appreciated for all he did, and all he wished to do for our lives, but the terrible fact of life was that the greater the need, the more likely it will be rejected, and I rejected him (sometimes with cause, more often without) as no father should have been rejected by a son. Quite simply, I looked at him and saw my own weakness, my own need for affirmation, my own desire to be pleasing, and in that distorting mirror that was my father, it appeared ridiculous and grotesque.

There was a well-developed choreography to these rages. He reached for the belt, I began my run for the bathroom door, opening it and turning the bolt just before he could reach it and demand that I come out and take my punishment. Then there were the muffled voices of my mother and father in their furious argument, and finally a silence, followed by my mother assuring me that it was safe to come out now. But only in those rages—those Mount Etna eruptions that came without warning—was he able to lash out at me with the tip of his swinging leather belt, wielded like a lariat by a crazed cowboy as punishment for some crime that he believed required immediate punishment. And that crime was often the betrayal of my discontent.

I was not above deliberately provoking these rages, for once the fire had started there was a certain perverse pleasure in feeding it, fanning those leaping flames, and watching as my mother arrived to throw cold water on it. I knew what I was doing but I did not know what compelled me to do it. It was not courage; it was my own fierce pride. Today I can see that I was seeking a reason not to reciprocate his love, and testing my power to move him to that very rage that justified my boyhood contempt for him. We were not so unalike, both of us wanting to be loved for what we most prized in ourselves—me for my artistic ambitions and he for his unending generosity—and yet neither of us capable of offering the other that longed for appreciation.

For me to express an opinion about the "dumb" radio show he was listening to with such a show of pleasure, or to refuse to be picked up at the skating rink at Rockefeller center by Jerry, his hunchbacked man of all jobs, or worse yet to show an indifference to some toy he had purchased for me, was enough to set him off with a violent explosion of noise that soon translated to action. Prevented from fulfilling his paternal task of punishment by my mother, he depended upon her, as I did, to step between us and command him to "stop the craziness, Nat." And he would, although I knew the odds favored him getting in a few licks while she was out shopping or visiting with her sister. The times when she was not about and I had provoked a rage, I usually made it to the bathroom and locked the door. After huffing and puffing and failing to blow the door down, he walked away and my sister would sound the all clear. I would then return to my room and my art work.

My mother, my constant defender and greatest advocate, found only the best in me, even in my worst moments. She was also the one who found it hardest to express her love for me. Some old world superstitions stood between her and the expression of love for her children. To betray the depth of that love in a public or private fashion was to put the child at risk. An angry God might view such love as a pride that had to be taken down—as she had been taken down for her love of her dead mother and her lost sister and brother. She could not risk that with her own beloved children, so there was never a kiss, and hugs were given only when a child had fallen and needed the closeness of a mother to recover from the crying that followed the accident.

And so it was my father who would show me *all* the affection I would know as a child, except for that which Uncle Frankie and Cousin Bella bestowed upon me during their visits. And yet for all his claims of loving me, my father was my personal bogeyman, for I never went to bed at night knowing for sure if I would be alive in the morning, since it was clear that this man of coins, toys and kisses could and might eventually kill me; that he might see something on my forehead which would provoke him into murdering me. Little did I suspect then that my sister, for all her triumphs in being the perfect daughter, felt the same nightly terror.

It was clear to me that this man—so generous and loving, so often sweet-natured—could easily murder me as I slept, and none would be the wiser for it. If it was a fantasy it was one grounded in genuine fear. Knowing that his presence was such a burden to my life, I concluded that I was just as much a burden to his. What a source of pain I must have been to him, having to endure the failure of his only son to love him as he wished to be loved, as he needed to be loved. As a child I understood that my crime—failing to love my father—one that God and the Bible asserted to be among the worst of sins, was one that might be punishable by my death. How easy it would be for him to smother me with a pillow and have the ever-obliging Dr. Jackson view my death as the result of a fatal asthma attack.

My father's rages were now family lore, indulged, laughed at, dismissed with a wry smile as "that's Nat;" rages that in a poor man might have been looked upon differently. Police might have been called. But he had the power of Zeus, which in his case meant his excellent earnings, and even my Mother was unwilling to sacrifice that. Her modeling days were long gone and with them her ability to survive on her own. Even worse, a divorce was a blemish she could not live with in her pursuit of a spotless life. She would laugh a small insincere laugh when she discussed him, and if she ever mentioned him to us, it was clear that behind that laugh was an apology for what she had brought down on our lives in her desperate youthful search for security.

At the time I was growing up there were cartoon drawings titled "What's wrong with this picture?" in which it was necessary to identify the several "wrong" creatures or objects hidden among the ordinary (a tree whose fruit grew upwards in a park where a cat was riding a tricycle). The goal was to find all of them, some securely hidden in a forest or a sky. I knew that something was very wrong with my family picture, but I could never solve that puzzle. Why the boy could not love his father was part of that upside down world, and at seven I had no answer for it.

And now there was the train set that had become a reproach to my boyhood abilities, and a confirmation to my father of my stubborn, immutable inadequacy. Given the magnitude of the gift and my clear inability to master its complexities, my life now depended upon my ability to get that train set up and running for my birthday the following day. Anything less would be a monstrous show of ingratitude that would bring on a rage as monumental as the train set itself.

My mother recognized that her husband had made a dreadful mistake in buying that train set, yet it was her son who was bound to pay for that mistake. And so when her brother, my beloved Uncle Frankie came by that morning with his weekly laundry delivery, my mother showed him the train set in all it's terrible jumble, with words that expressed this latest impulsive act that her *meshuggah* Nat had imposed upon our lives. And she spoke in her own code, one that Frankie understood. "Who could expect a child to put this monster train set together except someone like Nat?" The question contained its own answer and its own request.

Although there was a truckload of laundry that Frankie had to deliver that day, he knew his first obligation was to his sister and to his nephew. "The hell with the laundry," he declared, as he studied the tracks and the trains. "Let it wait." He placed a call to his Italian friend Tomasino Marinara, called "Tomato Sauce" by Frank in honor of his friend's last name. Tommy was Frank's boyhood friend from the lower East Side who, like Frank, had moved to the Bronx. Within a minute Frank was summoning Tomato Sauce to come to his sister Lilly's nearby apartment where there was a family emergency. I had once seen the men together at Uncle Frankie's small apartment calling each other "dago" and "wop," "sheeney" and "kike" with so much affection that they seemed the secret words of lovers rather than street toughs. Tommy was a superintendent in a nearby apartment house, but he had been apprenticed to an electrician in his youth, later working as a radio repairman who could also rewire a lamp or fix a vacuum cleaner, a job he held until the Depression had closed down his small shop and wiped out such employment. Within the half hour, Tomato Sauce arrived and immediately set to work.

I will forever be grateful to the memory of Tomato Sauce, first for solving the puzzle of the train set, and second for later helping me deal as a college student with the poetry of T.S. Eliot. I had failed to admire the majesty of Eliot's arid masterpieces *The Wasteland* and *The Love Song of J. Alfred Prufrock,* or his *Four Quartets*, and recoiled at their modernist obscurities and their mean-spirited anti-Semitism, which I took personally. When told that they were the greatest poetical works of the Twentieth Century, I managed to put them in their proper place by thinking of the prissy faux-English poet with Tommy's initials as Tomato Sauce Eliot. But that was years later, and the Tomato Sauce who put together those tracks and set up the machinery to run them was a model of rough, splintery kindness and sterling loyalty, something a child would always remember.

There was only one trouble faced by Tomato Sauce as he put together the train set. The tracks went on forever. There was no end to them. Clearly, they were custom made with extra tracks to be set up in vast rooms of a great house where the spawn of a Merchant Prince might play before riding his pony on a vast lawn. A set made to order for an Astor's mansion, not a Yellen's commodious but limited Bronx apartment. Nevertheless, the ingenious Tomato Sauce, assisted by Uncle Frankie, found a way to use all the tracks. He started laying them down in the entrance hallway, then moved them into the parlor room under the piano, threading them around the piano legs, and connecting them with the ease of a man who could think big thoughts with his huge hands. Then he looped them through the dining room under the table, back into the hallway, traversing door jambs with their numerous bridges, into my room by way of a short detour into my parent's bedroom and ending their journey just short of my small desk where he set up the last of the train stations. My sister and I delightedly set up the trees and the livestock, as Uncle Frankie planted the surrounding Alps and the heavier scenery.

My mother said nothing as Tomato Sauce finally produced a small transformer that replaced the European one and plugged that into the hallway outlet. He sat at the controls with Uncle Frankie and the train came chugging into magnificent life. The two grown men argued over who would take turns as engineer running the trains, but they soon realized that I was waiting and cleared a path for me. No trip on the Orient Express could have been as thrilling as the one that that train made through our apartment at 1810 Loring Place. There was not only the splendid click-clack and chug-a-chug of the train on its tracks, the wonder of its disappearance through mountain tunnels, its rising high on an elevated bridge, but the magic of smoke coming from the engine (a fine acrid smell that filled the apartment) caused my mother some concern that the train, together with the excitement, might bring on an asthma attack. But all it did that day was plant in me the desire to see the real world, the larger world that those toy passengers were experiencing, one that would take years for me to realize.

During my later years in Hollywood, I had an agent who had a similar train set in his beautifully furnished wine-cellar basement; model trains he had purchased in Berlin when he was a major in the army during WWII, at a time when he met his German war bride. But years had passed and the Second World War was behind us, and when I looked at the train I thought little about that train set of my eighth birthday. I could only think of those real German trains with their cattle cars that transported the Jews to their deaths, and I saw the trains as a malign reminder of what had happened to so many innocents. But none of that existed at the time when Uncle Frankie and Tomato Sauce had set up the splendid train set in our Bronx apartment.

On the eve of my eighth birthday, we waited together for the return of my father from his work in Manhattan, eager to show him that the railway had been completed, as eager in our own way as the builders of any trans-continental railway might have felt. When my father finally returned home from work that night, Frankie and Tomato Sauce were long gone and I was alone with my sister still operating the amazing set. My father looked at my mother as he smiled the smile of the just. She shrugged, saying, "It's a miracle they weren't killed by it," as if these were real trains on real tracks that might snatch up our young lives as they made their majestic journey through the apartment which had now become a canton of Switzerland. She told my father that it took half a day for me to put it together. She, who had never lied; she, who had made truth her religion, had just told my father a whopper, and my sister and I were amazed at her ability to do so, and at his willingness to believe her, which was another lie, for he didn't. She polished it off with just the right finishing touch, declaring that this was the most ridiculous gift that a man could give to a boy, even one as brilliant as I was, yet he heard little of that as he watched me and Simone shouting and playing, so filled with happiness that this disastrous gift had been turned into a joyful miracle of movement, scenery and splendor.

We all knew that it would have to be taken apart the following day and stored in the basement for special occasions, that this was a short-lived time of happiness when my father's gift—that Trojan horse that was to confirm both his generosity and my ineptitude as a boy—had turned into a glorious family event. The following day I invited my friends Eugene and Marty to come to my apartment to see the trains before they were retired from use until my next birthday—which of course meant forever—and we spent a few more hours of glorious play before my mother came in and instructed our maid, Polish Mary to pull the plug. "The stench of that steam engine is too much for me, and God knows it could bring on one of his asthma attacks," she said, and soon Mary and my mother began to pack up the trains, the tracks, and the glory of Switzerland, and place them all in the boxes to be stored in the building basement from which they would never emerge again.

"You're one lucky guy," my friend Eugene said. "You gotta have the best father in the world." And since I survived my childhood and that train set, I suppose that in that world, I did.

A Polish Postage Stamp

One argument between my parents ran in and out of our lives like a musical theme. It was the leitmotif of our family opera that announced my mother's dislike for my father's family, the Yellen *schnorers*, and her belief that he was putty in their hands; that he could not resist their greedy blandishments or refuse their secret appeals for more and more money, something that would someday bring us all to ruin.

I can recall a day in the late 1930s when my father returned home from his office in a foul temper. He usually arrived cheerful only to turn angry as he confronted his family at home. Having discovered that all the bills were missing from his wallet while out for lunch, he had barely enough change in his pocket to buy a sandwich and take the subway home. He accused my mother of rifling through his pockets and she did not deny it. My mother, who rarely if ever judged others, never judged her own behavior. She was not a reflective woman, and she believed firmly in her own impeccable instincts when it came to her family. When it related to my father, she knew she was in the right. She explained that she knew that Little Grandpa was coming by the office for a visit that day; my father had let that slip over dinner the night before, and she suspected that the old man was now the designated petitioner for the Yellen *schnorers*. The conspirators—lead by his Sister Ruthie and her followers, his younger brothers Manny, Ben and Harry—knew that Nat could never refuse his elderly father. If she, Lillian, removed the money from his pockets it was to save her own children from the impoverishment that would surely come to all of us if the Yellen *schnorers* were allowed to bleed him dry. Nat denied all of this while his mouth assumed his singular liar's lip-quiver and his anger rose in noise level as he spoke, as if his outraged innocence grew with the rising level of his voice.

How strange it seems to me today that he did not turn to my mother and say, "I earn this money. What do you lack in your life? My family's poor. We're in the middle of a Depression. Ruthie's husband is in prison and she has two small children to raise, just as you do. I will help them any way I can." But all this was lost in his shouts, and my mother left the scene of that argument triumphantly believing that she had struck a small if temporary blow against the infamous Yellen *schnorers*.

The hatred that his sister Ruthie evoked was unusual in my mother, who mainly took a benign view of the world. It had come as the direct result of Ruthie's ingratitude, her failure to thank my mother after she had cleaned Ruthie's house without even being reimbursed for the necessary cleaning supplies.

This dislike was only compounded by Ruthie's fawning manner to my father, and the fact that her two small children were always in her company, ready to kiss "Uncle Nat's" cheek and proclaim their love for him; young *schnorrers* in training. Worse still was my father's handsome younger brother, "Manny the Bum," the one who had joined the peacetime army in the early 1930s, a sign of moral weakness ("Too lazy to look for real work"), and was divorced from his *shiksa* bride before he was thirty. He was unemployed and yet still dressed to the nines, a sure sign that he, too, was living off my father's industry. In no other way could my mother imagine their surviving. These two had aroused in her the contempt that began early in her marriage and was now so great she felt it necessary to spread it over the entire Yellen clan, even though some of them were hard-working and lived self-supporting middle-class lives.

The strife in the great world outside ours was different. My sister and I were sheltered from Hitler as much as possible—the radio news reports were lowered or shut off when we entered the living room—in much the same way as we were sheltered from polio (kept out of crowds) and snowstorms (kept inside the house). If there were woolen hats, rubber boots and fur-lined mittens that could have kept the bad news coming from Europe away from us, my mother would surely have purchased them. But one could not avoid the bits and snatches of conversation about European events overheard in my parents' conversations or on the radio coming from the maid's room, or in the newsreels which we sat through as we waited impatiently for the feature film—*Captain Blood* with Errol Flynn—to begin at the Park Plaza Theater.

It was at this time that I lost interest in collecting painted lead soldiers and I had thrown myself—with all the passion that my six years could summon—into collecting stamps. My collection started with a Christmas gift, the usual large, red cloth-covered album with its clearly marked spaces for stamps and a cellophane envelope filled with cancelled stamps from all over the world, purchased cheap in a five and dime. The world knew that FDR was a great stamp collector—philatelist and philanthropist were confused and conflated into one word in describing his hobby and his virtue. And once the passion for stamps had taken hold, I was obsessed by everything to do with stamps and I could not let go. I loved the sweet taste of the little transparent flaps of the stamp fasteners on my tongue, flaps that one licked to attach the back of the stamp to its proper place in the album. My album was soon heavy with U.S., British and French stamps, but I seemed to lack all those of the smaller Eastern European countries, Poland and Czechoslovakia. And the stamps that contained Hitler's visage seemed to be screened from those cellophane bags by some anti-Fascist factory worker.

My friends and I talked endlessly about the rare upside-down airplane stamp known as the "inverted Jenny," a twenty-four cent U.S. postage stamp that featured a World War I training aircraft, seven hundred of which were misprinted and subsequently discovered and destroyed by the Post Office, leaving behind roughly one hundred copies circulated inadvertently. The Post Office destroyed its mistakes with a savage cruelty from a boy's point of view in order to keep that stamp out of the hands of boys like me who were clinging to the hope of finding one and becoming a child millionaire.

By this time, we had moved from the large house on Andrews Avenue to the rental of an eight-room apartment on Loring Place, a building no longer in existence, having later been a victim of the burning of the Bronx in the 1970s. In it's heyday in the 1930s, the building housed many aspiring teachers and writers. Our upstairs neighbor was a young City College student Nathan Glazer, later the Harvard sociologist famed for his groundbreaking report on poverty.

This sturdy apartment house had a row of brass mailboxes with the apartment numbers engraved on each box. My desire for stamps was so great that I begged my mother to allow me to take in the mail every day, at each of its three deliveries, so that I could be the first to see the stamps pasted on the envelopes. Usually, the stamps were of no particular value or interest; perhaps one or two in a week might fill a space in my album, and these were carefully monitored by my mother who made certain that my tongue did not touch the back of that cancelled stamp.

One day we received a letter that carried a stamp depicting a beautiful woman in a long white robe, her capacious arms outspread sheltering three workers, one a miner with a pickaxe, the other two merely blurs under the postmark, but no doubt figures representing other tradesmen embraced by Mother Poland. My first thought was that it closely resembled my mother, a woman who would shelter those who needed her help under her generous cloak of kindness. Alas, the stamp was so hideously cancelled that one had to squint to find the details in the artwork, but the printed writing on the top of the stamp, Poczta Polska, alerted me to the fact that it had come all the way from overseas, and it did not take much for me to connect the Polska with Poland.

I rushed upstairs with my trophy and presented it to my mother. The letter was addressed in a shaky hand to Nathaniel Yellen. It had the proper address on it except that the Bronx was written as Bronk, easily translated by the Post Office of that time. She examined it warily, clearly debating whether to leave it for my father to read or to open it and discover its mysterious foreign contents. My mother sat down in a club chair—one covered by Cousin Bella in a toile pattern fabric of brown birds and blue flowers, an elaborate pattern that might incorporate a spot of dirt or a child's ink mark without anyone noticing—and made her decision.

As my mother tore open the letter I stood over her shoulder begging for the stamp as she read the message inside, and to my surprise she ignored my request. I could see that it was written in English in a spidery foreign script, not the elegant loops that my parents used to write their letters. The letters and numbers seemed to be crossed in a haphazard fashion; some words were crossed out in the desperate effort of the sender to make his appeal clearer in a language that was not his own. I got no further than "Dear Cousin Nathaniel, I am the son of your great Aunt Essie and in great need of your..." when my mother became aware of my presence. She shooed me towards the kitchen and told me to pour a glass of chocolate milk for myself. It was Mary's day off and we were obliged to fend for ourselves when my mother could not do so.

I stood my ground, demanding the stamp, refusing to leave the room without it. What was chocolate milk to this wonderful, unexpected stamp? My mother hastily tore the corner of the envelope with the stamp on it and gave it to me. As she did so she cautioned me about removing it from the envelope and pasting it in my book in any way that required that my lips touch the stamp. "It's taken a long trip on its way from Poland. Who knows what germs are on it? What sickness on the lips of the poor people who sent it," she observed.

The fact that this stamp—unlike the others—had taken its journey to 1810 Loring Place made it particularly precious for me. At the same time, I could see that this letter was unique. My mother was not a woman of indecision. I may not have known the word at six years old, but what I saw could only be understood as hesitation, or deliberation, something alien to her nature. I watched as she tossed the letter in the woven wire wastebasket after reading it, but when I returned to the room with my glass of chocolate milk I saw that she had retrieved it from the basket and was re-reading it. Finally, she crumpled the letter in her fist, crushing it as if it contained a cockroach inside, and walked to the kitchen, placing the letter in a brown paper bag that contained the potato shavings of the boiled potatoes that were being prepared for tonight's dinner. She then deposited the paper bag in the dumbwaiter in the kitchen that carried the trash to the basement below, opening and closing the lid of the dumbwaiter with a force that I had never observed before, determined that it would leave our apartment with as much speed as possible.

That night I could barely wait for my father to return home from work to show him the Polish stamp. As ever he pretended to an interest in the hobbies that obsessed me, asking cheerful but perfunctory questions in an attempt to bring us closer together, never realizing that these were the very questions that set us farther apart.

"Nice looking stamp. Worth anything? Where'd you get it?" he queried, eager to get away from the boring stamp as he picked up his evening *Tribune* and neatly folded it so that he reached the sports pages while creating creases so fine they could rival those of a Japanese Imperial fan.

"It came in a letter for you," I said. Although my mother had never asked me to keep my knowledge of the letter from my father, I knew at once that I was doing wrong, betraying my mother as I spoke, but finding it necessary in order to get to the bottom of the question: why had she destroyed the letter to the Cousin Nathaniel to whom it was addressed? My curiosity exceeded, at the moment, my concern about my mother, should this enrage my father.

My mother, unlike my father, would never have asked me to lie for her. Lies were now outside the borders of her moral universe; they had been necessary for her survival in her childhood, but as a woman, secure in her world, she put them aside as one would put aside toys and jump ropes, as no longer needed. Evasions, however, were perfectly acceptable, you owed no one a hard truth, but lies were something that the poor, the ugly, or the temperamentally disabled like my father were obliged to indulge in.

I can only determine that she felt that I would not recall the arrival of the letter by the time my father returned from his work, that I would be so absorbed in Jack Armstrong or some other radio program as I surveyed my stamp collection, my books, my art work, my handwriting exercises due as homework the following day, that the matter was as good as closed. Knowing her as I did, it would have been inconceivable for her to ask me to lie about that stamp's origins. More important to her was that I worship the same god of honesty that she cherished, more important than avoiding a quarrel with my father.

"Sherman tells me that I got a letter from Poland," my father stated at the dinner table. "Where is it?"

"Oh, that?" she said. "I threw it out."

"You did what?" he said, not as a question, but as the start of an angry conversation.

"It was garbage so I threw it out with the trash. It was from some so-called second or third cousin in Poland you never heard of—a Cousin Ezra—so why trouble yourself about it?"

"That was for me to judge," he said. "What did he want? This Cousin Ezra?"

"What they all want. Money. He got your address from your sister Ruthie who apparently writes to him from time to time. That figures. Not only is she the queen of the *schnorers*, but a meddler who passes other beggars on to you. Only this one wanted more."

"More of what?" my father asked, the anger rising, reddening his cheeks as he raised his voice. He knew that she felt no guilt for having disposed of his letter in her way.

"You were supposed to agree to support him so he could get a visa to come to America. His plan—or was it Ruthie's?—was that he would live with us until he got a job and a place of his own, but you were supposed to be responsible for any debts he might incur, and agree that he would not become a burden to the country. That's what the American consulate told him he needed. He swore he would not be in the way, he and his wife would help with the children, wash the dishes, and make the beds, and... oh yes, they had a boy, Emanuel, who was just Sherman's age, or so Ruthie had told him. How dare she tell him about our children? Or that we had a large apartment that could easily hold him and his family in one of the maid's rooms. The woman never stops. She's shameless."

"She just wanted to help a poor man," my father protested.

"Then why didn't she offer to do so herself? No, it's as if there weren't enough American *schnorers* in your family already that she had to import some for us from Europe. Ruthie assured him that you would do this although you never met the man, or his family. Yet your wonderful sister—not satisfied with having you support her while her crook of a husband serves out his jail sentence, now wants you to support half of Europe."

"You know what's happening in Europe, Lil?" he asked. She cast a glance towards me and my sister—both of us intrigued by the newness of this conversation with its fresh subject, not the stale stuff of the Brooklyn Yellens—as if to say that the conversation was not to be had before the children.

"This was wrong. Very wrong," my father said. It was the first time that I had ever heard him accuse her of wrongdoing. Stubborness? Always. Willfulness? Yes. But wrongdoing? Never. The accusation did not seem to trouble her. She refused to assume the role of the guilty party when it came to his family. What had she, Lillian, done other than protect him and their children from these strangers? She had no doubt that these unknown foreign *schnorers*, if allowed, would disturb, if not destroy, our hard-earned lives with their debts and their sickness.

"Okay, you want them to move in. Fine. We'll move out, the children and me so you will have lots of room for them. Nat, be sensible. We have no space for them here, and who knows what terrible diseases they bring with them from Vilna? Head lice are the least of it. Sherman has been sick enough with his asthma, Simone catches every cold in sight, and you would endanger them by bringing in this Ezra and his wretched family. They are probably coughers who don't know how to use a handkerchief!"

I was amazed. This was not the mother I knew. This was not the woman on the stamp, embracing the poor workmen with her outstretched arms. This was not the Lillian who gave twenty dollar bills to the Salvation Army, who could never pass a beggar without giving him money, who was always stuffing envelopes with five dollar bills for the March of Dimes, who overpaid the women who worked for us, who championed the black women who worked in Uncle Mike's laundry, and who cautioned my sister and me against the great crime of selfishness; this was an altogether different Mother than I had ever seen before.

She had clearly viewed this Ezra and his family as a threat to her own children's lives, and to our very security. And the fact that it was the despicable Ruthie who had given them our address, and who had tried to conscript these would-be refugees into Ruthie's private army of *schnorers*, fomenting a secret invasion of beggars to invade our lives, was enough for my mother to close her generous heart to this desperate family. Late into the night I could hear her repeat her litany about this family as she reassured my father of the rightness of her act.

"Nat, stop brooding. You never met them. You don't even know them!"

"And now I never will," my father said, his voice breaking as he began to weep. "What if I were in Europe and someone here in America..."

"Shush!" She commanded. "You'll wake the children."

Years later we were to learn through my Aunt Ruthie that second cousin Ezra had died in Auschwitz, but that his family had survived and emigrated to Israel. My father would send them a substantial check in Israel and my mother did not protest. It was a chapter of her life that she had wanted to close and to forget. Her work raising funds for displaced refugees after the war was honored by the Hadassah with a laminated plaque, and as a survivor of her own life she had long ago learned that what could not be corrected was better not recalled.

As a grown man I began to understand my mother's actions, controlled as they were by the limits of her imagination. If these desperate refugees had suddenly appeared at her doorstep, hungry, weary, penniless, she would have offered them food and shelter and possibly found work for them. But they were abstractions—faceless— an extension of the Yellen *schnorers* who had clung to my father through his life and, in her mind, threatened the well-being of her family. Such were the German and Eastern European Jews to most Americans at that time, beggars to be ignored by the Depression-weary, including Roosevelt who was beloved by American Jews in the 1930s. It took an Anne Frank to put a face on the Holocaust—the millions of second cousin Ezras died faceless.

By the time I entered High School, I had abandoned my stamp collection. It had been passed along to my Uncle Frank's young son, my Cousin Jeff, and the Polish stamp had ultimately disappeared with the collection into a local flea market where Jeff later worked up a lively business.

The other day I read that the "Inverted Jenny" stamp had sold for $825,000. I hope it had passed through the hands of a boy who once treasured it. I had long since learned that stamps could carry with them grief and doubt as well as joy. That Polish stamp with its sheltering woman, arms outstretched welcoming the workers who stood beneath her, was not my loving mother, but an early lesson in the complexity of life. No longer could I believe that all goodness resided in one person. I had finally understood that the love of family, the most primal and important love, might have no room in it for a desperate stranger.

Finding Myself in an
Italian Tablecloth

I t is strange how a combination of events and objects can bring the past home again, spanning long periods of time in a moment. I'm hardly the first to recognize this: Marcel Proust wrote a masterpiece, *Remembrance of Things Past* based on this notion. Listening to the release of some private Nixon tapes, rife with anti-Semitic virulence, and observing the recurrence of anti-Semitism in Europe today, somehow fused with a gray organdy tablecloth hidden away in a linen closet in our apartment, and brought about some sort of time travel into my own past. I won't glorify it by calling it an epiphany, but in a funny way it was akin to one.

My wife and I have been trying to simplify our cluttered lives by giving away, selling, or donating to charity "stuff" that fills our closets and no longer has a place in our everyday life. We came upon the tablecloth as we investigated the back of that linen closet which contained some broken antique lamps, ancient perfume bottles, and other never-to-be-used-again items. The tablecloth was wrapped in fine tissue paper and seemed as crisp, and new as the day it had been purchased. It had seen little if any use during its 50-odd year history. My wife observed that nobody uses such tablecloths anymore, least of all organdy ones with white hand sewn flowers on them. Together with its 12 matching napkins it had been bought by us as a gift for my mother-in-law in 1953 when my wife and I were on our honeymoon in Florence, Italy. It had come into our possession a few years ago when my mother-in-law died in her early nineties. Somehow, we couldn't add the tablecloth to the pile of giveaways. As I studied it I knew at once that it had a special meaning for me and the reason could be traced to a dinner party in a dilapidated villa in Fiesole, outside of Florence many years ago.

We were on our wedding trip when we arrived in Florence without hotel reservations—my lifelong bad habit, and, after checking into a modest railway hotel, we visited the museums, saw the required

Michelangelo and Botticelli, we purchased inexpensive gift shop reproductions of Fra Angelica saints, gilded and glued on to wooden panels, together with some hand-tooled leather goods as souvenirs for our families back home. The dollar was strong in the fifties, nothing cost a great deal for an American in Europe, one could live comfortably there on 10 dollars a day, or so the guide books told us. Leaving a museum, we came upon a small linen shop where we hoped to purchase some table linens for my wife's mother who had asked us to buy her a new table-cloth in Florence.

The woman who owned and ran the shop introduced herself as the Contessa Montevello, or Montebello, I don't quite recall, but Contessa she surely was. She was an elegant gray-haired woman in her late forties who spoke English with an Oxford accent, ever so faintly tinged with an Italian rhythm. It was evident that she was not by birth or custom a shop-keeper; this was the result of the war which turned royalty into peddlers, long before the arrival of the Ralph Laurens, the Tommy Hilfigers, and the Diane von Furstenbergs who turned peddlers into royalty.

The Contessa showed us a variety of hand-made cloths she had for sale, treating each item with the reverence reserved for the very best merchandise made for the very best clientele. My wife selected a muted gray and white organdy table-cloth and napkins knowing that this would please her mother's simple taste. "A wise choice," the Contessa declared, commending my wife for her judgment which had rejected the brightly embroidered linens. As she wrapped the tablecloth in tissue paper and ribbon, the Contessa then asked me what I did in the world and I told her that I was a recent college graduate, a writer, or at least an aspiring one. "Wonderful!" she exclaimed. You must meet Jamie Hamilton. He's visiting me with his wife, my cousin, the Contessa Pallavicino. You'll adore Yvonne and Jamie, and they will love you," she assured us, looking with approval at my beautiful bride. She went on to explain that Jamie was better known as Hamish Hamilton, the successful British publisher and one-time Olympic rowing champion, the publisher of such authors as Jean Paul Sartre and Albert Camus; just part of his long list of literary luminaries. I had heard of this man and I was impressed. More than that, I entertained the hope that someday he might publish my work in England should I ever write a novel.

"You'll come to dinner tonight?" the Contessa asked, less a request than a command. The Contessa took down our address so that she could send her driver to pick us up. When she discovered that we were staying in the railway hotel she declared it fit only for whores and anarchists, not for a charming young couple and suggested a beautiful but inexpensive pension nearby into which we moved as soon as we returned to the hotel. We packed our heavy leather wedding-gift luggage, placing the tablecloth carefully inside, encased in the tissue paper to keep it from creasing.

Early that evening we were picked up at the pension by an elderly man in chauffeur's livery. He held the door open to a large, ancient, gleaming, black Bentley with enormous bug-eyed headlights, ushering us inside where we sat on deep maroon leather upholstery. It was like being seated in a fine old theater rather than an automobile. So this was Europe! The real Europe, where struggling aristocracy managed to keep up the appearance of luxury by living on pride and willpower alone. We were having a Henry James adventure; a young American couple on their first time abroad, dining with an impoverished Italian countess, and who knew where this could take us? Intrigue awaited as layers of motivation would be peeled away and we would see the worldly heart of old Europe. Better than that, we were Zelda and Scott without the drinking, the breakdowns or the despair. Being in our very early twenties, everything seemed possible. One day you're living in a fleabag hotel, that same night you are on your way to a Contessa's villa in a luxury auto to meet a famous British publisher and his aristocratic Italian wife.

It was dusk as we drove through the Fiesole woods in that enormous black vehicle, down a long gravel driveway bordered by conifer trees towards a villa with just the right amount of peeling stucco and faded geraniums in old stone pots, where the Contessa stood waiting to welcome us in her pre-war silver lame evening gown. She hooked her arms between ours and led us inside the villa to meet the other guests. The great drawing room was furnished with ancestral paintings, old tapestries and tattered sofas and chairs, many of which had horsehair stuffing peeping out of the torn upholstery, betraying the aristocratic indifference of the owner as much as her poverty. The Contessa explained that the Germans had requisitioned her villa during the last days of the war and that they had done much damage to it, damage she could not afford to repair. She was currently renting out a whole wing of the villa to some rich Americans; and noisy and disagreeable as they were, she would rather do that than sell this home, one that had been in her late husband's family for hundreds of years. "The war took everything, you know," she said, without further explanation. We assumed that the "everything" she referred to included her husband, her wealth, and her former life. It was less than seven years since the end of World War II, and we understood that not only working class Italians but many in the Italian aristocracy had suffered much from Mussolini's fascism, and the Allied bombing of Italy.

Jamie Hamilton proved to be as charming and erudite as the Contessa had claimed he would be. I won his approval by praising an inexpensive edition of *Middlemarch* that he had published several years before; one with colorful, marbleized end papers. I owned a mildewed copy of that book which bore his company's trade name, having picked it up in a second-hand bookshop in Bermuda during a school holiday. His lovely, aristocratic Italian wife had a warm, welcoming smile and a genius for putting a self-conscious young couple at their ease, advising us as to what we should see, where we should eat, and what we should avoid in Firenze. We were seated near the Hamiltons when halfway through the meal Jamie Hamilton asked me, "Have you read many Italian writers?" I replied that I had enjoyed the works of Italo Svevo, Carlo Levi and Alberto Moravia, hoping to impress him with my knowledge of European literature, while in truth I had just exhausted the names of the only three Italian authors I knew. It was then that my hostess, the Contessa laughed, as if she was about to betray a wicked secret, remarking, "You mean Schmitz and Pincherle?" I looked confused. She went on; "Those are their real names. They are all Jews, hiding behind distinguished Italian names, all except Levi who couldn't conceal his wretched origins no matter how hard he might try. No Italian is deceived by this. The Jews will do anything to hide their true heritage. It's quite disgusting, but fortunately they are always found out.

Communists—all of them. If I can forgive the Germans anything, which is not easy after what they did to Italy, I can forgive them for getting rid of so many Jews." I waited for Jamie or his wife to respond, to argue with her, to contradict her statement, but no one said anything. They went on eating and drinking undisturbed as the Countess ended her diatribe and flashed her smile at me, satisfied that she had improved my education in the true nature of Italian writers.

Although I had been raised with the knowledge that my family was Jewish, my parents provided only a minimum of religious education. If we had any larger identity other than as a family, it was as New Yorkers. Growing up in the City, I had never come up against any anti-Semitic remarks. This was during the early '40s in America, a time of Father Coughlin and Charles Lindbergh, vicious anti-Semites who had a wide following during the Depression and years after. Hardship, I've learned, doesn't often make people better, it just makes them harder. And hard times seek out easy victims for blame, and the Depression was one of those times. But growing up in a cosmopolitan city, a city with a large Jewish population, had sheltered me from overt signs of bigotry, although once as a 10-year-old on vacation in Miami with my family we passed a sign on the Kennelworth Hotel reading "No Jews or dogs allowed." When I asked my father about it he simply said that these people were idiots and I should pay no mind to that sign. And I didn't.

When I was a small child my mother had made the mistake of renting a beach house in a Long Island resort town that she later learned was "restricted." I was told years later that we children were shunned by the neighbor's children when an elderly immigrant aunt of ours had come to visit, her presence revealing our Jewish origins. But never before in my personal life had I heard anyone make an anti-Semitic remark. I was neither ashamed nor proud of my background. I saw no reason to be proud of anything you didn't create like your religion, your race, or your appearance. But I was not so naïve as to think they didn't matter in the world. My wife who was also Jewish had that Swedish, Garbo-like beauty that was so admired in America and elsewhere at that time, and beauty, great beauty often trumps bigotry. And I did not "look Jewish" in the parlance of the day—a horrible expression—but true for those who had preconceived notions as to how Jews, the most varied of people, actually looked. Many took me for a young Italian, even in Italy people first spoke to me in Italian, something that pleased me, and disappointed them when I replied in English or opened up my small phrase book to reply. I wanted more than anything to blend in wherever I was so I could watch and listen and take mental notes for the future masterpieces I was sure to write. And here I was in this villa in the Fiesole, when all the artifice of civilization was peeled away like the villa's rotting stucco, and I was staring into the face of a deep, ugly racial hatred.

I didn't plan it. Without thinking I rose from my chair and turned to my wife saying, "We have to go, love." Everyone looked up at us surprised. The Contessa asked if I was ill. I replied, "No, not ill, merely Jewish." She looked stunned. I repeated my remark in a more direct way. "I am a Jew. My wife and I—we're both Jewish."

I don't recall if it was the Contessa or Jamie Hamilton who responded, "Really, I thought you were Canadian." On any other night I would have laughed at the absurdity of that remark but this was no night for laughter. I realized that I never wanted to be defined by anything but my own character and my own talents, and I believed that I had gone beyond race and religion when I immersed myself in world literature, but I had been faced by a challenge that night for which there was only one reply, identifying oneself with the despised group.

The Contessa offered us her driver to take us back to the pension but I refused her in a steely show of controlled outrage and independence. I would not be beholden to her for anything, not even a lift back to Florence. We nodded goodbye to Jamie Hamilton and his wife without the customary handshake and made our way out of the villa. It was now a very dark, starless night and I realized soon after we reached the end of the driveway that we would have to make our way through a road in the woods to the main highway, and that road had many forks and turnings. Need I add that we were soon miserably lost in those woods? We were Hansel and Gretel without the trail of bread-crumbs. It took us two hours to find our way to the nearby main highway when I finally saw the distant lamplights on the roadway through the trees and we headed towards the lights. We finally flagged down a bus and made our way back to Florence.

Somehow, looking at that tablecloth again, and hearing the Nixon tapes and the TV news of anti-Semitism in the "new" Europe, brought this whole misadventure back to me with such clarity. It seems that anti-Semitism often sleeps late, but it always awakens and it never dies. I have spent a lifetime believing that I am a part of the family of man, and avoiding the formal religious aspect of life, finding the beliefs of others something I accept with ease but without any desire to partake of those beliefs. I realize that for many this reveals my great limitations of mind and spirit; and that for them my life is narrow and circumscribed, without spiritual comfort or the hope of redemption. Since religion is to me so divisive, it seems responsible for much of mankind's misery as much as it offers comfort, and I regard all organized religion as a drowning pool in which I don't want to swim. But on that dark night in the Fiesole outside of Florence I knew that I was a Jew, and that I could not live with myself if I did not declare it openly in response to that ugly table talk, the kind of talk that had previously led to the death of millions of my fellow Jews. I knew that I would not have been spared by my love of books or my wife's beauty had I lived in Europe during the war years, certainly not by the likes of that Contessa. That night I was no New Yorker, and I was certainly no hero. I was simply someone who had found a moment of clarity, a discovery that would stay with me for life; and all because we had purchased that organdy table cloth in Florence. And so, the other day, I decided to keep the table cloth as a reminder of times past, a time when I learned that I was not Scott Fitzgerald, not Italian or even a Canadian, no citizen of the world, but that I was simply, inexorably me.

Afterword

I recognize that I have left out much of what went into the making of the man I would become. I had hoped that in these pages I could be found by my observations on the people and events that touched my young life. But perhaps a summing up is needed.

Fiercely ambitious, yet with a deep hatred for injustice, prone to anxiety and despair yet absurdly overconfident, these qualities of mine are often at war with each other. I can only attribute my fierce love of my own created family, my wife of sixty years, my two sons and my three granddaughters, to a genetic disposition to love and protect inbred in both my mother and father and passed on to my sister and me. Someone asked me recently where I developed my love of theater, and I doubt if it came from those early school plays, or even from the first professional theater I saw as a boy. Shakespeare may not have been the first to notice it, but he was the first to remark that "all the world's a stage." My world as a boy was nothing *but* theater. Our various apartments were the stage. I suspect that my training in drama came from observing my father, who not only loved all forms of entertainment, but in his own vivid and theatrical actions turned every event in our lives into a performance, a drama or a comedy, one in which he starred with my mother, my sister and me in supporting roles, a drama of love, anger, guilt, despair, and equally a comedy in which he tripped over himself in an effort to please everyone, particularly my mother, and we were all his audience.

Violent, but never vicious, loving but needing more love than any of us could provide, we rarely knew what to expect when the curtain went up on one of his productions. Would a loving father appear, or a madman chasing us around the apartment flourishing his belt like a lariat, and his rage turning to hilarity as his pants fell down revealing his skinny legs in his long underwear? Lon Chaney as Laurel and Hardy. Or when the curtain would go down on the final act, a tragedy that did not end with my sister's death by leukemia or my mother's death by accident. My mother spent a lifetime trying to deal with the realities that she was obliged to face, laughing at some events, stoically facing others, seldom weeping or allowing herself the luxury of outrage, but from her I inherited my love of stories and a certain collection of her memories that would lead to my sense of the connectedness of so many disparate events, a connectedness I tried to bring to my writing. I have also left out of this narrative so many of the battle stories that one has in building a life and a career, in which the teller or the writer is always the hero, despite. That is for another time, if there *is* enough time in my future to recover that part of my past.

About the Author

Sherman Yellen, playwright, librettist, screen-writer, lyricist and now memoirist, was nominated for a Tony Award for his book for the 1970 musical *The Rothschilds*, with a score by *Fiddler on the Roof* songwriters Jerry Bock and Sheldon Harnick, which he and Harnick have recently reimagined as *Rothschild & Sons*. Sherman wrote the libretto for the Will Holt and Gary William Freidman musical *Treasure Island*, winner of the Broadway World Best Regional Musical Award (2012). Among his many theater works is his satirical sketch "Delicious Indignities" which appeared in the New York and London revue *Oh! Calcutta!* His straight plays on and off Broadway include *New Gods for Lovers, Strangers*, and *December Fools*.

Sherman was librettist and lyricist for *Josephine Tonight*, an original musical he wrote with the late composer Wally Harper about the early life of Josephine Baker, which *The Chicago Sun-Times* called "a shining new musical" and which the DC press praised for being "so hot that it sizzles."

In his youth he worked as a librettist with legendary composer Richard Rodgers. Together with Sheldon Harnick they recently revised the Rodgers-Harnick musical *Rex* about Henry VIII. This new version had a successful premiere in Toronto.

His teleplays have won him two Emmy Awards and a Peabody Award, first for his *John Adams, Lawyer* in the PBS series *The Adams Chronicles*, and later for *An Early Frost*, a groundbreaking drama about AIDS in America broadcast on NBC, as well as an Emmy Nomination for his *Hallmark Hall of Fame* version of *Beauty and the Beast* starring George C. Scott. Sherman's screenplay adaptations of classic novels range from *Great Expectations* to *Phantom of the Opera*. He has received awards in Arts and Letters from Bard College, and he is a frequent contributor of essays on the arts, literature, and politics to online publications such as *The Huffington Post*.

Sherman recently published his autobiographical novella *Cousin Bella – The Whore of Minsk*, available in a volume which also includes his holiday short story *A Christmas Lilly*, and a collection of three plays, *December Fools and Other Plays (December Fools ● Budapest ● Gin Lane)*.

Sherman is married, the father of two sons, Nicholas and Christopher, and has three much loved granddaughters. He has lived in London and Los Angeles, worked in Berlin and Budapest, but home was, is, and always will be New York City.

A GUIDE TO THE BACK COVER JIGSAW PUZZLE

1. Simone Yellen, sister, age 19; 1947.
2. The author and his wife Joan Fuhr at their wedding in 1953.
3. Nathaniel "Nat" Yellen, father, age 26 in 1925.
4. Joan Fuhr Yellen, wife, age 16, freshman year at Bard College.
5. Maryasha Horowitz, the Tante Mary, sister of maternal grandfather, Meyer Horowitz.
6. The infant Sherman, 1932-33.
7. Lillian Horowitz, 1918.
8. Nat Yellen holding Sherman, age 2, with Sherman's disapproving sister, Simone, age 6.
9. Sherman, age 15, photo portrait by Fabian Bachrach, 1947.
10. Lillian Horowitz, circa 1922.
11. Sherman in P.S. 26 school play, a sailor for Columbus.
12. Simone Yellen Feldman, sister, 1972.
13. The infant Sherman in carriage, 1932.
14. Grandfather Meyer Horowitz with second wife, Augusta ("Gussie").
15. Horowitz family studio portrait; circa 1916. Top row from left: Aunt Rebecca, 16; Grandmother Sarah, 43, Aunt Ida (a.k.a. Anndida) 20; Tall Uncle Sam, 18; Patriarch Meyer, 48; Sherman's mother Libby/Lilly age 13. Bottom row: Uncle Frankie, age 4; Uncle Al, age 5.
16. Simone Yellen, age 4, clowning at Coney Island.
17. Sherman, age 3, with sister Simone in the great garden on Andrews Avenue.
18. Sherman, age 12; standing far right at Camp Robin Hood with bunkmates Martin and Alvin; the tormented and the tormentors.
19. Young Simone looking through a kaleidoscope, 1937.
20. Infant Nicholas Yellen, son of Joan and Sherman.
21. Cousin Ida (called Bella in *Cousin Bella – the Whore of Minsk*); infant Sherman in her arms, 1932.
22. Sherman, age 9, dressed in Native American ("Indian") costume for class play, 1940.
23. Ageless Uncle Frankie with sister Simone.
24. Sherman, age 17, Freshman at Bard College, 1949.
25. College roommate Larry Hagman, far left; Sherman seated far right in Bard College production of *The Cherry Orchard*, 1950.
26. Sherman, age 3, standing in Lillian's "Dutch Schultz" gardens on Andrews Avenue.

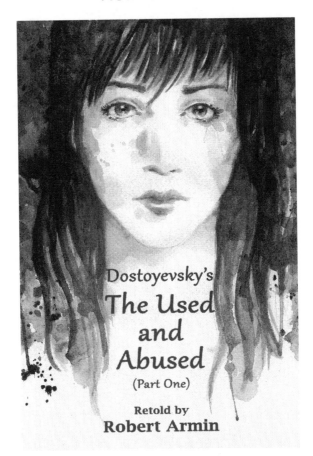

From the pen of one of America's finest painters and illustrators, James Montgomery Flagg, best remembered today for his iconic recruiting poster of Uncle Sam ("I Want YOU for U.S. Army"), this delightful collection of comic poems and cartoons takes a tongue-in-cheek look at the many justifications people come up with to wed. First published in 1906, this volume features newly reset and more legible text, and crisp, detailed illustrations reproduced directly from a rare first edition copy of the original.

Trade Paperback ISBN-13: 978-0996016933 Paperback $6.95

MORECLACKE PUBLISHING

New for 2016

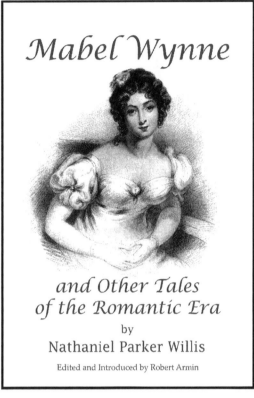

Mabel Wynne

and Other Tales
of the Romantic Era
by
Nathaniel Parker Willis
Edited and Introduced by Robert Armin

Mabel Wynne and Other Tales of the Romantic Age is a selection
of short romantic fiction and poems by Nineteenth Century
American writer, editor, journalist and international travel
correspondent, Nathaniel Parker Willis (1806-1867), newly
edited and introduced by novelist Robert Armin. Beautifully
illustrated with rare etchings and decorative drop cap
lettering all reproduced from vintage books of the period.
Also included are five essays by Willis on the American
Woman, as originally published in the *New York Mirror* and
The Home Journal.

Trade Paperback ISBN-13: 978-1499187229 Paperback $9.95
Also Available in **Kindle eBook** and **Audiobook**

MORECLACKE **PUBLISHING**

Also Recommended

"Yellen has given us the Jewish-American immigrant experience more vitally and persuasively than any writer since Isaac Bashevis Singer."

Christopher Davis

Bonus Story - Sherman Yellen's Holiday Classic
A Christmas Lilly

COUSIN BELLA
THE WHORE OF MINSK

Sherman Yellen

Cousin Bella – The Whore of Minsk recounts the life of a young Jewish woman in Tsarist Russia who was sold into prostitution, rescued by the author's indomitable grandmother, and then immigrated to America where the most extraordinary drama of her life was yet to unfold. Written by Tony® nominee and two-time Emmy® winning screenwriter, Sherman Yellen. Also included is Yellen's holiday classic, *A Christmas Lilly*, a tender, poignant memory of a Jewish family's first Christmas tree in 1939, celebrating the author's wise and compassionate mother.

Trade Paperback ISBN-13: 978-1495290435 Paperback $8.95
Also Available in **Kindle eBook** and **Unabridged Audiobook**

MORECLACKE PUBLISHING

Also Recommended

The Flash of Midnight
By Robert Armin

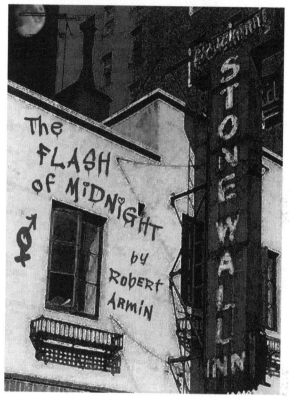

Taking its inspiration from Voltaire's *Candide*, Robert Armin's novel *The Flash of Midnight* recounts the bisexual escapades of Laurie Norber, a young woman who steadfastly believes that true love is just around the corner, never imagining that in June of 1969 she will become the spark that ignites a sexual revolution at a Greenwich Village bar called the Stonewall Inn.

Trade Paperback ISBN-13: 978-1463508074 Paperback $12.95
Also Available in **Kindle eBook** and **Unabridged Audiobook**

MORECLACKE PUBLISHING

Also Recommended

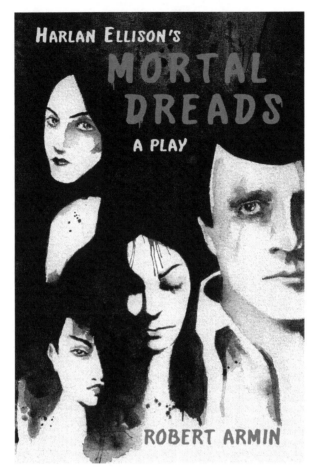

Welcome to *Harlan Ellison's MORTAL DREADS*, an anthology play by Robert Armin, featuring dramatic adaptations of six short stories (including *Shatterday* and *Paladin of the Lost Hour*) by acclaimed fantasist Harlan Ellison. Six extraordinary tales that tear through the fabric of space and time and reveal the gaping hole which opens onto Some Other Place. If you find these dark dreams troubling, maybe it's because they're your dreams!

Trade Paperback ISBN-13: 978-1478310884 Paperback $11.95

MORECLACKE **PUBLISHING**

Also Recommended

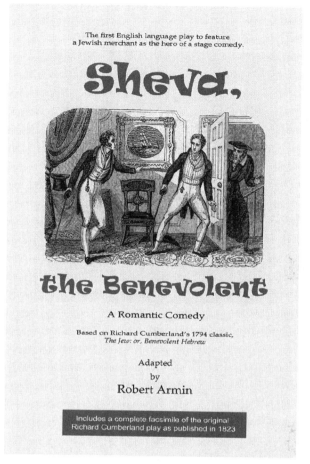

The first English language play to feature a Jewish merchant as the hero of a stage comedy.

Sheva, the Benevolent

A Romantic Comedy

Based on Richard Cumberland's 1794 classic, *The Jew: or, Benevolent Hebrew*

Adapted by Robert Armin

Includes a complete facsimile of the original Richard Cumberland play as published in 1823

Sheva, the Benevolent is a faithful adaptation of Richard Cumberland's 1794 comedy, *The Jew: or, Benevolent Hebrew*, featuring Sheva, the first Jewish moneylender to be portrayed as the hero of a stage comedy. Includes a Preface by playwright Robert Armin, an introduction by 18th Century theater scholar Jean Marsden, and a high quality facsimile of the original play as published in 1823.

Trade Paperback ISBN-13: 978-0615663166 Paperback $11.95
Also Available in **Kindle eBook** (without facsimile)

MORECLACKE PUBLISHING

48506832R00151

Made in the USA
San Bernardino, CA
27 April 2017